PRACTICAL RECIPES

FOR THE

HOUSEWIFE

A BOOK

OF

PRACTICAL
RECIPES

FOR THE

HOUSEWIFE

PUBLISHED BY

DETROIT TIMES

DETROIT, MICHIGAN

Manufactured in U. S.A. by the
John F. Cuneo Company
Chicago

The pages which follow were compiled with a view to supplying dependable recipes.

Grateful acknowledgment is hereby made to more than 13,000 housewives, ready and willing to contribute their favorite recipes and thereby help to make this Cook Book possible.

Detroit Times.

Table of Contents

TABLE OF WEIGHTS AND MEASURES

Weight

16 ounces	1 pound
2 cups meat	1 pound
4 cups flour	1 pound
2 cups granulated sugar	1 pound
2 cups butter	1 pound

Wet Measure

2 cups	1 pint
2 pints	1 quart
4 quarts	1 gallon

Dry Measure

8 quarts	1 peck
4 pecks	1 bushel
1 peck potatoes	15 pounds
3 teaspoons	1 tablespoon
4 tablespoons	1/4 cup

All measurements in this book are level.
Level contents of cups and spoons with a knife.

Table of Food Content

Organic Matter

Protein: builds up the tissues and cells burned up throughout the day's activities.
Eggs, meat, fish, milk, cheese, beans, peas, nuts, grains, and gelatines.

Fats: lubricate the body and furnish energy.
Butter, cream, olive oil, nuts, meat and vegetable oils.

Carbohydrates: starches and sugars.
Furnish heat and energy.
Cereals, lima beans, lentils, peas, corn, potatoes.
Fruits, syrups, sugars.

Vitamines: for growth and health.
Fresh fruit juices, eggs, butter, milk, coarse grains, greens and fresh vegetables. Especially citrus fruits.

Inorganic Matter

Mineral Salts: to build bone in children, to aid digestion and to make food palatable.
Salt, good water.
Spinach, carrots, onions, greens, raw lettuce and raw vegetables.

HOUSEHOLD HINTS

Wash the sink and drain pipes with boiling water every day and once a week, wash and drain with strong solution of washing soda (sal soda).
The drain of the icebox may be kept free in the same way.

To Remove Stains

Blood Stains: Wash in cold water, then in warm water and naphtha soap.

Bluing: Wash in boiling water using a little vinegar. If the stain persists, try oxalic acid or 10% solution acetic acid.

Coffee: Stretch material with spot over a bowl and pour boiling water through it from a height of two feet.

Cocoa or Chocolate: Try cold water and soap. If not effective, soak in cold water and borax and pour on boiling water as for coffee stain.

Grass: Weak solution of ammonia and water—1/4 ammonia to 3/4 water. Use cleaning fluid on non-washable materials.

Grease: Saturate French Chalk with benzin and paste over spot. Lay a blotter over the spot and rest a warm iron on the blotter for half an hour. Remove the iron, dust off the chalk and the spot should be removed. The grease goes into the chalk from the heat.
If other chemicals or acids are in the grease, try cleaning fluid.

Ink: Use salt and lemon and sunshine for white goods. Use alternately drops of ammonia and oxalic acid on colored materials.

Iron: Lemon and salt followed by sunshine are often effective. Moistening with hot water and laying oxalic crystals on the spots should be effective.

Medicine: Soak in alcohol.

Mildew: For old stains treat alternately with potassium permanganate and oxalic acid.

Milk: Wash in warm water and soap suds.

Paint: Fresh paint should come out with water and yellow soap. Turpentine, gasoline and benzol are best for silks.

Perspiration: Try weak solution sodium hydrosulphite and wash in water. If material is nonwashable the stain is hopeless to remove.

Water Spots: Steam the spot, shake dry and iron.

Cleaning Out the Coffee Pot: Boil up one tablespoon washing soda in the coffee pot full of water. Boil for fifteen minutes. Wash several times with fresh water and stand in the direct sunshine to dry.

Cleaning Stained Knives: Scour with sand-soap and raw potato. Rub with a moistened cork.

Cleaning Piano Keys: Wash piano keys with a soft cloth dampened with alcohol.

Flowers: To keep flowers as long as possible, stand them during the night in a cool, dark place in a tall vase so that the water reaches almost to the heads. Cut the stems a little every morning.

A small quantity of salt or a five grain aspirin tablet keeps the flowers fresh.

Wild flowers should be put in boiling water as soon as they are picked. Allow the water to cool and keep the flowers in this water.

Roses will absorb moisture from wet waxed paper if it is placed as a cap over the bouquet at night.

Beverages

Hot and Cold

HOT DRINKS

Coffee

Never make coffee in a tin coffee pot.

PERCOLATED COFFEE

Put grounds in the coffee compartment of the percolator. Average 1 heaping tablespoon of ground coffee to one cup of water. Put cold water in the bottom of the percolator. Boil for five minutes. Boiling is figured from the time the water first trickles over the coffee grounds. After coffee has boiled violently for 5 minutes, turn off flame completely and allow coffee to stand for another five minutes in a warm place. Serve.

BOILED COFFEE

6 heaping teaspoons ground coffee
6 cups boiling water
1 egg
1 cup cold water
Pinch of salt

Scald the coffee pot. Place coffee in pot, add pinch of salt, six tablespoons of egg water. Stir well and add one-half the boiling water (3 cups). Allow to boil for three minutes, add the remaining three cups of boiling water. Keep warm but do not boil further.

Egg water is made by beating one egg while pouring on 1 cup cold water. This may be kept in the icebox and one tablespoon of egg to one cup of coffee used.

Milk

Kettles used to boil milk must be kept scrupulously clean. Wash first in clear, cold water, then with warm water and borax and after rinsing should be carefully dried and if possible stood in the sun for a time.

Always keep milk in a cool place for it is very quick to spoil. In summer, milk for infants and children should be sterilized twice a day.

To Pasteurize Milk:

Boil bottles to contain sterile milk for twenty minutes in pure water. Fill clean bottles nearly full of milk, cork them with cotton that has previously been baked in an oven and not handled by hands, place suspended on rings in a deep pan of cold water so that the water in the pans just covers the milk in the bottles.

Place the pan on the fire and heat until you see small bubbles form on the top of the milk in the bottles. Lessen the amount of heat, but allow some heat for about one-quarter hour. Then chill as quickly as possible and when the milk is cold, remove the bottles from the pan of water and set them in the icebox. In very hot weather even this treatment only keeps the milk sterile for about twelve hours.

Tea

2 cups freshly boiling water   4 teaspoons tea

Scald the china teapot; put in the tea, pour on boiling water; let stand to steep for two to three minutes. Strain when serving. The secret of well-brewed tea is to use fresh actively boiling water.

Russian Tea

1 cup boiling water	Clove in slice of lemon
1 loaf sugar	Rum drops
1 preserved cherry	1 tablespoon strong tea
Canton ginger	

The tea is brewed and allowed to stand until very strong and almost black in color. Pour the boiling water over the strong tea and allow to stand two or three minutes. The sweetening and trimmings are placed in the bottom of the cup or tall glass and the tea poured over them.

Chocolate

1½ ounces bitter chocolate	3 cups milk
1 cup boiling water	4 tablespoons sugar

Melt the chocolate in a saucepan; add sugar and gradually the boiling water. Stir smooth, allow to come to a boil and add the milk, scalded.

Beat well together and serve with salted wafer.

Cocoa

2 teaspoons cocoa	1 cup boiling water
1 cup milk	2 teaspoons sugar

Pour the boiling water onto the cocoa; stir until the cocoa dissolves. Boil about five minutes until cocoa thickens. This paste may be kept and when cocoa is wanted, use 1 teaspoon paste to one cup hot milk. Stir and serve with sugar to taste.

Hot Lemonade or Orangeade (for colds)

Juice of 4 lemons	3 whole cloves
1 quart cold water	Bit of cinnamon bark

Boil together water, sugar and spices. Simmer for five minutes and then strain. Serve as hot as may be sipped.

Hot Malted Milk

3 teaspoons malted milk	Salt and white pepper
1 cup hot milk	1 tablespoon boiling water

Mix paste of malted milk and boiling water. Stir in hot milk and add seasoning. Celery salt and a dot of butter make a palatable addition.

Hot Egg Malted Milk

2 tablespoons malted milk	2/3 cup hot milk
1 egg	Grated nutmeg
Boiling water	

Make a paste of malted milk in boiling water. Beat up egg light and add to malted milk. Stir smooth, add nutmeg and serve.

Hot Chocolate Malted Milk

Add one tablespoon melted sweet chocolate, to one cup hot milk. Sprinkle grated nutmeg on top of beverage.

COLD DRINKS

Chocolate Sauce (For Ice Cream and Puddings)

2 ounces bitter chocolate
2 cups sugar
1 quart water

2 tablespoons cornstarch
2 teaspoons vanilla
1/4 teaspoon parafin

Make a syrup of the sugar and water. Add the chocolate, parafin and the cornstarch which has been dissolved in a little cold water. Cook three minutes. Add vanilla, cool and keep in a jar in the icebox for use over ice cream and over certain puddings.

Frosted Chocolate

Make sufficient quantity of hot chocolate for needs. Cool and chill in icebox. Serve in tall glasses with plenty of cracked ice.

Frosted Cocoa

Same as for frosted chocolate.

Frosted Russian Chocolate

2 cups strong boiling black coffee
2 ounces chocolate
1/2 cup sugar

2 cups scalded milk
1 tablespoon cornstarch
Cinnamon
Nutmeg grated

Dissolve cornstarch in coffee and cook in double boiler with coffee, chocolate, spices and sugar. Then add the milk to this thickened liquid. Stir well and boil for one quarter hour. Serve chilled with some cracked ice in tall glasses.

Maple Float

2/3 cup milk
2 tablespoons maple syrup

1 egg yolk
Whipped cream

Beat egg yolk. Add syrup and milk and beat or shake. Pour into glass; add whipped cream. Serve with sweet wafers. Especially liked by children; a wholesome, nourishing drink.

Iced Tea

Pour strained fresh made strong tea into glasses one-half full of ice cubes. Sweeten to taste and decorate with one slice of lemon. The quicker the chilling, the better the flavor.

Iced Coffee
Strain boiled coffee, add sugar to taste, chill and add cream. Serve in tall glasses with ice.

Lemonade
1 lemon   4 tablespoons sugar
2 cups water
Squeeze out juice of one lemon. Dissolve sugar in lemon juice and then add water. Serve with ice cubes and decorate with one slice lemon and sprig of mint.

Orangeade
Same as for lemonade.

Limeade
Juice of three fresh limes   2 tablespoons sugar
Cold water   Sprig of mint
Place all ingredients in tall glass of cracked ice.

Mint Squash
Four sprigs of mint   1 tablespoon powdered
Juice of one lemon   sugar
                                   Ginger ale
Bruise all but tip of one sprig of mint in a glass. Add strips of lemon rind, juice of the lemon, sugar and chill. When ready to serve, fill glasses with ice cubes, pour over ginger ale and serve with sprig of mint on top of ice.

Black Cow
Place four tablespoons of vanilla ice cream in a tall glass; pour over strong root beer and serve.

Cider Punch
1 quart cider   Juice of two oranges
1 quart white grape juice   Juice of two lemons
2 quarts water   1 cup sugar
Grate part of orange and lemon rinds.
Dissolve sugar in fruit juices; pour in cider and add grated rinds. Pour over lump of ice for use in a punch bowl.

Citrus Punch

Juice of 6 lemons
Juice of 6 oranges
½ cup green maraschino
  cherries
½ cup red maraschino
  cherries

1 cup sugar
1 cup pineapple shredded
2 quarts charged water
2 cups water

Make a syrup of the sugar and water; boil for five minutes.
Cool and when cold add the fruit and fruit juices. When
perfectly cold pour in charged water and serve over ice.

Lemon Ice Punch

Place one quart of lemon ice (or orange ice) in a punch bowl.
Stir in ginger ale. When made thick, may be used with a meat
course; when thin, serve as a cold drink.

Bread, Biscuits & Rolls

Bread, Rolls, and Muffins

Since flour must be kept dry to bake well, it is often advisable to heat it in the oven just before using it. Bread after baking should be kept in a dry place.

Scald the milk and cool it before making bread. Use only lukewarm liquids with yeast as hot water kills the yeast plant. Use only fresh yeast.

Wheat flour may be substituted by other flours:

1 cup wheat flour equals:	¾ cup cornmeal
1½ cups rolled oats	¾ cup potato flour
¾ cup rice	
¾ cup buckwheat	

Butter may be substituted by other fats:

1 cup butter equals:	¾ cup cotton seed oil
1 cup butterine	¾ cup peanut oil
1 cup nut butter	

By using ¼ quantity substitute with ¾ wheat flour, a very satisfactory product may be made and an economy accomplished.

Bran Health Bread

4 cups bran flour	1 cup dark molasses
4 cups white flour	2 teaspoons salt
4 cups milk	½ cup raisins
4 teaspoons baking soda	½ cup nut meats

Mix molasses and milk; add bran. Sift the white flour into the salt and baking soda. Add to the liquid and mix thoroughly. Place in greased low pans and bake one hour in a moderate oven.

Buttermilk Bread

1½ cups buttermilk
4 cups flour
1 egg
¼ teaspoon salt
1 teaspoon sugar
1 teaspoon soda
2½ teaspoons cream of tartar

Mix the dry ingredients, add the egg beaten well, and mix all thoroughly. Place in bread pan and bake in a moderate oven for one-half hour.

Corn Bread

¾ cup cornmeal
1¼ cups flour
5 tablespoons sugar
1 cup milk
½ teaspoon salt
2 tablespoons melted butter
1 egg
5 teaspoons baking powder

Sift together the dry ingredients. Beat the egg, pour in the milk and add the melted butter. Beat all together well and bake in low pans for one-half hour in a hot oven.

Serve split with dots of butter and maple syrup or corn syrup.

Gluten Bread

6 cups gluten flour
1 cake compressed yeast
3 cups milk
1 egg
½ teaspoon salt
2 tablespoons butter, melted
2 tablespoons sugar (unless for diabetic patient)

Dissolve yeast in warm milk. Mix flour and milk and allow to stand and rise. Add salt, butter, sugar, egg beaten well and more flour to knead. Shape into loaves and bake in a moderate oven (350 degrees F.) for about one hour.

Quick Raisin Bread

1 cup raisins
2½ cups graham flour
1 teaspoon salt
4 teaspoons baking powder
1 cup milk
¼ cup sugar
1 tablespoon shortening

Add dry ingredients to the milk and mix thoroughly. Add shortening and raisins. Beat together well.

Turn into greased baking pan; let rise in warm place and bake for one hour in a moderate oven.

Boston Brown Bread

2¾ cups graham flour
½ cup molasses
½ cup sugar
1 egg

2 teaspoons soda
1 cup sour milk
1 teaspoon salt

Add sugar and molasses to beaten egg. Mix with rest of ingredients. ½ cup raisins may be added.

Place in three one-pound baking powder cans, well greased. Steam for two hours or more. See that can covers fit very close.

Dark Bread

1½ cups graham flour
¾ cup wheat flour
¼ cup nuts, chopped
1/3 cup dark molasses

½ teaspoon salt
1½ cups sour milk
1½ teaspoon soda

Mix dry ingredients with the milk, add the molasses and last the nut meats. Stir well. Place in a greased bread pan and bake in a moderate to low oven (325 degrees F.) for one hour.

Graham Bread

3 cups graham flour
1 cup wheat flour
¾ cake compressed yeast
¼ cup sugar

2 tablespoons butter
1 teaspoon salt
1½ cups lukewarm water

Dissolve the yeast in lukewarm water.

Mix flour, sugar, butter and salt in mixing bowl. Knead lightly and place dough in warm place to rise. When dough has risen, knead once more and then place in floured pans. Allow to rise once more and bake in a moderate oven (350 degrees F.). This dough is very light and should be beaten well to get in plenty of air bubbles. If a very soft dough is desired, more wheat flour may be used and dough poured into pans after thorough beating.

Light Nut Bread

½ cup nut meats, chopped
2½ cups flour
1 egg
½ teaspoon salt

½ cup sugar
1 cup milk
4 teaspoons baking powder

Beat the egg into the milk, add the dry ingredients and let stand fifteen minutes in a greased bread pan.
Bake in a moderate oven (350 degrees F.) for one-half hour or more.

Nut and Raisin Bread

1½ cups flour
2 cups corn meal
½ cup brown sugar
1 teaspoon salt
4 teaspoons baking powder

¾ cup chopped nuts
1 cup milk
½ cup molasses
¼ teaspoon soda

Sift together all dry ingredients, add nuts and raisins, add milk and mix well, then add molasses and soda which have been mixed together. Bake in two small greased loaf pans in moderate oven about 45 minutes.

Oatmeal Bread

1½ cups rolled oats
1 cake compressed yeast
5 cups wheat flour

¼ cup sugar
2 teaspoons salt
2 cups hot water

Dissolve yeast in additional ¼ cup warm water.
Soak oats in boiling water, add salt and sugar and let cool to tepid temperature. Add the dissolved yeast, then the flour. Knead well until dough is smooth. Cover and allow to rise to twice its bulk. Shape into loaves and place in well floured pans (should make two loaves). Allow again to stand and double bulk. Bake in a moderate oven (350 degrees F.) for one hour.

Whole Wheat Prune Bread

2½ cups whole wheat flour
¼ cup sugar
4 teaspoons baking powder
1 teaspoon salt

1 cup milk
1 tablespoon shortening
1 cup prunes

Wash prunes, soak several hours, drain, stone and chop. Mix and sift flour, sugar, salt and baking powder; add milk and beat well. Add prunes and melted shortening. Put into greased bread pans. Allow to stand 20 to 25 minutes in warm place, and bake in moderate oven 1 hour. Dates, raisins or nuts may be used instead of prunes.

Spoon Bread

½ teaspoon baking powder
1 cup yellow cornmeal
2 eggs
2 cups milk

1 tablespoon butter
1 teaspoon salt
2 cups boiling water

Pour hot water over cornmeal, stir well and allow to cool off. Beat eggs well and add melted butter, salt and milk. Stir well. Pour into baking dish and bake three-quarters of an hour in a moderate oven. Serve from the dish with a spoon.

Raisin Bread

¼ cup raisins
1 pint hot milk
1 egg
8 cups flour

1/3 cup butter or substitute
½ cup sugar
1 teaspoon salt
1 cake compressed yeast

Dissolve yeast in ½ cup lukewarm milk. Place butter, sugar and salt in mixing bowl and add rest of hot milk. Allow to cool to tepid temperature then add beaten egg and the dissolved yeast.

Add flour and turn out onto a floured board. Knead well, adding raisins. Return to the bowl, cover and allow to stand in a warm place to rise. Form into loaves and bake in a moderate oven (350 degrees F.) for three-quarters of an hour or until the loaves are nicely browned.

Wheat Bread

6½ cups flour
½ ounce compressed yeast
2 cups scalded milk or
  boiling water

1 tablespoon sugar
1 tablespoon salt
1 tablespoon butter or substitute

Makes two loaves

Dissolve yeast in ½ cup lukewarm water. Place sugar, salt and butter in large mixing bowl; pour on the hot milk. Add five cups flour to the yeast paste and stir well. Add last cup of flour and knead the dough until soft and pliable.

Return to the bowl, cover and allow to stand in a warm place until the dough rises to almost twice the original size. Place on floured board, divide the bulk in two and knead each part. Shape into loaves and place in floured bread pans.

Stand once more in warm place and allow to rise again to twice original bulk. Test the oven: if a piece of paper turns dark brown within five minutes, the oven is "hot" and the right temperature for baking bread. Bake the bread for one hour at constant temperature.

Remove loaves from pans and let stand in current of air to form hard crust.

Light Nut Bread

¾ cups sugar	1 egg
1 teaspoon salt	2 cups milk
4 cups flour	1 cup nuts, cut small
4 teaspoons baking powder	

Mix dry ingredients, add egg and milk and bake in moderate oven.

Whole Wheat Bread

4 cups whole wheat flour	1 cup wheat flour
1 cake compressed yeast	2 teaspoons salt
1 cup boiling water	2 tablespoons sugar
1 cup milk	

Dissolve yeast in a little lukewarm water.

Mix hot water with milk and add enough flour to make a thin batter. Beat this well to let in air bubbles. Add sugar and salt. Let stand in warm place until dough rises. Stir in more flour, knead well, making a light dough. Mold into loaves, place in buttered pans and allow to stand in warmth to rise once more.

Bake in a moderate oven (350 degrees F.) for about 1½ hours.

One half cup nuts and one half cup raisins may be added to the batter if desired.

Old Fashioned Johnny Bread

1½ cups white flour	4 tablespoons sugar
1 cup white or yellow corn-meal	1 egg
	1½ cups milk or water
5 teaspoons baking powder	3 tablespoons shortening

Mix and sift dry ingredients. Add unbeaten egg, milk or water and melted shortening. Mix thoroughly and quickly, keeping spoon on bottom of bowl and stirring in ever-widening circles. Pour into well greased shallow pan and bake in a moderate hot oven (375 degrees) 35 to 40 minutes.

Quick Brown Bread

1½ cups graham flour
1½ cups white flour
1½ cups buttermilk or plain
  sour milk

¼ cup granulated sugar
1 teaspoon salt
1 scant teaspoon baking soda

Stir well and bake one hour in moderate oven. Recipe makes
one loaf.

Rye Bread with Caraway

4 cups rye flour
2 cups wheat flour
1 cake compressed yeast
1 tablespoon salt
1 teaspoon sugar

1 cup riced potatoes
1 pint water drained from
  potatoes
1 teaspoon caraway seed

Dissolve yeast in ¼ cup of lukewarm potato water; add sugar
and place with rest of hot potato water and milk in a mixing
bowl. Stir in the salt, flours and caraway seed. Knead well
on floured board. Return to bowl, cover and allow to rise in a
warm place. Form into loaves, place in floured pans and allowed to rise further. When size has almost doubled, bake in
a hot oven (375 degrees F.) for one hour or more.

Pumpernickel

Follow the same directions as for Caraway rye bread, but use
rye graham instead of the rye flour. Use smaller pans and
bake very thoroughly.

Freshen stale bread by dipping it into cold milk and placing
it in a pan in the oven until it is thoroughly warmed through.
The moisture goes into the bread.

Stale bread crumbs should be kept in tight jars so that they
will not mold.

BAKING POWDER BISCUITS

Use two teaspoons baking powder for one cup flour. Less
baking powder is needed if eggs are contained in recipe.

Bake soft doughs in a very hot oven (450 degrees F). Stiff
doughs for quick biscuits should stand in a warm place to

rise for fifteen minutes and then baked. Have the oven heating while mixing the ingredients.

4 teaspoons baking powder   2 tablespoons shortening
2 cups white flour   1 teaspoon salt
1 cup milk

Work the flour into the butter with a fork; add the milk gradually until enough milk has been added to make the dough easy to handle and shape. Add the sifted dry ingredients and roll out about ½ inch thick on a lightly floured board. Cut round with a cooky cutter or the top of a water glass. Bake quickly in a very hot oven (450 degrees F.) for about ten minutes.

Serve very hot with butter and jam.

Baking Powder Biscuits for Shortcake

4 teaspoons baking powder   ¾ cup milk
2 cups white flour   ¼ cup shortening
1½ tablespoons sugar   ½ teaspoon salt

Work flour into butter, then the other dry ingredients. Add the milk gradually to make a soft dough. Pat and roll on a lightly floured board and cut with a very large round cutter or spread flat in flat cake pans. Bake in a very hot oven for fifteen minutes.

Split and use for shortcake. Crush strawberries or peaches and slice bananas. Sweeten to taste, and use either whipped cream or heavy unwhipped cream. Place biscuits on plate with split sides up, one on top of the other with the fruit between and on top.

Soda Biscuits

½ teaspoon soda   ¾ cup sour milk
2 cups white flour   2 tablespoons butter
1 tablespoon baking pow-   ½ teaspoon salt
    der

Work flour into butter thoroughly. Add the dry ingredients and then pour on the milk gradually. Roll out and cut into rounds or drop into greased muffin pan.

Bake about fifteen minutes in a hot oven (400 degrees F.).

Quick Tea Biscuit

2 cups flour

2 tablespoons baking powder
  ing powder

2 tablespoons lard

2 teaspoons sugar

1 cup sweet milk

Pinch salt

Stir well and drop from spoon in buttered gem pan. Bake in hot oven.

Never Fail Biscuit

3 cups of flour

3 teaspoonfuls of shortening

3 teaspoonfuls of baking
  powder

1 teaspoonful salt

¾ cup sweet milk

Mix dry, cut shortening in with knife. Add milk and mix quickly. Do not roll.

Cheese Biscuits

Sift together two cups flour and three teaspoons baking powder; add three-fourths cup grated American cheese and one-half teaspoon salt. Add two tablespoons butter and mix in thoroughly with steel fork. Add one cup milk. Drop from spoon in small portions on baking sheet. Bake 15 minutes in moderate oven (375 degrees). Makes about eighteen small biscuits.

Quick Parker House Rolls

6 teaspoons baking powder

4 cups white flour

1½ cups milk

2 tablespoons shortening,
  melted

1 teaspoon salt

Sift together the baking powder, flour and salt. Add the milk and melted shortening slowly to the dry ingredients. Stir all together until smooth. Roll to ½ inch thickness on a lightly floured board. Cut round with a glass or with a cookie cutter. Fold over the finger and pinch down the edges. Stand in a pan in a warm place and allow to rise. Separate rolls if necessary after rising. Paint tops with butter and bake for fifteen minutes in a very hot oven (450 degrees F.).

Serve warm with butter.

Blueberry Gems

1 cup blueberries	1 egg
2½ cups flour	¼ cup sugar
4 teaspoons baking powder	¼ cup shortening or butter
1 cup milk	½ teaspoon salt

Mix ½ cup flour with the blueberries and allow to stand for one hour.

Cream the butter with the sugar and add the beaten egg. Sift the flour with the salt and baking powder. Add ½ cup milk to the berries and ½ cup milk to the sifted flour. Mix all the ingredients adding the berries last.

Bake for one-half hour in a hot oven in greased muffin tins.

Cinnamon Rolls

½ teaspoon cinnamon	2 tablespoons citron
2 cups flour	2 tablespoons sugar
3 teaspoons baking powder	½ cup raisons or currants
2 tablespoons butter or sub-stitute	½ cup milk
	½ teaspoon salt

Mix flour with butter and add milk, baking powder and salt. Mix thoroughly and turn out onto floured board. Roll quite thin and paint with melted butter. Spread raisins and citron which have been chopped, cinnamon mixed with sugar and roll over and over like a jelly roll.

Cut into pieces an inch thick and arrange on flat side in greased pans. Bake in a hot oven for one-quarter hour.

Bran Muffins

1 cup bran flour	2 tablespoons molasses
2 cups graham flour	1 teaspoon soda
1½ cups milk	½ teaspoon salt

Mix milk and molasses, add the dry ingredients. Bake in a very hot oven for one hour. This recipe should make a dozen muffins.

Cheese Rolls

¾ cup grated American cheese	1 cup milk
2 cups flour	2 tablespoons butter or sub-stitute
4 teaspoons baking powder	1 teaspoon salt

Work flour into butter, add the other dry ingredients, then stir in the milk gradually. Mix well and add the grated cheese. Pat and roll to one-half inch thickness on a lightly floured board. Cut with round cookie cutter and bake in a greased pan for fifteen minutes in a hot oven.

French Rolls

4 cups flour	½ cup butter
1 cake compressed yeast	½ teaspoon salt
3 cups lukewarm water	1 egg
½ cup sugar	

Dissolve the yeast in a little warm water.
Beat the egg, and add to the dissolved yeast. Cream butter with the sugar. Add the flour and the rest of the warm water. Knead well. This should be a stiff dough; add more flour if necessary. Let stand in a warm place to rise. When bulk has doubled, turn out on a floured board. Roll or braid into small rolls; put into greased or floured pan and let rise again to double the bulk. Bake in a very hot hoven (400 degrees F.) for about fifteen minutes.
If kept in an icebox this dough will keep and requires only to be kneaded, risen and baked.

Parker House Rolls

1 quart sifted flour	1 teaspoon salt
½ ounce compressed yeast	1 tablespoon butter
1 cup warm milk	2 eggs
¼ cup sugar	2 large baked potatoes

Dissolve the yeast in a little warm milk.
Mix the butter, milk, salt and sugar. Crumble the potato while still hot and knead into flour, yeast and liquid ingredients. Roll out thin on a floured board and cut with a small round biscuit cutter. Fold over the finger so that edges lap. Set close to one another in a greased pan, allow to rise and then bake in a moderate oven (375 degrees F.) for fifteen minutes. Serve warm, with butter.

Light Rolls

1 medium size potato (mash)	¾ cup shortening
½ cup potato water	1 teaspoon salt
1 cup warm milk	6½ cups flour
1 cake yeast	⅓ cup sugar

Bake 20 minutes in a medium oven.

Potato Rolls

1 cup milk	2 eggs
1 cup mashed potatoes	1 yeast cake dissolved in hot
¾ cup sugar	water
¾ cup lard	5 cups flour
1 teaspoon salt	

Mix the potato, sugar, lard, and salt, and then add the milk (scalded). When lukewarm, add the eggs, yeast, and one cup of flour. Beat well, then let stand two hours in a warm place. Add four cups flour and let stand two more hours. Make into rolls, using as little flour as possible. Do not kneed. Let stand one hour and bake in hot oven.

Delicious Breakfast Rolls

4 cupfuls of flour	½ cupful of any kind of
2 teaspoonfuls baking	shortening
powder	Enough milk to make a stiff
¼ teaspoonful salt	dough
2½ tablespoonfuls sugar	

Sift the dry ingredients together. Cut in the shortening. Add the milk. Toss on a floured baking board, roll half an inch in thickness. Cut with biscuit cutter. Place a small piece of butter on each. Fold in half. Place in a slightly floured baking pan. Bake from fifteen to twenty minutes in a moderate oven.

Rye Bread Rolls

4 cups rye flour	1 tablespoon shortening
6 teaspoons baking powder	6 teaspoons caraway seed
1½ cups milk	1 teaspoon salt

Mix shortening and milk and add the sifted dry ingredients, using half the caraway seed. Turn out on a floured board and knead well. Shape into small rolls and arrange on a greased pan a few inches apart to allow for rising. Let stand for twenty minutes.

Paint with beaten yolk of egg; sprinkle caraway seed on top and bake in a hot oven for one-half hour until thoroughly baked.

Cornmeal Muffins

1 cup cornmeal   2 cups white flour
4 teaspoons baking powder   1/3 cup butter
2 eggs   1/2 cup sugar
1 cup milk   1/2 teaspoon salt

Sift the baking powder, flour, cornmeal, salt. Cream the butter with the sugar and add the beaten eggs whole. Beat all thoroughly and then add to the dry ingredients. Add the milk gradually. Bake in greased muffin tins for fifteen minutes in a hot oven.

Southern Corn Pone

2 cups yellow cornmeal   2 cups boiling water
2 teaspoons fat   1 teaspoon salt

Mix cornmeal, salt and melted fat. Pour on boiling water. Beat very well and allow to cool. Mold into thin cakes and bake in a hot oven (400 degrees F.) for one-half hour, until crisp and brown.

Serve warm with butter.

Oat Cakes

Mix 1 tablespoon butter, 1/2 teaspoon salt and 1/4 teaspoon baking soda with 1 cup boiling water. Stir in enough oatmeal to make a stiff dough. Knead well and roll out thin, cut into squares and bake on a frying pan or griddle. Dry out in a warm oven.

Serve with butter and syrup.

Graham Flour Muffins

1 cup graham flour	1 cup milk
½ cup white flour	1 egg
3½ teaspoons baking powder	¼ teaspoon salt

Beat the egg well. Sift the flour to remove any coarse bran flakes. Mix with salt and the baking powder. Add the egg and pour in enough milk to make a stiff batter, beat well and bake in buttered muffin tins for fifteen minutes in a hot oven.

Popovers

1⅓ cups milk	2 eggs
½ teaspoonful salt	1⅓ cups flour.
½ teaspoonful sugar	

Beat eggs thoroughly. Add sugar and salt. Slowly add one and one-third cups of milk and one and one-third cups of flour (the more you beat this the lighter it will get). Fill muffin pans half full, bake about thirty minutes. This makes twelve good-sized popovers.

Popovers

Sift one cup flour and ¼ teaspoon salt together. Beat one egg and add 1 cup milk to it. Stir this gradually into the flour to make a smooth thin batter.

Beat hard with an egg beater whipping in the air bubbles. The more beating, the higher the popovers will rise.

Fill greased, heated muffin pans half full of the batter. Bake in a very hot oven (450 degrees F.) for one-half hour, then reduce heat to about 350 degrees F. for fifteen minutes when popovers will be "popped" and brown.

Serve hot and at once, with butter and jam or honey.

Potato Flour Muffins

½ cup white potato flour	1 tablespoon sugar
3 teaspoons baking powder	¼ teaspoon salt
2 eggs	3 tablespoons ice water

Sift the flour and baking powder twice.

Beat the yolks, add the sugar and salt. Beat the whites until

very stiff. Add the beaten whites to the beaten yolks and add the dry ingredients.
Beat all together thoroughly and add the ice water last. Bake in greased muffin tins in a hot oven for fifteen minutes. Serve hot with butter.

Whole Wheat Muffins

½ cup whole wheat flour
1½ cups white wheat flour
3 teaspoons baking powder
1 tablespoon butter or substitute

1 egg
1 cup milk
½ cup brown sugar
½ teaspoon salt

Beat the yolk and add to the milk. Sift the dry ingredients and work into the butter. Stir all together until smooth.
Fold in the beaten white. Turn into heated, greased muffin pans and bake in a very hot oven (450 degrees F.) for fifteen minutes.

Scones

1 cup flour
½ teaspoon soda

½ cup buttermilk
¼ teaspoon salt

Mix the flour, salt and baking soda. Add enough sour milk to make a soft dough. Mix well.
Roll onto a lightly floured board to about ½ inch thickness. Cut round with a cookie cutter and bake on a griddle. Brown on both sides and serve hot with butter and jam.

Corn Muffins

2 cups corn meal
1 cup flour
2 tablespoons sugar
1 teaspoon salt
2 tablespoons sugar

1 cup sour milk
¼ teaspoon soda
3 tablespoons melted shortening
2 teaspoons baking powder

Pour ½ cup scalding water over corn meal. Let stand until cool. Mix all other ingredients with corn meal except flour and baking powder and beat well. Add flour and baking powder. Bake in hot oven until brown.

Raspberry Muffins

Three tablespoons of butter	½ teaspoon of salt
¾ cup of sugar	1 teaspoon of cinnamon
1 egg	1 teaspoon baking soda
1½ cups of flour	1 cup raspberries

Cream the shortening and sugar together. Add the beaten egg and milk alternately with the flour, salt, cinnamon and soda sifted together. Flour the raspberries with an additional two tablespoonfuls of flour, add them to the batter, and bake in greased muffin tins, in a hot oven for 25 minutes.

This mixture also makes delicious cakes for tea when baked in patty tins, or may be served as a sweet with lemon sauce.

Blueberry Muffins

Sift and mix thoroughly 1½ cups flour, 1 cup sugar, 2 teaspoonfuls baking powder. To the above then add 4 tablespoons melted butter, 2 eggs well beaten, 1 cup milk, and 1 box blueberries that have been dredged in ½ cup flour. Bake in hot oven 12 to 15 minutes.

Quick Muffins

8 tablespoons flour	1 egg
1 tablespoon sugar	1 cup milk
3 teaspoons baking powder	3 tablespoons melted butter
½ teaspoon salt	

Sift dry ingredients into mixing bowl; drop egg in center, add milk, a little at time, and beat until smooth. Add melted butter the last thing. Bake in greased muffin tins about fifteen minutes.

Dry Toast

Place slices of bread close to the flame in broiling oven. When golden brown on one side, turn and toast on other side. Serve hot with or without butter.

Melba Toast

Cut bread as thin as possible and toast very crisp. Serve with jelly at tea or dry with soup course.

Milk Toast

Melt two tablespoons of butter, add one tablespoon flour and brown. Stir in two cups of milk and one-half teaspoon salt. Stir and heat until this thickens slightly. Pour over slices of dry toast. Serve very hot.

Cinnamon Toast

Toast bread in broiling oven. Butter quickly and sprinkle on a mixture of one-third cinnamon and two-thirds sugar. Return to oven and allow sugar and butter to soak in. Serve with afternoon tea.

Sweet Milk Griddle Cakes

1 cup milk

1 egg

1 cup flour

2 teaspoons baking powder

1 teaspoon butter

¼ teaspoon salt

Beat the egg well, add the milk and the butter melted. Sift the flour, baking powder and salt and stir all together to make a smooth, thin batter. If batter is too stiff, add a little more milk.

Heat and grease an iron griddle. Spoon off batter into hot griddle. Bake until the cake is full of air bubbles, turn over with a pancake turner and brown on other side. Remove all drippings after each cake is browned and wipe griddle off with waxed paper or greased cloth.

Serve hot with butter and syrup.

Sour Milk Griddle Cakes

Mix 2½ cups of flour, ½ teaspoon salt and 1¼ teaspoons baking soda. Add 2 cups of sour milk, one beaten egg and 1 teaspoon butter. Beat all together to make smooth batter.

Spoon off batter onto a heated, greased iron griddle. Brown on one side and when filled with bubbles, turn and brown on other side.

Serve with butter and syrup or with butter and sugar.

Buckwheat Cakes

3½ cups buckwheat flour	1 quart water
½ cup white flour	1 teaspoon salt
½ ounce compressed yeast	1 teaspoon sugar
2 tablespoons molasses	

Dissolve the yeast in a little tepid water. Add the sugar and the rest of the water, also tepid. Mix with the buckwheat and white flours and salt to make a light batter.

Raise over night, add the molasses and bake on a greased, heated iron griddle browning well on both sides.

Serve steaming hot with butter and syrup or sugar.

Cheese Cookies

1 pkg. Philadelphia cream cheese	¼ lb. butter
	¼ cup sugar
Yolk one egg	1 cup flour

Cream butter and cheese with yolk of egg, flour and sugar and mix well—put in ice box over night. In morning, roll out, cut into shapes—spread each cookie with beaten white of egg—then cinnamon and sugar mixed together. Place a nut into each cookie and bake.

Crisp Corn Sticks

1 egg	¼ teaspoon salt
½ cup milk	1 tablespoon baking powder
2 tablespoons sugar	
¼ cup canned corn	2 tablespoons butter or other fat, melted
1 cup hard wheat or bread flour (measured after sifting)	

Beat the egg, add milk, sugar and canned corn, stir until well mixed. Measure the flour, salt and baking powder, add these ingredients through a sifter to the egg mixture. Mix well. Then add the melted fat. Beat until the ingredients are thoroughly blended. Grease bread-stick pans, fill each section of the pan about two-thirds full. Bake at 400 degrees for 25 minutes. Serve hot with soup or salads.

Yield: Twelve sticks, about seven inches long.

Rye Drop Cakes

1 egg, well beaten	½ level teaspoon salt
2/3 cup rye flour	½ cup milk
2½ teaspoons baking powder	2 tablespoons molasses

Sift together flour, baking powder and salt. Add gradually, milk, molasses and the egg. Drop by spoonfuls into new hot fat; drain on brown paper and serve hot.

Twenty Minute Coffee Cake

1 cup sour milk	2 tablespoons butter
½ teaspoon soda	1 cup sugar
2 cups flour	1¾ teaspoons baking powder
1 egg (well beaten)	½ teaspoon salt

Mix soda and milk. Add egg, salt, sugar, butter, flour, and beat very hard; then add baking powder. Sprinkle on top granulated sugar, cinnamon and bits of butter and nuts. Bake in moderate oven about 20 minutes.

Pfeffermisse (Pepper Nuts)

1 pound flour	1 nutmeg (grated)
1 pound sugar	1 teaspoon cinnamon
4 eggs	1 teaspoon cloves
3 ounces citron	1 teaspoon baking powder
1 ounce lemon rind	⅛ teaspoon salt

Beat eggs, add sugar, and then mix in spices, citron and lemon peel cut fine. Add flour, to which baking powder and salt have been added, and mix thoroughly. Drop by spoonful on cookie sheet and bake in a moderate oven for 15 minutes.

Cheese Dainties

½ pound cottage cheese	1 egg
1 box soda crackers	1 tablespoon water

Spread some of the cheese, about one-quarter inch thick, between two buttered crackers. Beat egg and add water. Dip sandwich in egg. Butter pan and fry until brown on both sides.

Philadelphia Cream Cheese Cookies

½ pound sweet butter
2 cakes Philadelphia cream
    cheese, creamed with the
    butter

2 cups flour
2 tablespoons sugar
2 teaspoons baking powder

Mix and sift dry ingredients and work into cheese and butter.
Roll out to ¼ inch, top with poppy seed or cottage cheese or
prune jam. Bake in quick oven 20 minutes.

Pimento Sandwich Filling

(1) Chop fine ¼ pound
      cheese
    1 can pimentos and
    2 hard boiled eggs

(2) ½ cup cream
    1 egg beaten
    3 tablespoons vinegar
    1 heaping tablespoon
      sugar and flour
    A little butter and salt

Cook in double boiler until it thickens, then add to part (1)
while hot.

Pop-Overs

1 cup flour
1 cup milk
½ teaspoon salt

2 eggs
1 tablespoon melted butter

Mix salt and flour, stir in milk gradually, add eggs beaten until
light, add butter, beat two minutes using egg beater.
Bake 30 minutes in very hot buttered pans.

Potato Doughnuts

Cream three tablespoons of butter, add three-fourths cup of
sugar, the yolks of three eggs and one white—one cup of
freshly mashed potatoes, one-fourth cup of milk, two and one-
half cups of flour, three teaspoons of baking powder, one-half
teaspoon of salt; flavor with grated nutmeg.

Cream the butter, add sugar, then the eggs; stir in the potato which has been lightened with the egg white, beaten stiff. Add milk and flour gradually. Chill on ice before rolling out. The less flour used, the more moist will be the doughnuts.

Cheese Straws

2 cups sifted pastry flour	1 egg
2 teaspoons baking powder	½ cup milk
1 teaspoon salt	¾ cup dry grated cheese
½ cup butter	
¼ teaspoon paprika or red pepper	

Mix flour, salt, baking powder and red pepper and sift three times. Put in mixing bowl, chop in butter and drop in egg without beating. Add cheese and milk and mix together; turn out on molding board; roll out ⅛ inch thick; cut 4 inches long and ¼ inch wide sticks. Bake in moderate oven until light brown.

Cheese Turn-Overs

2 packages cream cheese   ½ pound butter

Mix well. Knead in 2 cups sifted flour. Let stand in cold place several hours or over night. Roll out thin. Cut in squares. Put jam in center and turn over. Bake about 15 minutes.

Pancake

Beat two eggs well. Add ¾ cup flour, one cup sweet milk and ½ teaspoon salt. Heat spider in the oven, melt 2 tablespoons butter in it and pour in the batter.

Return to hot oven, allow to bake for twenty minutes, gradually lessening heat. Serve quickly on hot platter with sugar, cinnamon and lemon juice sprinkled on top.

German Pancakes

½ cup milk
½ cup flour
3 eggs

2 tablespoons butter
½ teaspoon salt

Use a ten inch spider.

Beat the eggs thoroughly with a whirling egg beater. Add the flour, salt and milk beating all the while.

Take a cold spider, spread on butter, turn in the batter and bake in a hot oven for one-half hour gradually reducing heat. The pancake should behave much like a large popover. It should puff up and become brown and crisp, but will fall upon being removed from the oven.

Place on a hot plate and serve with sugar, apple sauce or lemon juice.

French Pancakes

3 eggs
1 cup flour
1 tablespoon butter

1½ cups milk
½ teaspoon salt

Beat the eggs well. Add the milk and then the sifted flour and salt. Heat an iron spider, melt one teaspoon butter into spider, spoon in a little batter and allow to spread thin over spider. When brown turn with a pancake turner and brown other side.

Spread thin jelly on each pancake, roll up and sprinkle with powdered sugar. Serve hot as breakfast or lunch dish.

Potato Pancakes

6 raw potatoes

Peel potatoes and soak two hours in cold water. Grate and drain. Beat two eggs and mix with about two tablespoons flour, one teaspoon salt and ⅛ teaspoon baking powder. Moisten with a little milk and beat up with grated potatoes. This will make a thin batter.

Spoon onto a hot greased spider. When pancakes brown, turn with a pancake turner and brown on other side. Serve hot with sugar or apple sauce.

Squash Pancakes

Wash the squash, remove the seeds, and then grate the squash. To one grated squash weighing about ½ pound, add ½ cup water, ½ cup flour, one egg, and a little salt. Mix thoroughly and drop on a well greased skillet with a spoon. This will make between fifteen and twenty medium sized pancakes. Sprinkle these pancakes with a little sugar before serving.

Rice Waffles

4 eggs	1¼ pints of flour
1 teacup boiled rice	1 tablespoon butter
1¼ pints of milk	2 teaspoons baking powder

Beat eggs, whites and yolks together until very light. Stir in a teacup of boiled rice, then the milk; sift the flour and add gradually the butter (melted) and the baking powder. Bake in greased waffle iron.

Waffles

1 cup sour cream	1/3 cup butter
¼ cup flour	4 eggs
½ teaspoon salt	

Cream the butter, add yolks of eggs one by one, then slowly the flour and the sour cream. Stir well and when well mixed, fold in egg whites beaten stiff and a little vanilla.
Heat and grease the waffle iron.

Spoon off batter into center of each section of the waffle iron, allow to run, bake first on one side, turn iron and bake on other side. Remove drippings and crumbs after each waffle is made.

Serve hot with syrup.

Aluminum waffle irons do not require greasing.

No. 2

1 cup sweet milk	2 eggs
1½ cups flour	1/3 cup butter
1½ teaspoons baking powder	½ teaspoon salt

Separate and beat the eggs. Melt the butter. Sift flour and salt with baking powder. Add to egg yolks. Fold in the beaten white and bake in a greased waffle iron.

To Make Syrup from Maple Sugar

Break up the maple sugar, place in a saucepan and cover with boiling water. Heat over flame, stir only until the sugar has entirely dissolved, then boil until a clear amber color and cool for use on griddle cakes and waffles.

English Muffins

4 cups flour	3 tablespoons butter
1 cake compressed yeast	1 teaspoon salt
2 cups hot milk	

Dissolve the yeast in a little warm milk.

Cool milk and when lukewarm, add butter and salt. Mix with yeast paste. Mix the flour with this liquid and let stand for several hours in a warm place.

Grease a dozen muffin rings. Fill the rings half full of the batter. As dough starts to rise place muffins with rings on heated, greased griddle. Let bake slowly.

When golden brown, turn with a pancake turner and bake slowly on other side until done. Do not bake too well. When cool, split in two, toast on the cut side, butter generously and serve with marmalade or honey or maple syrup.

Italian Bread Sticks

4 cups flour	¼ cup butter
1 cake compressed yeast	2 tablespoons sugar
½ teaspoon salt	1 white of egg
1 cup hot milk	

Dissolve yeast in warm milk.

Add butter, sugar and salt to the milk; cool and add flour, beaten white of egg and dissolved yeast.

Knead well, stand in warm place and allow to rise. Roll with the flat of the hand into long thin sticks. Place in a floured pan quite a distance apart and just before baking, brush with beaten yolk of egg. Let stand to rise, then bake until very crisp in a hot oven (400 degrees F.).

Tea Biscuits

1 ounce compressed yeast	2 tablespoons sugar
1 cup milk	1/2 cup butter
2 eggs	1 1/2 teaspoons salt
1 1/2 cups flour	

Dissolve yeast in a little lukewarm milk.

Add flour to milk and pour over yeast paste. Beat well. Allow to stand in a warm place. Add beaten eggs, sugar, salt and butter. More flour may have to be added in order to knead the dough. Knead well and allow to stand and rise. Shape into narrow rolls and line up close together in floured pan.

Bake in a hot oven for fifteen minutes.

Rice Cakes

2 cups hot boiled rice	2 cups flour
2 eggs	3 teaspoons baking powder
1 pint milk	1 teaspoon salt

Mix flour, baking powder and salt. Beat the yolks and add to the milk; add the dry ingredients and beat well. Fold in the stiff whites and prepare as griddle cakes.

Serve hot with butter, sugar or jelly.

Drop Doughnuts

Beat three eggs until light, gradually add one cup sugar, then one cup boiled and cooled milk, one teaspoon vanilla.

Fold in the following dry ingredients: (sifted four times).

3 cups flour
2 heaping teaspoons baking powder
1 teaspoon salt

Drop by spoonful in hot fat and fry till brown. Sift powdered sugar over them.

CANDY

Fudge

Grat four squares chocolate, add to one pound powdered sugar, with one tablespoon butter and a small can of evaporated milk. Bring to boiling point and boil for ten minutes, stirring constantly to prevent sticking. Remove from fire and add the contents of a small can (five ounces) marshmallow whip—beating until creamy. Pour into a buttered pan and mark in squares when cool.

Cream Caramels

2 cups sugar	2 cups evaporated milk
2 cups corn syrup	1 teaspoon vanilla
½ cup butter	¼ teaspoon salt

Put sugar, syrup, salt and butter into sauce pan and place on fire. Stir till it boils to a clear thick consistency; stir in gradually so as not to stop boiling the evaporated milk. Stir constantly, cook to the firm ball stage. Add vanilla and pour into buttered pans. When cold, cut and wrap in waxed paper. Makes two pounds.

Nut Caramels

Mix together—

1 cup granulated sugar	1 ounce of bitter chocolate
1 cup white syrup	(small pieces)
½ pint sweet cream	1 tablespoon butter
Pinch of salt	

Boil for ten minutes, stirring almost constantly, as chocolate burns quickly; do not beat, however, as this will make it granular. Add gradually another half pint of cream, until a few drops of the syrup in cold water form a rather firm ball, that is, just a little firmer than the soft-ball stage. Add vanilla and half a cupful of nut meats before removing from fire. Pour into small buttered tin so that layer will be three-quarters of an inch thick.

It is best not to cut this candy until twelve hours after cooking. Cut in squares and wrap in wax paper.

Nut Creams

3 cups granulated sugar   1 cup broken nut meats
1 cup rich cream   ½ teaspoon vanilla

Boil sugar and cream over slow fire, stirring frequently. Remove from fire and place pan in cold water. When cool add nut meats and beat until creamy. Turn into an oiled pan and cut in squares.

Peanut Butter Fudge

2 cups sugar   3 tablespoons peanut butter
1 tablespoon cocoa   1 rounded teaspoon butter
3 tablespoons white syrup   2/3 cup milk

Mix sugar and cocoa; add syrup and milk. Boil till it forms a soft ball in water. Remove from fire and let cool for about three minutes. Add butter and peanut butter and beat till thick. Pour in greased pans to cool and cut in squares.

Bologna Candy

2 cups sugar   ½ cup cocoanut
1 cup milk   ½ cup nuts
1 package dates

Boil sugar and milk until it forms a soft ball in cold water. Now add dates (which have been stoned and halved). Continue cooking until it leaves pan behind spoon while being stirred. Stir in nuts and cocoanut. Let cool. Pour out on cloth that has been wrung out of cold water, and roll up in the form of a bologna sausage. This is where it gets the name.

Peanut Bread

½ cup sugar
1 egg (beaten)
1 cup sweet milk
2 heaping teaspoons baking
    powder

1 cup nuts or ⅔ cup pea-
    nut butter
2½ cups flour

Cream sugar, egg and peanuts or peanut butter, then add milk and flour alternatively. Bake about 40 minutes. This is excellent bread for the children's luncheon.

Nut Candy

Use walnuts, peanuts, pecans or a mixture of nuts. After removal from shells, place on bottom of pans, previously greased, to the depth of about half an inch.
Boil two pounds of brown sugar, a half pint of water, and one gill of good molasses until a portion of the mass hardens when cooled. Pour the hot syrup on the meats and allow to remain until hard.

Penocha

1 cup brown sugar
1 cup white sugar
½ cup milk
1 tablespoon butter

1 tablespoon vanilla
1 cup walnut meats
Speck of salt

Boil all the ingredients, except the nuts, in a saucepan until a drop forms a soft ball in cold water. Remove from the flame, add the nuts and heat the mixture until thick and creamy. Pour into greased pan and allow to harden. Break into pieces.

Peanut Butter Candy

2 cups sugar   ½ cup milk

Cook seven minutes from time it begins to boil. Remove from fire. Add two heaping tablespoons peanut butter. Beat until it begins to thicken. Pour on buttered platter, cool, and cut in squares.

Sea Foam

2 cups granulated sugar   1 cup walnuts, broken up
½ cup cold water   1 teaspoon vanilla
⅓ cup white corn syrup   Pinch salt
2 egg whites, beaten stiff

Boil sugar, water and corn syrup until it forms ball in cold water. Have beaten egg whites and salt ready in large mixing bowl; slowly pour on boiling mixture, beating rapidly. Continue beating until mixture begins to granulate around sides of bowl. Add vanilla, then nuts. Turn out on buttered dinner plate and spread in circular motions with back of spoon, leaving it rough and foamy. Place in ice box for 20 to 30 minutes before serving.

CHEESE DISHES

Cheese is a cheap substitute for meat in the diet. It contains protein and fat and also the calcium of the milk from which it is made.

It is also valuable as a change from meat because of its sharp flavoring. For this reason it is used largely with such relatively tasteless foods as rice, spaghetti and bread.

Cheese is very highly concentrated and very tightly bound; therefore, do not use too often or in too great quantity.

Cheese Toast

½ cake cream cheese
1 snappy cheese
¼ teaspoon paprika
¼ teaspoon salt

1 tablespoon Worcester-
  shire sauce
12 slices bacon
2 eggs
6 slices of bread

Cream the two kinds of cheese together and add the seasoning. Beat the eggs lightly and mix with the cheese. Cut the bread thick and trim the edges a very little. Spread the cheese mixture thick on the bread and lay on each piece, two slices of raw bacon.

Brown in a hot oven until the bacon is crisp.

Cheese Souffle

3 tablespoons butter
2 tablespoons flour
½ cup milk
½ cup grated cheese

4 eggs
¼ teaspoon salt
Paprika

Heat the flour and butter in a double boiler. Stir in the milk, cheese and seasoning. Cook slowly to a creamy smooth consistency.

Beat the yolks of the eggs and add the mixture. Cool, then add the stiffly beaten whites.

Turn into a greased baking dish and bake in a moderate oven for forty-five minutes.

Serve at once so that the souffle will not fall.

Monkey

1 cup milk
1 cup bread crumbs
1 tablespoon butter

½ cup cheese, in pieces
1 egg
Salt and pepper

Soak the bread crumbs in milk. Melt the butter in a double boiler and then melt the cheese into it. Add the soaked bread crumbs, the beaten egg and the seasoning.

Cook through for a few minutes and serve on crisp crackers or toast.

Cheese Fondue

1 cup cheese
3 eggs
1 cup crumbs
1 cup milk

1 tablespoon butter
½ teaspoon salt
Mustard and pepper

Grate the cheese and mix with the beaten egg. Add the crumbs, milk and season.

Add butter melted.

Turn into a greased baking dish and bake in a moderate oven for fifteen minutes. Serve immediately. Very good with salad.

Italian Gnocchi

¼ cup butter
¼ cup flour
¼ cup cornstarch
2 cups milk

2 eggs
1 cup grated cheese
¼ teaspoon salt

Melt the butter and add the flour, cornstarch and salt. Stir in the milk and boil all together for five minutes, stirring continually to keep smooth.

Add the beaten egg, the salt and the grated cheese. Cook for a minute and turn into a low greased pan to cool.

Cut into small rounds with a cookie cutter, about one and one-half inches across. Arrange in a flat glass baking dish; sprinkle with grated cheese and brown in a hot oven.

Gnocchi

In a double boiler, boil 1 cup of farina, in a quart of rich milk, about 2 hours. Turn out in a bread pan mould, and let stand till cold and firm. Cut in thin slices.

Put a layer of this farina in a buttered baking dish, and a thick layer of grated cheese; add a second and third layer of farina and cheese and cover the top layer with plenty of grated cheese, and bake till the cheese melts and the top gets nice and brown.

The amount of cheese required is 1 pound of Swiss and ½ pound of yellow American cheese.

Corn and Cheese Souffle

½ green pepper chopped	1 cup chopped fresh corn
1 tablespoon butter	1 cup grated cheese
1 tablespoon flour	3 eggs
1½ cups milk	Salt and pepper

Simmer the chopped peppers and butter in a saucepan. When peppers are tender, add the flour mixed with the milk. Add the corn, cheese and seasoning, cooking all for ten minutes.

Beat the yolks of the eggs and add, heat a minute longer and remove from the flame. Beat the whitess tiff and add to the mixture. Set a baking pan into water in the oven, turn in the mixture and bake for half an hour at 350 degrees F.

Welsh Rarebit

1 pound cheese	Speck pepper
¼ teaspoon salt	½ cup water
¼ teaspoon paprika	1 teaspoon Worcestershire
¼ teaspoon dry mustard	Sauce

Use fresh cheese and cut into small pieces. Melt the cheese slowly in a double boiler. Do not have the water in the boiler boil but merely simmer. When cheese is melted add the seasoning and stir in the cold water and the Worcestershire Sauce.

Cook until smooth. Spread over crisped crackers or better, over crisp toast.

Combination Sandwich

Creamed roquefort cheese   White bread
White meat of chicken

Trim the crust from the buttered bread. Place a lettuce leaf on one slice and lay sliced white meat of chicken on it.

Cream the roquefort cheese with a tablespoon butter, paprika and a dash of Worcestershire Sauce. Spread this paste on the other slice of bread. Close together as a sandwich and toast each side.

Serve while the toast is still hot.

Club Sandwich

Directions given are for each sandwich.
3 slices hot buttered toast
3 leaves crisp lettuce
2 slices white meat of chicken
2 slices tomato
2 strips crisp bacon
1 tablespoon thick mayonnaise to which add a dash of dry mustard.

Put a lettuce leaf, a slice of chicken and a slice of tomato on one piece of toast. Spread mayonnaise on the tomato. Cover with another slice of toast. Lay on top of it, one leaf of lettuce, the bacon, chicken and tomato. Spread with mayonnaise and cover with the third piece of toast.

Hold together with toothpicks, if necessary. Serve while toast is hot and garnish with radishes, ripe olive and a sweet pickle.

Pastry

DESSERTS

Cakes and Cookies

Plain Cake

1/3 cup butter or shortening
1 cup sugar
2 eggs

1¾ cups flour
1¾ teaspoons baking
  powder
½ cup milk
1 teaspoon vanilla

Cream the butter and the sugar. Add the eggs, well beaten.
Sift the dry ingredients together and add alternating with
the milk. Add the vanilla and bake in layers for twenty
minutes in a moderate oven (375 degrees F.).

Fill and frost as desired. This recipe may be modified by adding nuts, cocoanut, spices, etc., and by frosting in an attractive way.

Plain Pound Cake

1 pound butter
1 pound sugar
1 pound flour

10 eggs
1 cup milk
½ teaspoon salt

Cream the butter and the sugar thoroughly together. Add
the well-beaten eggs. Sift the dry ingredients together and
add with the milk. Pour into buttered bread pan and bake
in a slow oven (320 degrees F.) for an hour and a quarter.

Fruit-Nut Loaf Cake

Add ¼ cup chopped blanched almonds, ¼ cup dried currants, ¼ cup chopped candied citron to the recipe for Pound

Cake. Trim the top with whole blanched almonds arranged in a pattern and bake with a paper cover for the last half hour of the baking.

Cocoanut Cake

2 cups flour
1 cup milk
½ cup butter

1 cup sugar
2 eggs
2 teaspoons baking powder

Cream sugar and butter, add slightly beaten eggs. Stir thoroughly. Add milk and beat together. Add sifted flour and baking powder mixed. Pour into buttered pans and bake in moderate oven twenty-five to thirty minutes.

Uncooked Icing

2 tablespoons butter
1 teaspoon vanilla

2 tablespoons cream

Enough powdered sugar to make desired consistency (about 2 cups).

Quick Coffee Cake

1½ cups sifted flour
2 teaspoons baking powder
½ teaspoon salt
¼ teaspoon mace or nutmeg

6 teaspoons sugar
2 teaspoons shortening
1 egg
½ cup milk or water

Sift dry ingredients, cut in shortening, add unbeaten egg and milk and stir to a smooth dough. Turn in a shallow pan and cover with top mixture.

Mixture to be sprinkled over the top of the dough before baking:

4 tablespoons sugar
2 tablespoons flour

1 teaspoon butter
¼ teaspoon mace or nutmeg

With a fork mix all ingredients thoroughly, scatter over top of coffee cake and bake in a hot oven over 400 degrees twenty-five minutes.

White Cake

½ cup butter
1¾ cups granulated sugar
¾ cup milk
¼ cup hot water
½ teaspoon almond flavoring

3 cups pastry flour
4 teaspoons baking powder
6 egg whites
1 teaspoon vanilla

Cream the butter, adding the sugar and a tablespoon of milk. Cream very well. Sift the flour and baking powder together several times for lightness. Pour the hot water on the milk and add the flour and milk mixture to the creamed butter, beating constantly. Add the almond and vanilla flavors.
Beat the whites stiff and fold into the batter.
Line two deep square pans with waxed paper and pour in the batter. Start in a low oven and when the cake has risen, increase the heat and bake for about three-quarter hour longer until the cake is done.

Frost and fill with caramel, white or fudge frosting. Or fill with jelly and frost with thin white icing

Orange Layer Cake

1½ cups sugar
½ cup butter or shortening
2 eggs
Juice and grated rind of one
  orange

2 teaspoons baking powder
3 cups pastry flour
½ teaspoon salt
¼ teaspoon soda
1 cup water

Cream the butter with the sugar; add the beaten eggs. Add one teaspoon grated rind of orange.
Add to the foregoing, the sifted flour, salt and baking powder. Dissolve the soda in the cup of boiling water and alternating with the orange juice add to the mixture. Stir until creamy. Bake in greased layer pans for twenty minutes in a moderate oven.

Top and Filling for Cake

Beat stiff the whites of two eggs and add two cups confectioners' sugar. Add the juice of two large oranges and the grated peel of one. Stir together well and spread thick over top and layers.

Chocolate Fudge Cake

1 cup butter	5 teaspoons baking powder
2 cups sugar	1/4 teaspoon salt
4 eggs	1 cup milk
3 cups flour	4 squares chocolate

Cream the butter and sugar. Separate the eggs and beat the yolks well and the whites stiff. Add the yolks to the butter and sugar. Sift the flour, baking powder and salt and add alternating with the milk.

Melt the chocolate and add. Fold in the beaten whites and bake in three layers in a moderate oven (350 degrees F.).

Frost with a thick fudge frosting. This makes a very rich cake.

Devils Food Nut Cake

2 squares bitter chocolate	1/4 cup shortening
2 cups brown sugar	1/2 cup sour milk
1/2 cup water	2 cups pastry flour
1 egg yolk	1/4 teaspoon salt
1 cup chopped nuts	1 teaspoon soda
2 whole eggs	1 teaspoon vanilla

Cook the chocolate, one-half cup brown sugar, cold water, and the egg yolk in a double boiler, stirring constantly until the mixture thickens. Add the nuts and stand aside to cool.

Cream the shortening and the remaining one and one-half cups sugar; add the well beaten eggs.

Sift the flour, salt and soda and add to the sugar mixture, alternating with the sour milk.

Stir together well and add vanilla. Last add the chocolate nut mixture and pour into a greased and floured cake pan. Bake for three-quarters hour in a moderate oven (350 degrees F.).

Lady Baltimore Cake

3 cups cake flour	1/2 cup butter
3 teaspoons baking powder	1/2 cup milk
Whites of three eggs	1/2 cup water
1/4 teaspoon salt	1 1/2 cups sugar

Sift baking powder, salt and flour three times. Cream butter and gradually add sugar until thoroughly mixed. Add the flour and milk alternately, stirring until smooth. Stir in one teaspoon vanilla and one-quarter teaspoon almond flavoring. Beat the whites stiff and fold in.

Bake in layers in a moderate oven (350 degrees F.).

Filling and Frosting

Make a syrup of two cups sugar and three-quarters cup water; cook to the soft ball stage. Pour over the whites of two eggs beaten stiff; beat until the mixture stands. Retain one-third for cake icing.

Grind one-quarter pound figs or dates with one-half pound raisins and one-half pound nut meats. Add the ground fruits and nuts to remaining two-thirds of mixture.

Spread between layers and on top of cake. Frost entire cake with plain icing.

Delicate Cake

½ cup butter   ½ cup milk
1½ cups sugar   4 egg whites
2 cups flour   2 teaspoons baking powder

Mix and sift the dry ingredients. Cream the shortening and sugar and add flour and milk alternately. Fold in the well beaten egg whites and bake in a thin sheet in a moderate oven 25 minutes.

Caramel Pineapple Cake (Skillet Cake)

Put three tablespoonsful of butter and a cupful of brown sugar in an iron frying pan. Let it simmer for a few minutes. Then add sliced canned pineapple just to fit pan. A medium pan requires about seven slices around and one in the middle. Then make a batter of three eggs, one and a half cups of sugar, one-half cup water, one teaspoon vanilla, a pinch of salt, one and a half teaspoons baking powder, one and a half cups flour.

Pour this batter over the pineapple; put frying pan into oven, leaving it in a hot oven for ten minutes; reduce heat and bake about fifty minutes. Turn out of the pan on a large plate. Serve with whipped cream.

Eggless Spice Cake

3 cups pastry flour
1 cup sugar
3 teaspoons baking powder
½ teaspoon salt
1 teaspoon cinnamon
½ teaspoon allspice

1 teaspoon mace
1 teaspoon cloves
½ cup liquid fat
1¼ cups water
1 teaspoon vanilla

Sift together all dry ingredients. Add liquid fat with water and vanilla and stir until well mixed. Bake in layers in a moderately hot oven 20 minutes; in a loaf in a moderate oven 45 minutes.

Fig Cake

1 cup sugar
½ cup butter
2 eggs
1 cup raisins

½ pound figs
1 teaspoon soda
1 cup of boiling water
2 cups flour

Cream butter and sugar, add eggs. Put figs and raisins through food chopper and add to boiling water; add soda; add pinch of nutmeg and cinnamon. Add flour. Bake in two layers in moderate oven.

Hasty Cake

1 cup sugar
1½ cups flour
2 teaspoons baking powder
¼ teaspoon salt
¼ cup melted butter or
  shortening

2 eggs
Milk
½ teaspoon vanilla

Mix sugar, flour, baking powder and salt together. Put butter in measuring cup, add the eggs and fill cup with milk. Add liquid to the dry ingredients and mix well. Pour into an oblong pan. Bake in a hot oven (400° Fahrenheit) 20 minutes. Cool and cover with any quick frosting.

Walnut Torte

7 eggs   ½ lb. ground walnut meats
7 tablespoonfuls sugar   Pinch of salt

Beat egg yolks till light. Add sugar, salt and ground walnuts. Stir. Beat egg whites till stiff and add to mixture. Mix all together and bake in slow oven 50 minutes. When cold serve with whipped cream. This recipe will serve 6 persons.

Eggless Chocolate Cake

2 squares chocolate   1 cup milk
1 cup sugar   1½ cups flour
1 tablespoon melted short-   1 teaspoon vanilla
  ening   ⅓ teaspoon salt
1 teaspoon soda

Dissolve the soda in a half cup of milk. Grate the chocolate and melt in the remainder of the milk. Mix together the sugar and shortening, add vanilla, salt, the soda dissolved in the milk, and the flour; beat thoroughly. Then beat in the milk, still hot, in which the chocolate has been melted. Bake in a loaf about fifty minutes in a moderate oven. This cake will keep moist for several days.

Apple-Sauce Torte

4 eggs   2 cups apple-sauce (un-
1 can evaporated milk   sweetened)
Juice of 1 lemon   ½ cup melted butter

Mix yolks of eggs, apple-sauce, lemon juice and milk together; add stiffly beaten whites. Line sides and bottom of torte pan with one package of ground graham crackers, mixed with scant cup melted butter. Bake in a slow oven.
Reserve some of the graham cracker mixture to sprinkle on top of cake. Serve with whipped cream.

Scotch Chocolate Cake

½ cup butter or shortening
1½ cups sugar
2 eggs
1 square chocolate dissolved
  in ½ cup of boiling water

½ cup sour milk
1 teaspoon soda, mixed with
  2 cups of flour
1 teaspoon vanilla

Bake in sheet or two layers about thirty minutes.

Graham Cracker Cake

½ pound graham crackers
  crush to powder form
½ cup butter
½ cup sugar
1½ teaspoons baking pow-
  der

Pinch soda
2 eggs
¾ cup sour milk
2 teaspoons vanilla

Cream butter, add crushed crackers, baking powder and soda, sugar; add egg yolks, stir; add sour milk. Stir constantly; add beaten egg whites, and vanilla. Pour in buttered cake tin; place in oven; bake.

Eggless Spice Cake

3 cups pastry flour
1 cup sugar
3 teaspoons baking powder
½ teaspoon salt
1 teaspoon cinnamon
½ teaspoon allspice

1 teaspoon mace
1 teaspoon cloves
½ cup melted shortening
1¼ cups water
1 teaspoon vanilla

Sift together all dry ingredients. Add shortening with water and vanilla and stir until well mixed. Bake in layers in a moderately hot oven (375 degrees) 20 minutes; in a loaf in a moderate oven (350 degrees) 45 minutes. When cool spread with maple icing:

1 tablespoon hot coffee
3 tablespoons maple syrup

Few drops of vanilla
Confectioners sugar

Mix together coffee, syrup and vanilla and beat in confectioners sugar until stiff enough to spread.

Caramel Cake

½ cupful butter
¾ cupful sugar
4 egg yolks, beaten light
Second ¾ cupful sugar
4 teaspoons baking powder

¼ teaspoon salt
1 cup milk
1 teaspoon vanilla
4 egg whites, stiffly beaten
4 cups flour

Cream shortening with ¾ cup sugar. Beat egg yolks until light and add second ¾ cup sugar, beating well. Add the egg and sugar mixture to that of the shortening and sugar, mixing well. Sift the flour, add the baking powder and salt and sift three times. Add this flour mixture and the milk alternately to the first mixture. Then add vanilla extract. Fold in the egg whites and bake in two layer cake pans in a moderate oven, 350° F. Put the layers together and cover cake with a caramel frosting.

1-2-3-4 Cake

1 cup butter
2 cups sugar
3 cups flour
4 eggs

1 cup sour cream
1 teaspoon soda
Spices

Cream butter and sugar; add eggs and stir until creamy. Add the sour cream and soda dissolved in cream and lastly the flour containing the spices.

Malted Milk Cake

Cream one-half cup butter, add one cup sugar gradually. Beat in one egg; then add three heaping teaspoons chocolate malted milk, one-half teaspoon vanilla, one-fourth teaspoon salt. Add one teaspoon soda to one cup sour milk and then add alternately with two cups sifted flour to the first mixture. Bake in buttered layer-cake pans. Put together and cover with white icing.

Banana Cream Cake

⅔ cup shortening
1½ cups sugar
2 eggs
1 cup mashed bananas

4 tablespoons of sour milk
2 cups flour
1 teaspoon soda
½ cup chopped walnuts

Cream shortening; add sugar gradually and cream again; add unbeaten eggs one at a time, beating thoroughly after each addition. Then add mashed bananas with sour milk; stir well. Fold in sifted dry ingredients and bake in layers in hot oven, 375 degrees F., 20 to 25 minutes. Makes 2 layers.

Poppyseed Cake

1 cup poppyseed
1½ cups milk
1½ cups sugar
½ cup butter

2 cups flour
2 teaspoons baking powder
4 whites of eggs, beaten
1 teaspoon vanilla

Grind poppyseed. Heat ½ of the milk; pour over poppyseed and let stand over night. Cream butter and sugar and add the poppyseed mixture. Add flour and baking powder mixed alternately with milk. Add the beaten whites and flavor. Turn in a well greased spring form and bake in moderate oven forty-five minutes.

Ginger Cake

½ cup sugar
½ cup dark molasses
Lard, size of an egg
1 egg
⅛ teaspoon salt

1 scant teaspoon soda
1 scant teaspoon ginger
1 large cup of flour
¾ cup boiling water

Add melted lard to sugar, then molasses and soda and beaten egg. Sift flour, salt and ginger and add the boiling water last. Bake in moderate oven about 25 or 30 minutes. (The mixture before baking is very thin.)

Pound Cake

1 cup butter   1¼ cups sugar

Cream butter and add sugar gradually, creaming mixture well. Add the yolks of four eggs, then the whites to which has been added 1 level teaspoon cream tartar; then add ½ cup of milk; then 2½ cups pastry flour; sift it three times with ½ level teaspoon baking soda.

1 teaspoon vanilla.

Bake in a slow oven about one hour.

Old Fashioned Raisin Cake

½ cup butter
1 heaping cup sugar
⅓ cup sour cream or milk
2 eggs
2 cups flour
2 level teaspoons b a k i n g powder

1 cup raisins
½ teaspoon vanilla
¼ teaspoon mace
¼ teaspoon cinnamon
¼ teaspoon ginger
¼ teaspoon soda in milk

Bake in square pan, in moderate oven, one hour.

Old Fashioned Hickorynut Cake

Cream together three-fourths of a cupful of butter and two cupfuls of light "C" sugar; add to this mixture one cupful of cold water, the well beaten yolks of four eggs, half a teaspoonful each of ground cinnamon and mace, and three cupfuls of flour into which has been sifted three teaspoonfuls of baking powder, and one-half teaspoonful of salt. Now add the stiffly beaten whites of the eggs, folding them in very carefully. Take two cupfuls of blanched hickorynut meats, chop them very fine, roll them in flour, and add gradually to the mixture, stirring well all the time. Pour into a loaf cake tin, cover with browned flour for the first half hour it is in the oven, or better still, with a piece of oiled paper—this merely to prevent its becoming too brown, before well done. Let bake for

an hour. When cool turn out of the tin, cover with boiled
icing, and decorate with whole nut kernels.

Would advise the using of oiled paper, rather than the flour,
for preventing its becoming brown too soon. There is danger
of the flour sinking into the batter and spoiling the delicacy
of the cake.

Date and Walnut Torte

6 eggs ½ pound dates (cut fine)
½ pound powdered sugar 2 tablespoons flour
1 cup walnuts (chopped) 1 teaspoon baking powder

Beat eggs very light and add sugar, nuts and dates. Lastly add
the flour mixed with baking powder. Bake in a slow oven,
one hour. Serve with whipped cream.

Fudge Cake

1 cup butter 1 teaspoon vanilla
2 cups of granulated sugar 1 cup of pecan nuts (cut
4 eggs fine)
3 squares of Baker's choco- 2 cups of flour
late

Mix in order given and bake in sheet pan on wax paper. Cut
in squares while hot, pieces to be about two inches square
and one and one-half inches thick.

Dorbas Torte

5 eggs 5 tablespoons flour
4 tablespoons powdered Pinch of salt
sugar

Beat the yolks with the sugar for half an hour, using a wood
spoon. Beat the whites stiff and add. Then the flour and salt
sifted together.

Mix all thoroughly.

Grease the outside bottom of a cake tin and bake the dough
in very thin layers, as many layers as possible, for ten minutes
or less in a moderate oven. The length of time for baking
depends on the thickness of the layer.

Cream one and one-half pounds unsalted butter with one and one-half cups confectioners sugar. Add the beaten yolks of two eggs and one quarter pound grated sweet chocolate. Stir into a smooth paste. Spread between the thin layers until it is all used.

Cover with a glaze made by cooking one cup brown sugar with one-quarter cup boiling water until it forms a brittle string when tested in cold water. Spread over the top and sides with a knife dipped in cold water.

Keep the torte cold until ready to serve.

Spice Cake

½ cup butter
1 cup sugar
2 eggs
2½ cups flour
¼ teaspoon salt
½ teaspoon ginger
¼ teaspoon ground nut-
  meg
¼ teaspoon ground cloves

½ teaspoon cinnamon
1 teaspoon chopped can-
  died citron
1 teaspoon grated lemon
  rind
½ cup raisins
½ cup currants
¾ cup milk
½ teaspoon soda

Cream the sugar with the butter. Add the beaten eggs. Sift a little flour over the fruit and sift the rest with the spices and salt. Add the spices and salt and flour to the egg-sugar mixture and stir well together.

Dissolve the soda in a little milk. Add to the mixture and then add the floured fruit alternating with the milk.
Stir all until smooth and bake in a deep cake pan for one hour in a moderate oven.

Sponge Cake

4 eggs
1 cup sugar
1½ cups flour

1 teaspoon baking powder
¾ cup water
1 teaspoon vanilla

Sift the sugar. Then sift the baking powder with one-half cup flour.

Sift the sugar and add gradually to the well beaten yolks, beating constantly. Add the flavoring, the water and one cup of the flour.

Sift the baking powder with one-half cup flour and add to the batter. Fold in the stiffly beaten whites. Pour into a special sponge cake pan, ungreased, and bake for thirty to forty-five minutes in a moderate oven.

When baked, invert the pan and cool. Remove from the pan and serve top side down, sprinkled with powdered sugar.

Sunshine Cake

1½ cups sugar
½ cup water
6 eggs

½ teaspoon cream of tartar
1 cup flour
1 teaspoon vanilla

Melt the sugar in the water in a sauce pan and boil until it threads off the end of the spoon.

Separate the eggs, beat the whites stiff and the yolks frothy.

Pour the sugar syrup very slowly into the stiff whites and beat until cool. Then add the frothy yolks.

Sift the cream of tartar with the flour and fold into the sugar-egg mixture. Do not stir or beat the mixture at this stage.

Turn into an ungreased sunshine cake tin with a tube in the center and bake in a moderate oven for forty-five minutes to fifty-five minutes.

When done, invert the pan and allow to cool. Remove the cake and serve.

Cup Cakes

1 cup sugar
¼ cup shortening
3 teaspoons baking powder
¼ teaspoon salt

1 cup milk
1 egg
1 teaspoon vanilla
2 cups flour

Sift and mix the dry ingredients.

Melt the shortening, add the milk, beaten egg and vanilla.

Mix the dry and wet ingredients and stir well. Bake in muffin tins for fifteen to twenty minutes in a moderate oven.

Strawberry Shortcake

2 cups flour	1 tablespoon sugar
4 teaspoons baking powder	1/4 cup shortening
1/2 teaspoon salt	2/3 cup milk

Mix dry ingredients, sift twice, cut in shortening and add milk gradually. Toss on floured board. Pat, roll out and bake in well-greased pan about twenty minutes in a quick oven about 450 degrees F. Cap, wash and sweeten berries to taste. Crush berries slightly and put between and on top of shortcake. Cover with whipped cream.

Pineapple Upside Down Cake

1/4 pound butter	1 medium can pineapple
1 cup brown sugar	

Melt butter slightly in heavy frying pan. Spread over this the brown sugar and then lay on pineapple.

(Batter)

3 eggs	1 cup flour
1 cup sugar	1 teaspoon baking powder
5 tablespoons pineapple juice	

Beat egg yolks, add sugar, pineapple juice, flour sifted with baking powder. Fold in beaten egg whites. Pour over first mixture and bake in moderate oven. When done place cake plate on top of pan and reverse. Serve with whipped cream. (Pan should be eleven inches in diameter—and three inches deep.)

Kisses

Use only strictly fresh eggs. Beat the whites of four eggs stiff and add two-thirds cup powdered sugar while beating. Beat until the foamy mixture stands by itself. Fold in one-third cup powdered sugar and drop into little mounds on tins. Leave about one-half inch between the mounds.

Bake until dry and lightly browned in a low oven for about three-quarters of an hour.

Add two ounces grated chocolate and a little vanilla to the beaten kisses for chocolate kisses.

Fold in one-quarter pound shredded cocoanut for cocoanut kisses.

Cornflake Kisses

3 cups cornflakes	1/4 teaspoon salt
1 cup dry chipped cocoa-nut	1/2 teaspoon vanilla
	1/2 cup corn syrup
2 eggs	1/2 cup sugar

Stir together all the ingredients and drop on buttered baking sheets. Use the equivalent of a heaping tablespoon for each "kiss." Bake for half an hour in a moderate oven.

Schaum Torte

Whites of 6 eggs	1 teaspoon vinegar
2 cups sugar	1 teaspoon vanilla

Beat the whites dry and stiff, adding the sugar a little at a time and then the vinegar and vanilla, beating constantly.

Use a spring form. Grease and pour in about two-thirds of the mixture. Form a circle of the remaining third around the edge of the tin. Bake three-quarters to one hour in a slow oven.

Serve filled with fresh berries covered with whipped cream; or with fruit ice cream, trimmed with whipped cream.

Ice Box Cake

Line the bottom of a melon or spring form with lady fingers, separated and with the curved sides toward the pan.

Place the filling on the layer of lady fingers, and arrange in layers until the form is full or the material used up. Finish the top with a few lady fingers laid in spokes from the center. Stand in the icebox for twenty-four hours. When ready to serve, remove the band of the form and serve on the metal bottom on the platter. Cover with sweetened whipped cream and chopped nuts or candied cherries, etc.

Filling:

Melt one-half pound sweet chocolate in a double boiler, add three tablespoons sugar. Beat yolks of four eggs and stir in three tablespoons water. Cook slowly with the chocolate in the double boiler until the sauce is smooth and thick; stir all the while to make smooth. Cool and add the white beaten stiff. Use this filling as directed above.

Such a filling will require two and a half dozen lady fingers.

Cream Puffs

½ cup butter	1 cup flour
1 cup water	3 eggs
½ teaspoon salt	Vanilla

Boil the butter and water in a saucepan. Add the flour and salt and cook for a minute, stirring constantly.

Remove from the flame, add the beaten eggs and the vanilla flavor. Stir all the while the eggs are being poured in.

Line the baking pan with waxed paper and drop the batter from a big spoon, heaping more dough in the center than on the edges.

Bake for half an hour in a hot oven (400 degrees) and cool. Split and fill with whipped cream; sprinkle powdered sugar on the top. Chopped maraschino cherries may be mixed with the whipped cream filling. Custard may also be used.

Brownies

2 cups sugar	1 pound walnut meats,
4 eggs	chopped or broken
1 cup butter	1 cup flour
3 squares grated chocolate	Pinch of salt

Cream the sugar and butter. Add the egg yolks, then the grated chocolate and the nuts. Stir and add the flour, salt and the stiffly beaten white. Spread on flat pan and bake in a moderate oven only until they are firm to the touch.

Remove from the oven, mark into squares or strips and allow to cool in the pan.

This makes a very rich fudge-like cookie

No. 2:

1 cup sugar	½ cup nut meats
1 egg	½ cup flour
¼ cup shortening	Salt
2 squares chocolate	

This makes a smaller amount of cookies that are not as rich.

Cocoanut Cookies

2 cups shredded cocoanut
1/2 cup sugar
1/4 cup shortening
1 egg
1/2 teaspoon lemon juice

1/2 cup milk
1 1/2 cups pastry flour
2 teaspoons baking powder
1/4 teaspoon salt

Cream the sugar and the shortening. Beat the egg and add. Then stir in the lemon juice, cocoanut and milk.

Sift the flour, salt and baking powder and add to mixture. Drop from a spoon on greased pan. Bake fifteen to twenty minutes in moderate oven (350 degrees F).

Chocolate Nut Drops

3 squares chocolate
1 cup broken walnuts
1/2 cup butter
1 cup sugar
1 teaspoon salt

2 eggs
2 cups flour
1/2 teaspoon soda
1/2 cup milk

Cream the butter and add sugar and salt. Stir in the eggs and then the nuts and chocolate. Sift the flour with the soda and salt. Add flour then milk gradually until all is mixed.

Drop the dough from a spoon and flatten out into cookies. Bake fifteen minutes in a moderate oven.

Lady Fingers

2 eggs
1/2 cup confectioners sugar
1 teaspoon vanilla

1/2 cup flour
Pinch of salt

Separate the eggs carefully and beat the yolks frothy and the whites until they stand alone.

Add the sugar and vanilla after beating the whites to complete stiffness. Add the frothy yolks and then the flour and salt sifted together.

Bake in lady-finger tins for ten minutes in a moderate oven.

Soft Molasses Cookies

1 cup shortening, melted
1 cup molasses
1 cup sugar
1 teaspoon ginger
1 teaspoon cinnamon
½ teaspoon salt

1 teaspoon soda
2 eggs
1½ cups raisins
1 cup sour milk
4 cups pastry flour
3 teaspoons baking powder

Mix the shortening, molasses and sugar; add the spices and salt and then the soda dissolved in a tablespoon cold water. Beat the eggs and add with the raisins and the sour milk.
Sift the flour with the baking powder and stir in. Drop onto buttered tins and bake fifteen minutes.

Scottish Shortbread

Cream one-half pound butter with one-quarter cup sugar and add one pound of flour and a pinch of salt.
Roll to about one-half inch thickness and prick with a fork. Cut into squares six inches long and lay on buttered baking sheets to bake for fifteen minutes in a hot oven.

Ginger Snaps

1 cup molasses
½ cup butter
3 cups flour

1 teaspoon soda
2 teaspoons ginger
1 teaspoon salt

Heat the butter and molasses. Mix and sift the dry ingredients and add to the molasses. Chill the dough. Roll very thin on a lightly floured board. Cut with a round cookie cutter, place on greased baking sheets and bake in a moderate to hot oven for fifteen minutes. Ginger snaps must be dry and crisp; but an excess of flour will make them too hard. Keep the bowl in which the dough is kept in a cool place and roll out only as much dough as you have pans to fill.

Oatmeal Cookies

¾ cup butter
1 cup sugar
2 eggs
2 cups flour
1 cup oatmeal
¼ cup milk

½ teaspoon soda
1 teaspoon baking powder
1 teaspoon cinnamon
½ cup raisins
½ cup chopped walnuts

Cream the butter with the sugar and add the eggs. Mix the remaining ingredients and stir in with the butter, sugar and egg mixture.

Use only enough milk to make a stiff dough.

Drop the cookies on a buttered pan allowing some room for expansion. Bake until lightly brown in a hot oven.

Frozen Cookies

2 cups melted shortening	4 cups flour
1 cup brown sugar	1 teaspoon soda
1 cup white sugar	1 teaspoon salt
3 eggs	Filberts, almonds or peanuts
1 teaspoon cinnamon	halved

Sift the dry ingredients and add to the others in the order given. Mold into a long roll and wrap in a clean towel. Let stand in a cold place to become hard. Slice thin and bake brown in a hot oven (390 degrees F.).

The dough may be kept indefinitely in winter weather or in a mechanical refrigerator and may be baked quickly whenever the oven is going.

Rocks

$\frac{1}{2}$ cup butter	1 teaspoon baking powder
1 cup brown sugar	4 tablespoons milk
2 cups flour	$\frac{1}{2}$ cup currants or seeded
Salt	raisins
1 egg	

Cream the butter with the sugar. Add the flour and currants. Beat the egg, add salt and baking powder and stir into a stiff dough. Drop by teaspoonsful on a greased pan an inch apart. Bake the rocks in a moderate oven to a light brown.

Molasses Cookies

$\frac{1}{2}$ cup butter	1 tablespoon molasses
$\frac{1}{2}$ cup brown sugar	$\frac{1}{2}$ teaspoon cinnamon
2 eggs	$\frac{1}{2}$ teaspoon ground cloves
1 cup chopped seeded	2 teaspoons baking powder
raisins	2 cups flour

Cream the butter, add sugar gradually. Beat the eggs and add with the molasses and raisins. Sift all the dry ingredients together and mix all thoroughly.

Roll the dough which is quite stiff, one-quarter inch thick and cut with a cookie cutter. Bake in a moderate oven for fifteen minutes.

Soft Molasses Cookies

¾ cup butter
1 cup sugar
1 egg
¾ cup hot water
1 cup molasses

4 cups flour
1 teaspoon cinnamon
½ teaspoon ginger
1 teaspoon soda
1 teaspoon salt

Cream the butter, add the sugar and the egg well beaten. Then the molasses and hot water and mix the sifted dry ingredients. Spoon onto a warmed greased pan and bake eight to ten minutes in a moderate oven.

By using less hot water, a stiff dough may be made, rolled out and cut with a cutter.

Blackberry Roll

1 pint flour
1 tablespoon butter

2 teaspoons baking powder
A small pinch of salt

Add milk enough to make the dough the thickness of biscuit dough. Roll about one-half inch thick and powder with flour and sugar mixed, half and half.

Drain from one pint to one quart of cooked blackberries, sweeten to taste and place on dough with bits of butter specked over berries. Roll quickly (to keep dough from splitting) and place in a deep pan into which a half pint of cold water has been placed. Dust top with two parts of flour to one part of sugar, place in hot oven and bake about thirty minutes.

Date Bars

1 cup sugar
1 cup dates
1 cup flour
¼ cup butter

1 cup walnut meats
1 teaspoon baking powder
2 eggs

RECIPES AND HOUSEHOLD HELPS 65

Cream butter and sugar. Beat eggs until light and add to butter and sugar. Beat hard. Sift flour and baking powder. Take half of flour and roll dates, also walnut meats, then add to butter and sugar mixture. Add remainder of flour. Mix well. Bake in square tin 20 minutes. When done cut in oblong pieces and roll in powdered sugar. This recipe makes about 24 bars.

Cherry Torte

¼ cup butter
¼ cup lard
4 tablespoons sugar
2 teaspoons cinnamon

2 egg yolks
½ cup flour
½ teaspoon baking powder

Line a form with this dough.

Strain the juice from one quart of cherries.

Make a custard:

4 eggs, yolks and whites
  beaten (separately)

¾ cup sugar
½ cup sour cream

Put chopped almonds on dough, then cherries, and then pour custard over all. Bake 45 minutes in slow oven.

Easy Cookies

¾ cup shortening
2 cups sugar
¼ cup milk
2 eggs

4 cups flour
1 teaspoon vanilla
3 teaspoons baking powder

Cream sugar and shortening. Add milk to beaten eggs and beat; add to sugar and vanilla; add flour with baking powder. Rolls easily cut with cutter. Sprinkle with sugar. Bake about fifteen or twenty minutes.

Cocoanut Macaroons

1 can condensed milk   9 oz. shredded cocoanut
Mix together and drop on greased pans and bake 15-20 minutes at 350 degrees.

Poppy Seed Cakes

Cream 1/3 cup butter scant, 1 cup of sugar, 2 whites of eggs well beaten. Put 1/3 cup poppy seed in bowl and pour over 2/3 cup of milk. Let stand while mixing the other part of cake. Add milk and 1½ cups of flour in which 2 teaspoons of baking powder is sifted. Beat well each operation.

Bake in a square shallow pan in a moderate oven. Cover with any desired icing and cut into squares.

Crumb Cookies

1 cup dry bread crumbs, ground or rolled fine
1 cup sugar
1 cup walnuts, pecans or peanuts, cut in pieces.
2 eggs, slightly beaten.

Mix all together and drop from a teaspoon on a greased tin. Bake in moderate oven 15 minutes only.

Grape Jelly Cookies

¼ lb. butter
1 cup granulated sugar
3 eggs
½ cup grape jelly
¼ cup milk
1 cup chopped nuts and raisins
1 teaspoon vanilla
½ teaspoon salt
3 teaspoons baking powder
About 4 cups flour

Cream butter and sugar. Add beaten egg, then add milk, jelly, nuts, raisins and vanilla and, last, fold in dry ingredients. Put in ice box to chill about one hour. Roll out about ¼ inch thick, cut with cookie cutter and bake in moderate oven about 20 minutes.

Swedish Ice Box Nut Cookies

Cream together ¼ cup boiling water, 1 cup brown sugar, 1 cup white sugar, 1 cup butter or substitute. Add 1 teaspoonful vanilla and beaten yolks of two eggs. Sift together 3½ cups flour, 1 teaspoonful salt, 1 teaspoonful baking powder, ¼ teaspoonful soda. Add 1 cup nut meats. Beat egg whites and add to first mixture. Lightly fold in the flour. Put in a greased bread tin and let stand in ice box over night. Turn out of pan and slice. Bake in moderate oven 10 to 12 minutes.

Sugar Cookies

3 tablespoons butter
1/2 cup sugar
1 egg
1 tablespoon milk

1 1/2 cups flour
1 1/2 teaspoons baking powder
1/8 teaspoon salt

Cream butter and sugar. Add egg and then milk. Sift flour twice. Add baking powder and salt, and beat with other ingredients. Chill dough. Then roll out on board, thin. Cut with cookie cutter. Bake from 15 to 20 minutes in moderately hot oven. Take out and sprinkle with powdered sugar.

A teaspoon of vanilla flavoring may be added when adding milk and egg, if desired.

Apple Roll

2 cups flour
4 tablespoons sugar
5 tablespoons shortening

2 teaspoons baking powder
1/2 teaspoon salt
2/3 cup sweet milk

Sift dry ingredients, then cut in the shortening, add the milk, stirring all together. Roll dough on board about 1/4 of an inch thick, keeping dough in oblong shape; spread with melted butter, then a generous layer of finely chopped apples and sugar. Sprinkle cinnamon over this and roll tightly into a long roll. Cut slices about 2 inches thick and place in greased pan. Keep slices close together; on top of each slice place 1/3 of an apple. Bake in oven until apples on top are brown. Serve hot with rich sauce.

Peanut Macaroons

1 egg white
1 cup powdered sugar

1/8 teaspoon salt
1 cup peanuts chopped fine

Drop from spoon two inches apart. Bake 15 minutes in moderate oven. Flavoring may be added if desired.

Drop Peanut Cookies

1½ cups light brown sugar
¾ cup shortening
1 egg
½ teaspoon soda
Cream sugar and shortening.

½ teaspoon salt
3 tablespoons milk
¾ cup ground peanuts
2½ cups flour

Add the egg well beaten. Sift dry ingredients and add the peanuts and milk. Drop batter in pieces the size of a walnut on a cookie sheet and bake in hot oven for 15 or 20 minutes.

Oatmeal Cookies

1 cup sugar
¾ cup shortening
1 egg
1 cup sour milk
½ teaspoon soda

2 cups rolled oats
½ teaspoon salt
2 teaspoons baking powder
2 cups flour

Mix in order named. Beat well. Drop by teaspoons on well greased tins. Bake in hot oven.

Banana Puffs

Take as many bananas as there are persons to serve. Roll in sugar and cinnamon, then roll each banana in thin pie crust. Bake in hot oven 15 minutes. Serve with whipped cream or lemon sauce. Puffs may be served hot or cold.

Lace Cookies

1 cup post toasties
1 cup cocoanut
⅔ cup sugar
2 eggs

1 cup oatmeal
1 teaspoon baking powder
Pinch salt
1 teaspoon vanilla

Mix dry ingredients and add to mixture of eggs, butter, and vanilla. Drop with a teaspoon on inverted tins and bake slowly.

English Apple Pie (No pastry)

2 very large mellow apples
1 cup sifted flour
½ cup brown sugar
Butter size of an egg

1 teaspoon white sugar
¼ teaspoon nutmeg
1 teaspoon lemon juice

Mix well the brown sugar, flour and butter
deep baking dish; put in all the apples sliced v
extra piece of butter about size of English w
and placed over apples; sprinkle over this whise
teaspoon water, nutmeg and lemon juice. Place on top of p
the dry mixture (sugar, butter and flour). Cover contents
thoroughly. Bake in moderate oven 30 minutes. Serve hot or
cold with whipped cream.

Dropped Peanut Cookies

2 tablespoons butter	¼ teaspoon salt
¼ cup sugar	1½ cups flour
1 egg	2 tablespoons milk
1 teaspoon baking powder	½ cup chopped nuts

Cream the butter, add sugar and cream again. Add the egg,
well beaten, and the chopped peanuts. Add the milk. Mix
and sift flour, salt and baking powder and add same to the
first mixture. Drop from a teaspoon on a pan about one inch
apart and decorate with half a peanut on each cookie. Bake
15 minutes in a slow oven.

Frozen Cookies

1½ cups butter or half but- ter and half shortening	4½ cups flour
1 cup white sugar	½ teaspoon salt
2 cups brown sugar	1 teaspoon soda
3 eggs	1½ teaspoons cinnamon
½ pound shelled almonds	¼ teaspoon allspice

Cream shortening; add sugar, gradually creaming until fluffy.
Add unbeaten eggs, one at a time, beating well after each
addition. Add coarsely chopped blanched almonds. Sift dry
ingredients together and cut into first mixture. Pack dough
into a buttered bread pan and chill in ice box over night.
Slice thin and bake in a hot oven (400 degrees) 15 minutes.

Almond Horns

½ pound flour
½ pound butter
¼ pound chopped almonds
1 teaspoon vanilla

Mix well together, roll out one quarter inch thick, cut and shape into crescents. Chill. Bake in hot oven 15 minutes. When they are cool roll them in powdered sugar.

Hard Tack

4 eggs
2 cups sugar
2 cups flour
2 cups dates, stoned
1½ cups nut meats
1 tablespoon water

Cream eggs, sugar and flour together, then add dates and nuts; also water. This makes a stiff batter. Spread over a waxed paper in a long biscuit pan, thin, and bake till it is a light brown all over. Turn out and cut in squares and dip in powdered sugar while hot.

Orange Crullers

2 eggs, beaten light
¼ cup sugar
2 tablespoons melted shortening
½ teaspoon salt
1 orange
2 teaspoons baking powder
3 cups cake flour
flour
¼ cup milk
Orange marmalade

Beat eggs until light, add sugar, then melted shortening. Sift flour, add salt and baking powder and sift again. Add the flour alternately with the milk to the first mixture. Then add grated rind of orange. Mix the dough. Roll the dough, only part at a time, on a floured board, into a sheet one-fourth inch thick. With a one and one-half inch biscuit cutter, cut dough into rounds. Put about one-half teaspoon of orange marmalade on a round of dough and cover with a second round. Wet the edges and press together closely. Fry in deep fat and drain on brown paper. Dust with powdered sugar.

Almond Roll

1 cake yeast
1 tablespoon sugar
1/4 cup water
1 cup milk
3 1/2 or 4 cups flour
1/2 of orange peel, grated

1/2 teaspoon almond extract
1/2 cup chopped almonds
3 tablespoons butter
1 teaspoon salt
1 egg

Dissolve yeast and sugar in lukewarm water. Scald and cool milk. Mix these with 1 cup of the flour. Let rise in a warm place until bubbly. Add beaten egg, melted butter, salt, extract, and flour. Work well into soft dough; let rise to double its height; roll out into a sheet, brush with melted butter, sprinkle peel and almonds on it and roll up; form into a roll and butter the top. Let rise again until light and bake 30 minutes at 400° F.

Corn Flake Cookies

4 egg whites
1/2 cup sugar

2 cups corn flakes
Nuts

Beat egg whites until stiff, then add sugar, corn flakes and nuts. Bake in moderate oven.

Cocoanut Jam Tarts

Crust:
1 1/2 cups flour
3/4 teaspoon salt

1/2 cup solid shortening
4 to 6 tablespoons water

Filling:
1 cup jam
3 egg whites
1/4 teaspoon baking powder

1/2 cup sugar
1 cup cocoanut

Sift flour and salt; cut in shortening with knife. Add water, cutting dough with a knife. Toss on floured board, pat and roll out.

Line tart tins with crust and put 1 teaspoon jam into each. Beat egg whites until frothy; add baking powder and beat until stiff, then fold in sugar and finely chopped cocoanut. Put 1 tablespoon cocoanut mixture on each tart and bake in a moderate oven (325 degrees) 25 minutes.

Spanish Bun

2 cups sugar
1 cup butter
1 cup sweet milk
2 cups flour
1/2 teaspoon salt
1/2 teaspoon allspice

1 teaspoon cinnamon
1 tablespoon cocoa
4 level teaspoons baking powder
1 cup raisins, seedless
1 cup nut meats

Cream butter and sugar. Mix dry ingredients and alternate with milk into sugar and butter. Add floured raisins and nuts to mixture. Pour into well floured loaf pan. Bake one hour in moderate oven.

Oat Meal Cookies

3 cups rolled oats
2 cups granulated sugar
2 cups flour
1 cup chopped raisins
1 teaspoon soda

1 teaspoon cinnamon
1/2 teaspoon salt
2 well beaten eggs
5 tablespoons milk
1 cup melted butter

Mix the dry ingredients thoroughly. Next add the eggs, then the milk and melted butter. Drop on greased pan, about the size of English walnuts, allowing room to spread. Bake in moderately hot oven.

Cream Puffs

1 cup boiling water
1/2 cup butter

4 eggs
1 cup flour

Boil butter with water until melted. Remove from fire and drop in whole eggs one at a time, beating well. Drop in buttered muffin tins. Bake in moderate oven 50 minutes. Remove from oven and cut open so steam may escape. When cold, fill with whipped cream.

Snowballs

2 eggs
1/2 cup sugar
1 cup milk

Pinch of salt
2 teaspoons baking powder
1 teaspoon vanilla

Enough flour so that they will drip from a tablespoon three-fourths full. Drop in hot shortening and fry like doughnuts. Sprinkle with powdered sugar.

Fruit Drop Cakes

1 egg
2/3 cups of sugar
2/3 cups of water
1¾ cups of flour
2 teaspoons baking powder
1/3 cup of milk
2½ tablespoons of butter

⅛ teaspoon salt
¼ teaspoon vanilla
¼ teaspoon cinnamon
¼ cup of chopped figs
½ cup of chopped nuts
¼ cup of chopped dates

Cream the butter; add the sugar, then the well beaten egg. Mix and sift the flour, baking powder, cinnamon and salt and add alternately with milk diluted with water to the first mixture. Add the vanilla, nuts, dates and figs. Mix well and drop from spoon onto a baking sheet and bake in a moderately hot oven. This recipe makes about twenty-eight cakes.

FROSTINGS

Divinity Fudge

2 cups white sugar
2/3 cup white syrup
1/3 cup water
2 egg whites

½ cup chopped walnut
  meats or raisins
1 teaspoon vanilla

Boil sugar, water and syrup until a few drops in cold water becomes hard and brittle. Beat egg whites stiff and add nuts and vanilla. When syrup is done pour very slowly into the egg whites, beating all the time. Beat until mixture will hold its shape when dropped from a spoon. Drop on buttered platters to harden, or use as rich frosting.

Boiled Frosting

Cook one cup sugar in one-half cup water until the sugar is dissolved. Stir to dissolve sugar. Without further stirring, cook the syrup until it forms a thread from the end of the spoon.

Stand to cool. Meanwhile, beat one egg-white stiff. Pour the syrup slowly into the egg-white, beating constantly. This will form a frosting thick enough to spread.

Brown sugar may be used with the addition of one egg-white and a little vanilla flavor.

If chopped nuts are to be added, stir them in just before spreading the frosting on the cake.

A quick frosting may be made by beating one white of egg and adding one-half cup powdered sugar, gradually. Beat until smooth and add one-half teaspoon vanilla. This makes a good frosting for cup cakes and pound cakes.

Chocolate Frosting

1 square chocolate
3 tablespoons sugar, granulated
1 tablespoon water
8 tablespoons powdered sugar
White of 1 egg
1½ teaspoons vanilla

Cook the chocolate, water and sugar together to make a smooth, shiny liquid.

Stir the egg but do not beat it. Add the powdered sugar and stir smooth. Combine the two mixtures and add vanilla.

Cool before spreading on top of the cake.

Chocolate filling:

½ cup sugar
1 tablespoon cornstarch
½ cup milk
½ cup grated chocolate

Mix the sugar, cornstarch and grated chocolate together and stir in the milk. Cook until thick, stir to make smooth and allow to cool. When cool add vanilla and spread between the layers of a cake

Boiled Frosting

2 cups of granulated sugar
½ cup water
1 tablespoon vinegar

Boil until it spins a thread; add above to three stiffly beaten egg whites. Any flavoring may be used. Vinegar prevents frosting from hardening or getting sticky.

Maple Icing

1 tablespoon hot coffee
3 tablespoons maple syrup
Few drops of vanilla
Confectioner's sugar

Mix together coffee, syrup and vanilla and beat in confectioner's sugar till stiff enough to spread.

Seven Minute Icing

1 egg white	12 marshmallows
1 cup sugar	1 teaspoon vanilla
3 tablespoons water	

Put egg, sugar and water in double boiler and set over rapidly boiling water. Beat constantly with an egg beater for seven minutes. Remove from stove and add vanilla and marshmallows, cut in small pieces. Beat until of the proper consistency to spread.

CARAMEL ICING

Cook 2 cupfuls light brown sugar with 1 cupful milk or water until it forms a soft ball when tried in cold water. Add 1 tablespoonful butter and 1 teaspoonful vanilla. Remove from fire; leave until cold, then beat until creamy.

Note: If sugar curdles the milk, add a pinch of baking soda.

Chocolate Icing

Take 1 can condensed milk, 2 squares of bitter chocolate, 1 teaspoon vanilla. Melt chocolate, add condensed milk and cook until it forms a ball and leaves sides of pan. Add vanilla.

Pies

Quick Pastry—Pie Dough

1/2 cup shortening	1/4 teaspoon baking powder
1/2 cup cold water	1/4 teaspoon salt
1 1/4 cups flour	

Melt the butter, add the water and mix in the dry ingredients to make a smooth dough. Roll on a floured board. Cut in two pieces slightly larger than the pie tin.

Pastry

1 1/2 cup flour	Cold water to make soft
3/4 teaspoon salt	dough
1/2 cup shortening	

Mix flour and salt, cut in shortening. Moisten to soft dough with cold water. Toss on lightly floured board and roll out, handling as lightly as possible.

Line two pie plates and partially bake.

Buttermilk Pie Filling

3 cups buttermilk
1½ cups sugar
3 tablespoons flour

3 eggs (yolks only)
Butter the size of a walnut
Juice of ½ lemon

(This makes two pies.)

Mix sugar and flour. Add buttermilk, egg yolks and butter.
Mix well. Cook in double boiler until thick, stirring constantly. After taking off stove, add flavor. Cool and pour in
baked shells. Beat whites of eggs until stiff, adding a little
baking powder and sugar. Place on top of pie and brown in a
moderate oven.

Deep Dish Apple Pie

4 tart apples

Slice the apples quite thin and put in a deep baking dish,
casserole or deep berry dish. Season with one cup sugar and
one teaspoon cinnamon. One teaspoon lemon juice and a little
grated rind improves the flavor of the apples.

If the fruit is very juicy, add two tablespoons flour.

Cover the dish with pastry rolled one-quarter inch thick. Cut
gashes in the crust, press the edges with a fork and bake.

Hot Water Pie Crust

1 cup lard
½ cup boiling hot water

3 cups sifted flour
1 teaspoon salt

Put lard into large mixing bowl; add hot water; work into
creamy mass; add about one-half the flour, mixed with salt,
and work in the rest of the flour gradually. Put on the ice
a short while before rolling out, and when baking a two-crust pie after putting in fruit filling, bake in a moderate oven
for 50 minutes.

Cream Date Pie

Scald one and one-half cups milk. Add two tablespoons cornstarch mixed with three tablespoons sugar. One tablespoon
butter, three egg yolks, one and one-half teaspoons vanilla.

Cook until thick. Chop one-half package dates in mixture. Pour into rich crust previously baked. Cover with meringue of three egg whites beaten stiff or whipped cream sweetened to taste.

Texas Pecan Pie

Use good pie crust.

Beat four eggs, conserving the whites of two for meringue. Add one cup of sugar, one bottle of whipping cream and one cup of broken pecans. Cook in double boiler, stirring constantly until it is thick. Beat up the whites with a little sugar and brown in oven after spreading on pie.

Cocoanut Cream Pie

2 cups milk
1/3 cup flour
1/2 cup sugar
1/4 teaspoon salt

2 egg yolks
1 teaspoon vanilla
3/4 cup grated cocoanut

Scald milk. Mix flour, sugar and salt. Combine with hot milk and cook in a double boiler 20 minutes, stirring until thick. Add hot mixture to slightly beaten egg yolks. Return to double boiler and cook 5 minutes, stirring to prevent lumps. Add vanilla and part of cocoanut. Pour into baked pastry shell and cover with meringue made of the two egg whites and sprinkle with remaining cocoanut. Bake in a moderate oven until meringue browns.

Raisin Pie

1 heaping cup of seeded
   raisins
1 cup of sugar
1 egg (beaten slightly)
1 cup of thick sour milk

1 teaspoon of flour
Butter, size of a walnut
1 teaspoon of nutmeg
1 teaspoon of cinnamon

Mix all ingredients thoroughly and bake with two crusts. Bake about 1/2 hour in a moderate oven.

Butter Scotch Marshmallow Pie

2 cups milk
1 cup brown sugar
2 tablespoons cornstarch
3 tablespoons butter
1/4 teaspoon salt

2 eggs
1 teaspoon vanilla
2 dozen marshmallows
Pastry crust

Scald milk in double boiler, mix sugar and cornstarch, add to milk, stir until thick, cover and cook fifteen minutes.

Add butter and salt and pour over egg yolks slightly beaten. Return to double boiler, stir and cook one minute; remove from fire and cool.

When ready to serve add vanilla and pour into a baked pastry crust. Cut marshmallows in pieces and put into a warm place until they are soft.

Beat egg whites until stiff, beat in marshmallows and spread over the top of the pie. Bake in the oven until delicately browned.

Butterscotch Pie

6 tablespoons butter
1 1/2 cups brown sugar
2 1/2 cups milk
2 eggs
Pie dough.

3 tablespoons cornstarch
4 tablespoons granulated
   sugar
1/2 teaspoon vanilla

Line a small pie tin with pastry, flute the edge.

Cook the butter and brown sugar together until it turns a rich brown. Add scalded milk and heat until the sugar dissolves.

Beat the yolks of two eggs slightly, add the cornstarch and pour the milk mixture over gradually, stirring continually. Flavor with one-quarter teaspoon vanilla and pour into the lined pie pan. Bake for ten minutes in a very hot oven (450 degrees F.) and then reduce the heat to a moderate heat (325 degrees F.) until the custard is firm.

Cover with the meringue made of the beaten whites to which the granulated sugar and one-quarter teaspoon vanilla are added gradually. Brown for ten to fifteen minutes.

Lemon Pie

1½ tablespoons cornstarch
1 cup water
1 tablespoon butter
1 cup sugar

1 lemon
White of 1 egg
2 tablespoons sugar for
   meringue

Mix cornstarch with a little cold water. Heat the cup of water and add the cornstarch paste. Cook until transparent. Add the butter, sugar, lemon juice and grated lemon rind. Set aside to cool.

Beat well when cool and turn into a pie pan lined with pastry. Cover with a meringue of the white beaten very stiff with the sugar. Brown the meringue but serve the pie cold.

Lemon Custard Pie

1½ cups sugar
4 tablespoons flour
5 tablespoons cornstarch
3 eggs
½ teasspoon salt
½ teaspoon vanilla

2¼ cups boiling water
½ cup lemon juice
Grated rind of one lemon
6 tablespoons granulated
   sugar for meringue

Stir boiling water into the mixed dry ingredients. Cook in a double boiler for fifteen minutes, stirring as the mixture thickens. Beat the yolks and pour the cornstarch mixture on slowly; stir in well. Return to the double boiler and cook two minutes longer. Remove from the flame, add the lemon juice and grated rind.

When cold pour into a baked pastry shell. Cover with a meringue of egg whites beaten stiff with the sugar and bake the meringue to a light brown for about fifteen minutes.

Lemon Meringue Pie

½ cup brown sugar
1 tablespoon cornstarch
2 tablespoons water

3 eggs
2 lemons
½ cup confectioners' sugar

Dissolve the cornstarch in the water and add to the melted

brown sugar. Beat the egg yolks and stir into the mixture.
Add the grated rind of one lemon and the juice of the two.
Cook for five minutes, stirring to make a smooth custard.

Line a pie dish with unbaked pastry. Fill with the lemon
custard and bake for fifteen to twenty minutes in a moderate
oven.

Make a meringue of beaten egg-whites and powdered sugar
added gradually. Cover the pie with this meringue and return
to the oven long enough to brown.

Mince Pie

Mincemeat as follows:

2 cups chopped lean beef	2 teaspoons salt
4 cups chopped tart apples	1 cup strong coffee
2 cups currants	1 tablespoon each of nut-
2 cups seeded raisins	meg, ground cloves, cin-
1 cup chopped suet or fat	namon and ginger
2 cups sugar	1 cup meat-stock

Boil the meat until tender, cool in the juice and chop fine.
Mix the materials in the order written. Simmer slowly; bottle
and seal while hot.

When making a pie, line a deep pie pan with crust, fill with
mincemeat, using one quart, pour over a tablespoon of cream,
a tablespoon of sugar and dot with a tablespoon of butter.

Put on the top crust and bake in a very hot oven (450 degrees
F.) for half an hour.

Serve hot with pieces of American cheese.

Mock Cherry Pie

1 cup cranberries	1 tablespoon flour
1/2 cup raisins	1 teaspoon butter
3/4 cup sugar	

Cut the cranberries in halves and the raisins into pieces. Mix
flour and sugar together and add to the cranberries and raisins.
Fill the lower crust with the mixture and dot over it with
butter. Bake between crusts.

Puddings

Bavarian Cream

2 teaspoons gelatine	5 eggs
¼ cup water	1 tablespoon vanilla
¾ cup sugar	Pinch of salt

Dissolve the gelatine in hot water.

Beat the yolks of the eggs, add sugar, vanilla and pinch of salt. Turn into a double boiler and cook until the mixture thickens. Add the dissolved gelatine and remove from the flame to cool. Beat the whites stiff and add to the mixture. Turn into a mold, chill and set on ice.

Serve with whipped cream. Any flavoring may be substituted for the vanilla.

Caramel Custard

4 eggs	½ cup sugar
4 cups milk	¼ teaspoon salt

Beat the eggs and add the salt; pour scalded milk slowly over the eggs and stir the whole.

Brown the sugar (or melt brown sugar) stirring to prevent burning. When browned, stir in the eggs and milk mixture.

Strain through a sieve into a greased baking dish. Bake in a pan of water in a moderate oven; do not allow the water in the pan to boil for this will toughen the custard. The custard will brown and set when done.

Serve cold with cream.

Individual custards may be made in cups, standing them in the water.

Floating Island

4 eggs	Pinch of salt
½ cup sugar	1 tablespoon vanilla
2 cups milk	

Put the yolks into a bowl with the sugar, milk, salt and vanilla. Beat thoroughly and turn into a double boiler. Cook slowly for ten minutes to form a creamy custard. Remove from the flame and cool.

Stand on ice when chilled; beat the whites stiff, adding a tablespoon of powdered sugar. The whites must be stiff enough to stand alone. Spread a little jam over the custard and then spread on the stiff whites in blobs to resemble islands. For chocolate floating island, add two squares of chocolate melted to the milk when hot.

Blanc Mange

2 cups milk
4 tablespoons corn starch
3 eggs

4 tablespoons sugar
1 tablespoon vanilla extract
Salt

Mix the corn starch with one cup of the milk. Scald the other cup of milk in a double boiler. Stir the cold milk slowly into the hot milk and cook together for fifteen minutes.

Beat the eggs, add sugar, salt and flavoring. Add to the milk mixture and cook for five minutes.

Strain through a fine sieve and place in a mold or into small forms. Put on ice to form. Serve with fruit or whipped cream on the top.

One-half cup grated chocolate may be substituted for the vanilla in the above recipe.

Canadian Pudding

1 cup chopped suet
1 cup molasses
1 cup bread crumbs
1 cup brown sugar
1 cup seeded raisins
1 cup finely chopped apples

1 cup sweet milk
1 cup chopped nuts
1 teaspoon each of cinnamon, cloves, nutmeg
2 teaspoons of baking powder in 2 large cups of flour

Steam or boil three hours. Serve with hard sauce.

Carrot Plum Pudding

1 cup grated raw potato
1 cup grated raw carrot
1 cup suet chopped fine
1 cup sugar
1½ cups flour
1 cup seedless raisins
½ cup currants

¼ cup citron, cut fine
2 eggs
1 teaspoon soda
½ teaspoon salt
1 teaspoon cinnamon
   (ground)
½ teaspoon nutmeg

Mix soda with potato and carrot; add sugar, suet, and eggs slightly beaten. Sift spices with flour and add to mixture. Lastly add fruit slightly floured. Steam three hours.

A Pound Plum Pudding

1 pound of suet
1 pound of currants
1 pound of seeded raisins
8 eggs
½ grated nutmeg
2 ounces of sliced candied
  peel

1 teaspoon of ground ginger
½ pound of bread crumbs
½ pound of flour
½ pint of milk

Chop the suet fine; mix with it the dry ingredients; stir these well together, and add the well-beaten eggs and milk to moisten with. Beat up the mixture well, and should the above proportion of milk not be found sufficient to make it of the proper consistency, a little more should be added. Press the pudding into a mould, tie it in a floured cloth, and boil five hours, or rather longer, and serve with sauce.

Note: The above pudding may be baked instead of boiled; it should be put into a buttered mould or pan and baked for about two hours; a smaller pudding would take about one and a quarter hours.

Graham Cracker Pudding

4 tablespoons butter
½ cup sugar
1 egg
1½ level teaspoonsful baking powder.

¾ cup milk
½ teaspoon vanilla
½ teaspoon salt
3 cups rolled graham crackers

Dates may be added, if desired.

Cream butter and sugar; add beaten yolk of egg and salt. Mix cracker crumbs with baking powder and milk. Add white of egg beaten stiffly. Put in mold and steam 1½ hours.

Date Pudding

1 pint boiling water
¼ teaspoonful salt
½ cup sugar

½ cup nuts
½ cup graham flour
½ pound dates (pitted)

Put sugar and salt into boiling water; add graham flour very slowly. Cook 25 minutes; stir in the dates (which have been chopped); turn off the fire and add nuts and vanilla. Pour in buttered pan and cool.

Serve in sherbet glasses with whipped cream.

Bread Pudding

3 cups bread	2 eggs
1 cup sugar	Nutmeg or vanilla
2 cups milk	

Beat mixture and eggs together; add milk. Pour mixture over moistened bread and stir. Add flavoring to taste.

Sauce for Bread Pudding

2 eggs	½ cup butter
1 cup sugar	1 teaspoon vanilla

Beat eggs and sugar thoroughly; add vanilla and put in double boiler; add butter. Do not boil.

Pineapple Rice

Cook one cup rice; when done add one cup sugar, one large can grated pineapple and cool. When cool add one-half pint cream whipped thick and put on ice until ready to serve. Garnish with whipped cream and cherries and serve.

Jellied Grapes

⅓ cup of rice	½ cup of water
2 cups of grapes	2 tablespoons of sugar

Sprinkle the rice and sugar with the grapes. Place them in a dish, pour on the water, cover close and simmer two hours, slowly, in the oven. Serve warm as sauce or cold as pudding. If served warm as pudding, increase slightly the proportion of rice and sugar.

Prune Pudding

½ pound prunes	Whites of 2 eggs
½ cup sugar	

Stew prunes until soft, then chop about the size of raisins. Beat egg whites stiff and add to sugar, then add to prunes gradually. Stir all well and bake 15 or 20 minutes. Serve hot or cold with cream or whipped cream. Vanilla may be added.

Marshmallow Rice Pudding

1 cup rice	½ cup sugar
3½ cups water	1 teaspoon lemon extract
1 teaspoon salt	½ cup milk
3 eggs	1 dozen marshmallows

Put salt in water and boil. When it begins to boil pour rice slowly and boil until tender. Then mix eggs, sugar, milk and extract together and add to rice. Put in a baking-dish and cover the top with marshmallows. Bake slowly until light brown.

Blueberry Pudding

½ cup sugar	2 cups flour
4 tablespoons oil	4 teaspoons baking powder
1 egg	½ teaspoon salt
1 cup water	½ teaspoon mace
2 cups blueberries	

Cream sugar, oil and egg together; add water. Stir in the sifted dry ingredients and blueberries. Turn in to a greased mold; cover tightly and steam two and one-half hours.

Baked Apple Pudding

½ cup water	½ cup milk
½ cup sugar	¾ cup flour
½ cup butter	1 teaspoon baking powder
1 egg	Pinch salt

Butter baking dish and put in 3 sliced and peeled apples. Cover with the water. Cream butter and sugar; add beaten egg, salt, milk, flour and baking powder. Pour over apples and bake 30 minutes or until apples are tender. Serve warm with cream.

Lemon Pudding

1 cup sugar	2 tablespoons flour
1 tablespoon butter	Yolks of 3 eggs
Add juice and rind of one lemon	1 cup milk

Fold in stiffly beaten whites last. Set bake dish in pan of hot water while baking. Bake in slow oven ½ hour. Serve with whipped cream. May be eaten hot or cold.

Indian Pudding

¼ cup cornmeal	1 tablespoon molasses
2 tablespoons sugar	¼ cup raisins or ½ cup figs,
⅛ teaspoon ginger	dates, or chopped apples
3 cups milk	

Put cornmeal in greased baking dish. Scald one-half of milk and pour over cornmeal. Stir this well. Add the fruit and seasonings. Add rest of milk cold and cook in slow oven for two hours, stirring three or four times during baking.

Rice-Corn Pudding

1 cup cornmeal	1 teaspoon baking powder
1 tablespoon rice	2 eggs
1 tablespoon butter	1 teaspoon salt
2 cups milk	

Boil rice in one and one-half cups water for ten minutes. Scald half the cornmeal with rice water, add eggs, well beaten, then the melted butter. Add the milk, rest of cornmeal together with salt and baking powder. Mix well and bake 40 minutes in a moderate oven.

Carrot Pudding

2 cups ground carrots	1½ cups flour
1 cup ground potatoes	1 teaspoon soda in 2 tea-
1 cup ground suet	spoons hot water
1 cup sugar	1 teaspoon nutmeg
1 cup raisins	1 teaspoon salt

Conserve all the vegetable juices during grinding. Mix all ingredients and steam in a greased pan for three hours. Serve with hard or foamy sauce.

Coffee Souffle

Mix one and one-half cups strong coffee, one tablespoon gelatine, one-third cup granulated sugar, and one-half cup milk. Heat in a double boiler, add yolks of three eggs slightly beaten and mix with one-third cup granulated sugar and one-fourth teaspoon salt. Cook until it thickens. Add the whites of the eggs beaten stiff, and one-half teaspoon vanilla.
Mold, chill and serve with whipped cream.

Banana Whip

(Serving of four)

2 bananas
2 tablespoons lemon juice
½ cup of sugar

½ pint bottle of whipping cream
Pistachio-nuts

Strain the pulp of the bananas through a sieve, add the lemon juice and sugar. Mix the ingredients, and place it on the stove letting it come to a boil. Then place it in the ice box until it is chilled. After it is thoroughly cooled, place two-thirds of a cup of cream in a bowl and whip it until it is firm to the bottom of the bowl. Then fold the cream into the banana mixture and place it into glasses, covering it with the remaining cream, which is also whipped, and then sprinkle the top with the blanched pistachio-nuts.

Blanched Pistachio-Nuts

Put the pistachio-nuts in a dish, covering with boiling hot water. Let stand for two minutes, after which remove the hot water and then cover with cold water. Drain the water and then remove the skins of the nuts.

Jelly Crescents

One large tablespoon butter, one of lard, rubbed into cup and a half of flour; add pinch of salt, yolks of three eggs, well beaten, and enough milk to roll out the dough. Cut in strips about two inches wide and three inches long, and put any kind of jelly, for a filling, and roll, pressing both ends. Form into crescents and bake about half an hour. When taken out of the oven dip in powdered sugar.

Peanut Brittle Whip

1 lb. peanut brittle (ground) or run through food chopper

½ lb. marshmallows (chopped)
1 pint whipped cream

Stir all together and chill for 4 hours before serving. Then serve with chocolate wafers.

Fruit Squares

1 package plain gelatine	4 cups granulated sugar
1 cup walnuts	Juice of 1 orange and lemon
½ cup candied cherries	Vanilla
1 package pitted dates	1 cup boiling water.

Soak gelatine for 15 minutes in ½ cup of cold water. Then add boiling water to gelatine and stir well. Then add sugar and juice of orange and lemon. Bring to boil and let simmer 15 or 20 minutes. Cut nuts, cherries and dates. Remove mixture from fire and add vanilla, nuts, cherries and dates. Wet pans in cold water, then pour mixture in ½ inch thick and let cool over night. Cut in squares and roll in powdered sugar.

Cinnamon Apples

Boil up one and one-half cups sugar, three-fourths cup water, one tablespoon red cinnamon candies.

Pare and core six tart apples, cut into quarters and drop into the liquid syrup. Cook slowly for three-quarters hour, basting with the syrup. Serve with whipped cream.

Apples need not be cut into pieces unless desired.

Maple Cream Whip

1½ cups maple sugar	½ teaspoon vanilla
2 cups hot water	1 cup pecans or English
⅓ cup cornstarch	walnuts
¼ cup cold water	Whipped cream
3 egg whites (beaten)	

Add the brown sugar to the hot water and bring to boil. Mix one-fourth cup cold water to corn starch and add to boiling syrup. Use double boiler and cook 15 minutes. After taking from fire let cool slightly. Then add egg whites stiffly beaten, vanilla and nuts. Put in sherbet glasses and chill.

Charlotte Russe

Whites of 4 eggs beaten light	Yolks of 4 eggs beaten light with ½ cup sugar
	1 pint cream, beaten stiff

Stir yolks into cream. Add the well beaten whites. One-half

ounce of gelatine dissolved in one-half cup warm water. Let gelatine become a little cool before adding to the cream. Line dish with thin slices of sponge cake or lady fingers. Pour on the Charlotte Russe. Let cool before serving. Garnish with maraschino cherry or angelica in small bits.

Rhubarb Individual Fanchonettes

1 cup sugar
½ cup strained orange juice
1 tablespoon powdered gelatine
1 piece orange peel

1 cup cream, whipped, flavored and sweetened
A number of individual pastry shells

Cut rhubarb in inch pieces. Place in baking dish in layers, sprinkling sugar between layers. Add two tablespoons water, one tablespoon lard and few thin strips orange peel. Place in moderate oven, cover and bake one hour. Dissolve gelatine in orange juice and when rhubarb is cooked, remove from oven and add this mixture to it. Let it get cold. When ready to serve fill shells with rhubarb mixture, heap with whipped cream and decorate with crystalized orange peel.

Dutch Cobbler

Into a pie tin put
3 cups apples, cut thin
1 tablespoon butter
1 tablespoon molasses
1 cup sugar
Top crust only.

1 tablespoon flour
Pinch salt, cloves
3 tablespoons hot water

Bake 40 minutes in hot oven.

Bananas En Casserole

6 bananas
2 tablespoons butter
4 tablespoons sugar

1 tablespoon maple syrup
Juice of 1 lemon

Cut bananas into halves lengthwise and place in a casserole, together with melted butter, lemon juice, sugar, and maple syrup, and bake slowly about 20 minutes, basting with the sweet syrup from time to time.

Prune Whip

⅓ pound prunes	½ cup sugar
Whites of 4 eggs	½ teaspoon lemon juice

Pick over and wash prunes; soak several hours in cold water to cover; cook in same water until soft; remove stones and rub prunes through a strainer; add sugar; cook 5 minutes or until consistency of marmalade. Cool. Then beat whites of eggs until stiff; add prune mixture gradually, folding in carefully; add lemon juice. Pile lightly in buttered pudding dish. Bake 20 minutes in slow oven. (Place pudding dish in a pan of hot water while baking.)
Serve cold with boiled custard.

Peach Cobbler

2 cups flour	¾ cup milk
2 tablespoons sugar	8 peaches
½ teaspoon salt	¾ cup sugar
4 teaspoons baking powder	¼ teaspoon salt
6 tablespoons fat	¼ teaspoon cinnamon

Mix and sift dry ingredients. Cut in fat, add milk and mix lightly. Toss on floured board and pat into shape.
Peel and slice peaches. Add sugar mixed with salt and spices. Place in bottom of buttered baking dish. Cover with dough and bake in moderate oven ¾ of an hour.

Peanut Brittle Trifle

Whip 1 cup thick cream until light. Fold in gradually ¼ pound peanut brittle which has been passed through meat chopper. Add 1 cup cooked rice (dry and flaky), 1 cup shredded pineapple, and 6 or 8 chopped marshmallows. Add 2 tablespoons pineapple juice and powdered sugar to taste. Pile lightly into glass serving dish, decorate with candied cherries and serve very cold.

Tutti-Frutti

1 cup maraschino cherries	2 teaspoons vanilla
1 cup marshmallows	3 cups whipping cream
1 cup nuts	¾ cup sugar

Whip the cream, add cherries, marshmallows, nuts, sugar and

vanilla. Put in ice box and freeze for 4 hours. Serves twelve people.

Baked Walnut Custard

Beat four eggs slightly. Add one cup of sugar, one-fourth teaspoon of salt, one quart of milk and three-fourths cup of chopped walnuts. Pour into greased ramekins. Place ramekins in a pan of boiling water and bake.

Fruit Cream of Wheat Custard

1 cup cooked cream of wheat	2 eggs
1½ cups milk	½ cup sugar
	½ teaspoon vanilla

Mix cream of wheat with milk, beaten eggs and sugar. Add vanilla. Pour mixture into buttered pan and bake one-half hour in moderate oven. Serve with cream and blackberries or any other fresh fruit in season.

Caramel Custard

One cup granulated sugar caramelized. Stir into one quart hot milk until dissolved; pour hot mixture into three or four well beaten eggs, add pinch of salt to eggs and bake.

Orange Charlotte

¼ package of gelatine	1 cup orange juice
⅓ cup cold water	Juice of 1 lemon and grated
½ cup hot water	rind of lemon and 1 orange
1 cup sugar	1 pint whipping cream

Pour cold water on gelatine, then add boiling water, sugar, orange, lemon juice, also grated rind. Put pan on ice and stir lightly until it begins to thicken. Stir in the whipped cream. Put in mould to harden.

Brown Betty

2 cups sliced apples	¼ cup melted butter
½ cup sugar	Juice and grated rind of
¼ teaspoon cinnamon	one lemon
2 cups bread crumbs	½ cup water or fruit juice

Alternate layers of sliced apples, bread crumbs, sugar and cinnamon mixed, and lemon juice until the baking dish is filled. Cover with crumbs and pour water over all. Cover and bake in a moderate oven for three-quarters of an hour and one-quarter of an hour longer with the dish uncovered.

Serve hot with Hard Sauce.

Peaches or rhubarb may be used according to season.

Baked Apple

6 large apples   ½ cup water
½ cup sugar

Core the apples, place them in a baking dish, pour on the sugar and water and bake in a hot oven until tender (about one-half hour). Baste every five minutes.

Pears and peaches may be baked in the same manner.

Baked Stuffed Apples

6 large baking apples   Chopped nuts
1 cup chopped cranberries   1 teaspoon cinnamon
1 cup sliced bananas
1 cup sugar (or maple
   syrup)

Remove the core of the apples and scoop out part of the pulp leaving a shell of about three-quarter inch thickness.

Mix the chopped fruits, sugar and cinnamon together and fill the cavities in the apples. Cover tops with chopped nuts and bake until tender in a hot oven.

Serve cold or warm.

Bread Pudding

12 slices stale white, raisin   ¼ cup currants
   or whole wheat bread   ½ cup sugar (brown or
¼ cup butter   white)
4 eggs   Pinch salt
1 quart milk

Cut the crust off the bread. More than one kind of bread may be used in the same pudding. Butter the bread thick.

Place a layer of bread in a pudding dish, sprinkle on a few raisins and moisten with the eggs, milk, sugar and salt beaten together. Cover with another layer of bread and so until the dish is full.

Bake in a moderate to slow oven for an hour.

Serve hot, plain or with Hard Sauce.

Vanilla Souffle

5 eggs
4 tablespoons powdered sugar

1 tablespoon vanilla
Pinch of salt

Beat the yolks and the white separately; the whites so they will stand alone. Add the sugar, vanilla and salt to the yolks and beat in. Add the whites to the yolks and beat together well.

Warm the baking dish and pour in the mixture. Bake in the souffle dish in a pan of hot water. Bake for five minutes in a moderate oven (325 degrees F.).

Souffle must be eaten immediately. It will fall if allowed to stand or chill.

Chocolate Souffle

Use two ounces grated chocolate melted in one-half cup water and cool. Add to the souffle in place of vanilla flavoring.

Tapioca Cream

1/3 cup tapioca
1 quart milk
1 egg
½ cup sugar

¼ teaspoon salt
1 teaspoon vanilla, orange or almond flavor

Scald the milk in a double boiler, add the tapioca, sugar and salt. Stir constantly and cook for fifteen minutes.

Beat the yolk of egg and pour into it gradually one-half cup of the milk mixture, stir in thoroughly.

Turn this into the double boiler and stir all vigorously. Cook until a thick custard is formed.

Beat the egg white stiff. Remove the custard from the boiler, add the flavoring and fold in the whites. Chill and serve as dessert or as a child's supper dish.

Serves six.

Fig Pudding

½ pound figs   2 egg whites
¼ cup powdered sugar

Soak the figs for two hours and then cook in a little water for
fifteen minutes or until soft. Mash the figs to a pulp.

Beat the whites and sugar together very stiff. Stir in the figs
and bake in a moderate oven for fifteen minutes.

Serve hot.

If dates are used instead of figs, the dates need not be soaked
previously.

Old Fashioned Plum Pudding

½ cup chopped almonds   1 tablespoon candied lemon
½ cup chopped citron   peel
½ cup chopped apple   ¼ teaspoon cinnamon
½ cup flour   ¼ teaspoon ground cloves
1 cup sugar   3 eggs
1 cup currants   2 cups bread crumbs
1 cup raisins   1 cup suet

Mix all the dry ingredients. Chop the suet and the apple fine
and add the eggs, yolks and whites beaten separately. Add
one-half cup brandy if available.

Stir the two mixtures together and blend well. Turn into a
tightly covered melon mold and steam for six hours at a constant temperature.

The pudding will keep indefinitely and if made for Christmas,
should be made a few weeks ahead, as aging improves the
flavor.

Marshmallow Pineapple Dessert

1 pound marshmallows   ½ pint cream
1 can sliced pineapple   ½ cup chopped walnuts

Pour the juice of canned pineapple over the marshmallows,
cut in fourths.

Cut the pineapple into pieces and add to the marshmallows
and liquor. Allow to stand for three or more hours.

Fold in the cream, whipped stiff, and stir in the nuts. Chill
and serve.

Serves eight.

Baked Indian Pudding

1/3 cup cornmeal	1 teaspoon ginger
½ cup dark molasses	1 teaspoon salt
5 cups milk	1 teaspoon cinnamon

Scald the milk. Pour it slowly on the cornmeal and cook for twenty minutes in a double boiler. Add molasses, ginger, salt and cinnamon. Set a buttered baking dish in a pan of hot water. Pour the mixture into the baking dish and bake for two hours. Serve with cream.

Prune Whip

1 cup prunes	3 egg whites
¼ cup confectioners' sugar	1 teaspoon vanilla

Soak the prunes over night in cold water.

Cook until soft (about one-half hour), stone and mash to a pulp.

Heat the pulp with the sugar in a double boiler for ten minutes. Cool. Beat the egg whites very stiff and when the prune mixture is cool, add the whites and the vanilla. Serve with whipped cream.

Any fruit may be made into whip. Nuts and marshmallows may be added to the prune whip also.

Chestnut Souffle

1 cup chestnuts	½ cup milk
2 tablespoons flour	3 egg whites
½ cup sugar	

Boil the chestnuts, drain and mash. Mix the sugar with the flour, add the chestnuts and then gradually add the milk. Cook for five minutes and stir constantly.

Beat the egg whites stiff and fold into the mixture. Bake in greased individual molds until firm.

Paradise Pudding

¼ lb. blanched almonds	1 doz. candied cherries
1 doz. marshmallows	½ doz. macaroons

Cut fine and stand aside in a cool place. Dissolve a package of lemon Jello in a pint of boiling water. When cold whip to the consistency of whipped cream. Fold in one cup of whipped cream, the cut fruit and one-quarter cup of sugar. Turn into a square pan and set in a cold place to harden. Serve in slices.

Cornmeal Souffle

Cook three-fourths cup cornmeal (white) in one pint sweet milk until well thickened. Add one-half teaspoon salt and remove from fire. When cold beat in yolks of four eggs, and last, the stiffly beaten whites. Bake in earthen dish, well heated and buttered. When light and nicely browned, serve at once from baking dish. This should bake about forty-five minutes.

Sally Lunn

Sally Lunn is an old southern dish and delicious for breakfast. Cream 1/4 cup butter with 3 tablespoons sugar. Add 2 well beaten eggs, 1 cup sweet milk, 2 1/2 cups flour, 2 teaspoons baking powder and 1/2 teaspoon salt. Bake in glass dish or muffin rings.

SAUCES

Hard Sauce

1/4 cup butter   1 teaspoon vanilla
1 cup powdered, brown or   Grated lemon rind
   maple sugar

Cream the butter well and work in the sugar and flavoring. Set in a cool place until needed. Cream and more sugar may be added for more sauce.

Foamy Sauce

1 cup confectioners' sugar   Hot water
1/2 cup butter   Vanilla
1 egg

Cream the butter and work in the sugar; add the beaten egg, and about two tablespoons hot water. Heat and mix over hot water until the sauce thickens. Add vanilla and serve.

Chocolate Sauce

1 cup sugar
1 cup water
3 tablespoons rich cream

2 squares bitter chocolate
Vanilla

Boil the sugar and water in a saucepan for five minutes and let partly cool. Melt the chocolate over hot water and stir in. Add vanilla.

Heat over hot water and when thickening add the cream.

If to be used as a sauce over ice cream, make with water instead of cream.

Thick Caramel Sauce

1 cup sugar
1 tablespoon butter
¼ cup water

1 tablespoon cornstarch
1 cup milk
Vanilla

Cook the sugar and water together in a saucepan until they are a golden brown. Heat the butter and cornstarch together in another pan and then combine the two adding scalded milk and last the vanilla. Stir constantly and make smooth and creamy.

A less rich sauce may be made with one cup hot water instead of milk.

Serve on bread pudding, Brown Betty, etc.

Lemon juice may be used instead of vanilla, but then use only hot water and no milk.

Apples in Casserole

Peel and remove core from six tart apples. Place in casserole; mix one cup sugar, one-half cup butter, one cup flour and one teaspoon cinnamon into crumbly mass; sprinkle on apples. Pour over all one-half cup water; place in oven and bake with cover on till apples are tender but not broken. Remove cover and brown slightly. Serve hot.

Sauce

To one pint of blackberry juice add three or four tablespoons cold water and let come to a boil. Add sugar to taste and butter the size of a walnut. Thicken with tablespoon of flour and cook till thick as desired and serve warm.

Any other berries may be used for this roll and is just as successful.

ICE CREAMS AND FROZEN PUDDINGS

In Making Desserts in a Mold:

Have the mold very cold before pouring in the mixture.

Fill very full so that mixture will be forced down into the mold when the cover is put on.

Smooth the top before putting on lid and cover the mixture with two layers of waxed paper, this will help to hold the lid tight.

Completely bury the mold in a mixture of three parts ice to one part coarse salt. Table salt will not give results and is wasteful.

To Prepare Desserts in the Pans of Iceless Refrigerators:

Thin ice creams with a small percentage of cream are not satisfactory in iceless machines since there is no opportunity for stirring the mixture and breaking up the little ice crystals. Rich ice creams are especially good when frozen in these pans. Beat the cream very stiff and add a small amount of dissolved gelatine to overcome the formation of ice crystals.

All desserts that are packed in ice ordinarily, may be made satisfactorily in an iceless refrigerator.

Desserts should freeze in from five to seven hours unless the machine is set below the average ice-cube forming temperature.

Vanilla Ice Cream

2 cups milk	1 teaspoon gelatine
1 cup sugar	1½ pints heavy cream
2 tablespoons flour	2 teaspoons vanilla
2 egg yolks	

Scald the milk in a double boiler and add the sugar and the flour mixed together. Cook fifteen minutes. Add the yolks, beaten, and cook for two minutes more or until the spoon coats.

Soak the gelatine in one tablespoon cold water for five minutes. Add the gelatine to the milk mixture and then chill.

Whip the cream stiff and fold into the cold mixture. Add the vanilla and a speck of salt. The salt brings out the flavor. Pour into refrigerator tray and stir every half hour until the ice cream starts to stiffen.

Chocolate Ice Cream

Melt three ounces of chocolate in one-quarter cup hot water and stir until smooth. Add to the vanilla ice cream mixture.

Crushed Fruit for Ice Cream

If the fruit is very juicy, add one-quarter teaspoon more gelatine to recipe.

If the fruit is bland, add juice of one lemon.

Mix the fruit with the Vanilla Ice Cream as much or little as desired.

Apricot Marshmallow Ice Cream

Drain one can apricots, put through food chopper. Combine with the juice of one lemon, add a dash of salt and one-half cup of sugar. Cook five minutes. Drop in ten marshmallows, cut in pieces, when cool fold in one cup cream whipped. Place in mold and pack in ice and salt.

Fudge Sauce for Ice Cream

1½ cups water	1 teaspoon vanilla
1 cup sugar	Pinch of salt
2 squares bitter chocolate	1 tablespoon cornstarch

Boil the sugar and water about two minutes and add the cornstarch dissolved in a tablespoon of cold water. Stir smooth. Melt the chocolate and add to the syrup; cook two or three minutes and add vanilla.

Serve hot over ice cream.

Butterscotch Sauce

1 cup brown sugar	Pinch of salt
4 tablespoons butter	¼ cup water
1 teaspoon cornstarch	1 teaspoon vinegar

Dissolve the cornstarch in cold water, mix with the sugar and boil all in a saucepan until a soft ball forms when a drop of sauce is put in cold water. Serve hot over ice cream.

Marshmallow Sauce

½ pound marshmallows	¾ cup sugar
2 tablespoons water	¼ cup milk

Stir the marshmallows with the water in a double boiler until smooth.

Boil the sugar and milk until the syrup threads. When nearly cold, beat until thick and white. Stand in boiling water and stir until thin enough to pour.

Pour the syrup over the melted marshmallows and beat the two together. Serve hot over ice cream.

Lemon Water Ice

1 teaspoon gelatine	2 cups sugar
4 cups boiling water	Grated lemon rind
¾ cup lemon juice	

Soak the gelatine in one tablespoon cold water for five minutes. Boil the sugar in the hot water for twenty minutes and add the gelatine.

When cool, add the lemon juice and gratings, strain and freeze either in ice or in mechanical refrigerator.

In freezing an ice, turn the freezer for five minutes, let the ice stand for five minutes and turn again for five minutes. Repeat until the whole is frozen.

Pineapple Mousse

2 cups canned shredded   2 tablespoons lemon juice
  pineapple and juice   2 cups cream
¾ cup sugar   2 teaspoons gelatine

Heat the pineapple, add the sugar, lemon juice and the gelatine which has been soaked for five minutes in two tablespoons cold water.

Cool the mixture. When it starts to thicken, fold in the cream beaten stiff. Pour into refrigerator pans and freeze without stirring.

Nesselrode Pudding

Add to two quarts of vanilla ice cream mixture
½ cup marrons chopped   1 tablespoon chopped pe-
¼ cup marron syrup   cans or walnuts
1 teaspoon citron
½ cup chopped red maras-
  chino cherries

Mix all the ingredients together and add to the ice cream mixture. Do not freeze too hard.

Serve with whipped cream sweetened with a little marron syrup or syrup from cherries.

Biscuit Tortoni

½ cup walnuts
6 macaroons
1 quart vanilla ice cream

Crush the nuts and macaroons as fine as possible. Mix with the ice cream and freeze in refrigerator pans.

Baked Alaska

Make vanilla ice cream in a melon mold.
Beat four egg whites very stiff with one cup confectioners
sugar. Cover the ice cream with this meringue and put in a
very hot oven just long enough to brown the meringue.
The meringue may be put onto the ice cream in fancy form
with a pastry bag.

Frozen Pudding

1 pint whipped cream
12 stale macaroons
½ cup sliced candied pineapple
¼ pound crystallized cherries or other crystallized
fruit

½ cup confectioners sugar
¼ teaspoon maraschino
syrup

Mix all together thoroughly and pack in a mold. Pack in ice
and let stand for four hours.

Such puddings may be packed in snow in the winter and the
freezing will be just as even as with ice. A little coarse salt
will hasten the freezing.

Frozen Rice Pudding

4 egg yolks
2 cups milk
1 cup cooked rice

3 tablespoons sugar
1 cup whipped cream
1 tablespoon vanilla

Heat the milk and egg yolks in a double boiler. Stir constantly until it thickens. Remove from flame and add vanilla,
sugar and the rice put through the food chopper.
When cold add the whipped cream. Turn into a tightly
covered mold and pack in ice and salt until frozen. Requires about one hour.

Banana Ice

Juice of 3 oranges	2 cups of sugar
Juice of 3 lemons	3 cups of water
3 bananas, mashed	

Dissolve the sugar in water. Mix fruit juices, and last, mash bananas and mix ingredients together. Put in freezer and turn freezer until the ice is hard. Let stand until ready to serve. Serves eight people.

Frozen Peaches

Take one can of peaches, remove paper wrapper and pack in bucket of ice and salt for two hours. Place can upright in bucket. To serve open can by dipping can in hot water. Slip contents out on plate. Slice one half inch thick and serve with cream and salad dressing.

Banana Ice Cream

1 quart cream	A few grains salt
4 ripe bananas	1½ tablespoons lemon juice
1 cup sugar	

Remove skins of the bananas and force through a sieve with lemon juice. Partly freeze the remaining ingredients and add banana-lemon pulp. Freeze.

Apricot Sherbet

1 can apricots	2 lemons
1 cup sugar	1 quart water
5 oranges	Whites of 3 eggs

Cook sugar and water to syrup. Rub the apricots through a sieve and mix with the syrup and fruit juices. Add the beaten whites. Put in a freezer and when thoroughly chilled add 1 quart of cream and freeze. Makes three quarts.

Peppermint Ice Cream

½ lb. peppermint sugar stick candy	2 cups milk
¾ cup granulated sugar	2 cups heavy cream

Melt candy and sugar with the milk; add heavy cream and freeze. Let ripen two or three hours. Makes one quart.

Eggs and Egg Dishes

Eggs

To test the freshness of eggs:

A fresh egg when placed in a glass of water will drop to the bottom. A stale egg will rise to the top of the water.

Try to cook eggs just below the boiling point of water. Boiling eggs destroys much of their food value and makes them tough and difficult to digest.

Putting Down Eggs in Water Glass

One part of water glass to ten parts of water.

Use only strictly fresh eggs as the water glass will preserve the eggs in exactly the state of freshness in which they are at the time they are put down.

Boil the water and allow to cool. Add to the water glass, which may be purchased at the drug store. Stir the water into the water glass thoroughly. Place eggs in layers in a stone crock and pour over the liquid, covering the eggs well. Place an old dish on top of the eggs to weigh them down. Keep in a cool place.

When eggs are wanted for use, take them out of the liquid and wash them in fresh water. New eggs may be added from time to time. The eggs must always be under the liquid or they will spoil.

Four Minute Soft Cooked Eggs

Boil the water, then slide eggs into the water and reduce flame so that water simmers for four minutes. Serve in egg cups.

Eggs may be started in cold water, brought to the boiling point and simmered.

Hard Cooked Eggs

Slide eggs into boiling water, reduce flame and allow to simmer one-half hour for complete hardness. Serve hot sliced in two with butter or mayonnaise.

Eggs au Beurre

Melt about one tablespoon of butter in a frying pan, slide in an egg and cook at medium heat until the white is firm and the edges brown a little. Turn over once being careful not to break but keep the egg intact. Use more butter if egg has tendency to stick.

Scrambled Eggs

3 eggs   ½ teaspoon salt
½ cup milk   Pepper
1 teaspoon butter

Beat whole eggs, add milk and salt and pepper. Place butter in frying pan, heat over low flame and pour in egg batter. Allow to cook until white begins to set, then stir and serve before the mass is dry. Serve on toast on heated plates. Garnish with parsely.

Fried Eggs

Heat tablespoon of butter or bacon fat in a frying pan. Slide in the egg. Let fry very slowly, basting with the butter or fat. The egg is fried when a thin white coating comes over the yolk.

Shirred Eggs

Grease a small glass or earthen baking dish and line with bread crumbs. Slide in the egg cover with crumbs, salt and pepper and bake in a slow oven until the white is well set. Serve in the baking dish. Grated cheese may be mixed with the coating of bread crumbs.

Ham and Eggs

If ham is very salty, soak in milk for fifteen minutes.
Trim off half the fatty edge of raw ham cut about one-quarter

inch thick. Use this fat to grease the frying pan. Have the frying pan very hot, fry ham quickly on one side then on the other until brown. Do not cook too long or flavor will be destroyed.

Slide eggs into pan with some ham fat remaining. Baste with ham fat and cook until yolk is covered with a thin white skin. Serve very hot; placing eggs on the ham and garnish with parsely.

Cheese and Egg Omelet

1 loaf stale bread	1 cup sweet milk
1/2 pound cheese	Pinch salt
3 eggs	

Butter pan well. Line with thin slices of bread, layer of cheese sliced thin, then alternate with layer of buttered bread. Beat the three eggs, salt and milk. Pour over the top and bake 10 minutes.

Chipped Beef in Scrambled Eggs

1/2 pound chipped dried beef	3 eggs
	1/2 cup milk

Pour hot water over the beef and simmer for fifteen minutes. Pour off any remaining water.

Mix milk and whole eggs and stir into the beef. Put one tablespoon butter in frying pan and scramble eggs and beef together.

Serve hot on toast. No further seasoning is required as dried beef is very salty.

A Change from Scrambled Eggs

2 tablespoons flour	Seasoning
1 tablespoon butter	1 egg for each person
1 cup milk	

Put milk on to boil. Moisten the flour and add it, with butter and seasoning, to milk. Cook gently for a few minutes. Gently break the eggs, and drop in one by one. When cooked serve on rounds of toast.

Poached Eggs au Gratin

Butter six sauce dishes, sprinkle salt, pepper and paprika in them and slide one egg in each. Sprinkle grated cheese over the egg. Place sauce dishes in a shallow pan of hot water and bake in the oven until the eggs set.

Brown for just a moment under the oven flame and serve hot on toast.

Eggs Scrambled with Tomato Sauce

Beat six eggs, add salt, pepper and one-half cup milk. Heat a spider, melt in it butter size of a walnut and pour in the egg mixture. Scramble and keep flame low to retain moisture. Stir in canned tomato and one-quarter pound grated American cheese.

Serve hot on toast.

Eggs Southern Style

6 eggs	1 tablespoon chopped green
1 cup tomato	peppers
1 tablespoon chopped onion	Butter
1 can mushrooms	
1 tablespoon chopped red peppers	

Stew the onions and chopped peppers in butter in a spider. Add the tomato and mushrooms. When heated, add the beaten eggs and scramble.

Serve on toast as a lunch dish.

Cold Deviled Eggs

4 hard cooked eggs

Slice eggs in two lengthwise and remove yolk. Chill the whites. Cream yolks into one tablespoon butter, season with one-half teaspoon dry mustard, one-half teaspoon salt, one-half teaspoon vinegar and one-half teaspoon Worcestershire sauce. Roll into balls and replace in each half egg white. Serve as a luncheon dish on lettuce leaves.

For picnics, replace yolk with paste and cover over with white of egg. Fasten in original shape with toothpick. Wrap in waxed paper.

Eggs au Gratin

6 hard cooked eggs
¾ cup grated cheese

¼ cup bread crumbs or
   cracker crumbs
2 cups white sauce.

Shell the hard cooked eggs, cut in two and cut off a little from
each tip so that the halves will stand up. Remove the yolks
and rub to a smooth paste with butter, cheese and a little dry
mustard.

Refill the empty white with this paste; sprinkle on more grated
cheese, seasoning and bread crumbs. Place in a shallow buttered dish and pour over the white sauce. (Tomato sauce
may be used instead.)

Serve hot on toast. Rye bread toast is very agreeable.

Curried Eggs

½ teaspoon curry powder
6 hard boiled eggs
1 cup milk

2 tablespoons flour
Salt and pepper.

Melt two tablespoons butter in a spider, add salt and pepper
and curry powder. Brown the flour and pour in the milk
slowly. Dice the hard eggs and baste with the hot sauce in the
spider.

Serve hot on toast.

Asparagus Omelet

(Chopped chicken, veal or ham may be used in place of
asparagus).

1 can asparagus
Make a plain omelet.

1 cup white sauce

Drain and wash the asparagus and add white sauce. Spread
half this mixture in the center of the omelet, fold over and
pour remaining half over as a sauce. Garnish with chopped
parsley.

Cheese Omelet

When making the Plain Omelet, add two tablespoons grated
American cheese to the yolks. Before folding over, sprinkle
with one tablespoon cheese.

French Omelet

3 eggs   Salt and pepper
3 tablespoons milk

Beat yolks and whites separately. Add milk, salt and pepper
to the beaten yolks.

Butter a hot spider. Fold white into yolk batter and turn in to
hot spider. Cook until it sets and browns lightly. Place
currant or strawberry jelly in center of omelet and fold over.
Serve hot on a warmed platter.

Spanish Omelet

Follow directions for French omelet.

Make the following sauce heated in a greased spider. Simmer
one tablespoon chopped onions, two tablespoons chopped
green olives, one small green and one small red pepper
chopped; when partially stewed, add one can tomatoes, two
tablespoons chopped mushrooms, salt, paprika and a few
capers. Cook this mixture until quite thick.

Pour one-quarter cupful in center of omelet, fold over and
pour rest of sauce over the omelet.

Milk Omelet

4 eggs   ½ teaspoon salt
¼ cup milk   Pepper
1 teaspoon butter

Beat eggs well. Add the milk and seasoning. Melt the butter
in the spider and turn in the egg mixture.

As edges cook, draw them toward the center with a knife
blade. When whole has set, fold once and serve on a hot
platter.

FISH AND SEAFOOD

Fish

Fish must be perfectly fresh and firm and must be kept cool. Wrap fish in a damp cloth, then in paper and keep on ice. Thaw frozen fish in **cold** water and use at once.

Clean a fish in cold water and sprinkle it with salt and pepper to bring out its flavor.

Trout, mackerel, whitefish, salmon, redsnapper, cod, halibut and haddock are in season throughout the year.

Oysters, scallops and muscles are in season only in fall and winter. Soft shell crabs are in season in summer.

Broiled Fish

Clean and bone the fish. Sprinkle with pepper and salt and dot with butter. Place as near flame as possible on broiling rack, flesh side up. As soon as flesh starts to brown, reduce flame and cook until white and firm. Turn on skin side with aid of pancake turner and broil until brown and crisp.

Remove to hot platter, garnish with parsley and lemon and serve with parsley butter poured over the fish.

Parsley Butter

1 tablespoon butter	¼ teaspoon salt
1 teaspoon chopped parsley	Pepper
	Paprika
1 teaspoon lemon juice	

Cream the butter, add seasoning and lemon juice. Spread over fish directly it is removed from fire.

Fried Fish

Clean fish and wipe dry. Sprinkle with salt and pepper. Dip in flour, cracker crumbs or cornmeal, then in egg, then again in flour. Fry in deep, hot fat until brown.

Boiled Fish

Cut fish into slices, rub with salt and let stand in salt for several hours.

Boil one quart of water with two tablespoons vinegar, one-half teaspoon whole pepper, one tablespoon each chopped onion, chopped celery, chopped carrot.

Drop the slices of fish into the boiling seasoned water and let cook slowly until the fish is tender. Remove the bones, strain and serve on a platter with egg sauce. Keep the fish stock if desired.

Sauce for Boiled Fish

1 cup brown sauce
2 egg yolks
Juice of one lemon

In making the brown sauce, employ the fish liquor. Beat the egg yolks and add the hot sauce. Stir until thick. Stir in the lemon juice just before serving.

Broiled Fish

Clean, bone and salt the fish. Grease the rack of the broiler and place fish, flesh side up, on it. Broil as near to the flame as possible. When edges crisp, lower the flame and cook until tender. Turn over carefully and brown on skin side.

Spread with parsley butter, garnish with parsley and lemon.

Baked Trout

3 to 3½ pound trout   1 can tomatoes
1 tablespoon flour   1 chopped onion
1 egg yolk   1 piece celery root

Salt the fish and let stand for several hours. Make a paste of the flour with a little tomato juice. Place fish in a dripping pan with tomatoes, onion, celery root and butter. Bake for one-half hour.

Drain and strain the sauce, thicken with the beaten yolk of egg, add a little cream, seasoning and serve over the hot trout.

Planked Fish

Use a hickory or oak plank. Have the fish boned and sprinkle with salt and pepper. Broil for five minutes on skin side. Then place on a heated, greased plank, skin side down. Paint with melted butter and put in a hot oven.

Bake until the fish is browned, then reduce the flame. Bake for fifteen minutes or until fish is quite tender. Press mashed potatoes thru a pastry bag to form a trimming around the fish; brown well in the oven, pour on melted butter, sprinkle with parsley and serve on the plank placed on a platter.

Baked Mackerel

3 tablespoons butter
1 cup bread crumbs
1 teaspoon chopped onions
1 teaspoon chopped capers
1 teaspoon chopped parsley

3½ to 4 pound mackerel
¼ teaspoon salt
⅛ teaspoon pepper

Melt butter. Add crumbs, onions, capers, salt, pepper, and parsley. Wash the fish and wipe with a damp cloth. Stuff and tie together. Sprinkle with salt and pepper, and spread with melted butter.

Bake in moderate oven (350 degrees F.) fifty to sixty minutes. Baste well.

Baked Mackerel

1 medium sized mackerel
3 slices bacon
2 cups stale bread crumbs
½ teaspoon chopped green pepper

1/3 teaspoon salt
½ small onion, chopped
1 tablespoon bacon, chopped

Have the mackerel dressed for broiling.

Mix bread crumbs, pepper, chopped onion and bacon, salt

and a little pepper. Lay stuffing in fish, cover with slice of bacon. Lay two strips of bacon on top of fish, place in baking pan, bake in a moderate oven basting with fat drippings.

Stuffing for Baked Fish

Beat one egg and use to moisten one and one-half cups bread crumbs. Add four tablespoons melted butter, season and mix well. Put the stuffing into the cleaned washed fish and sew in with thread.

Fish Baked on a Campfire

Build a hot fire of twigs and dry wood. Use when embers are red hot.

Remove head and entrails of fish, also its large fins but not the tail. Wrap in heavy paper and place in the hot embers. Let bake for half an hour unless fish is very large.

Rake out the fish, unwrap, sprinkle with pepper and salt and serve. The scales and skin will cling to the wrapping paper.

Fried Trout

Clean fish well, washed once only, drained, salted with about one-half teaspoon salt, then rolled in flour and corn-meal (half of each). For 2 lbs. of fish take ¼ lb. of salt pork, cut in thin slices and fried a crisp brown. Take pork from the pan and put in fish, having only enough fish in pan to cover the bottom. Fry golden brown on both sides. Serve hot with the salt pork as a garnish.

Creamed Shrimp

Wash and drain 1 can of shrimp. Put 1 tablespoon of butter and 1 tablespoon flour in a saucepan. When melted, add ½ pint of milk. Stir until boiling, season with salt and pepper. Add the shrimp. Serve on toast.

Halibut with Tomato Sauce

To one can of tomatoes add one onion, bit of bay leaf, few peppercorns, a little parsley, pepper and salt, a dash of red pepper, 1 teaspoon of sugar. Boil well together and strain. Put 2 tablespoons of butter into spider; add 2 tablespoons of flour; add the tomatoes; pour this mixture over a large halibut steak 2 inches thick, and bake ¾ of an hour. Baste often with the sauce.

Salmon Loaf

1 can salmon (2 cups)
2 eggs
1 cup cooked rice
¾ cup milk
¼ cup cracker crumbs

1½ cups white sauce
1 tablespoon butter
1 teaspoonful lemon juice
1 teaspoon paprika
1 teaspoon salt

Remove spines and bones; mix with cold rice, one whole egg, and white of one egg. Add milk and seasoning.

Grease loaf pan, turn in mixture, cover with crumbs and dot with butter. Bake at 400 F. for one-half hour.

Mix remaining yolk with white sauce, add lemon and serve as sauce. Makes an excellent luncheon dish.

Serves six.

Codfish a la Creole

2 cups codfish
4 boiled potatoes

1 cup canned tomato
2 pimentos

Wash salt codfish in cold water. Bone and shred. Cover with tepid water and allow to stand until fish is soft. Drain.

Place alternately layer of boiled potatoes, cold, then layer of shredded fish, one-half can red pimento cut in squares and season with salt and pepper. Pour over all one cup canned tomato, spread cracker crumbs on top and bake until crumbs turn brown.

Codfish Balls

Boil codfish thoroughly. Boil potatoes and mash the codfish and potatoes together. Add 1 egg, butter and cream, enough salt and pepper to season.

Fry in deep hot fat until nice and brown. Serve hot.

New England Codfish Balls

1 cup salt codfish

1 egg

½ tablespoon butter

2½ cups potatoes (raw)

Pepper, a speck

Wash the fish in cold water. Remove bones and shred. Pare and cut the potatoes in pieces. The fish and potatoes are cooked together in boiling water until potatoes are cooked soft. Drain dry, mash and add the butter. Beat the egg, add the seasoning and beat all together until well mixed. Shape in balls from the end of spoon and fry until brown in deep fat. Drain onto brown paper.

Should the balls break, add part of another egg to mixture.

Finnan Haddie

1 finnan haddie

1½ cups milk

1 small onion

1 green pepper

1 teaspoon salt

½ teaspoon paprika

4 tablespoons butter

2 tablespoons parsley

¼ teaspoon white pepper

Clean and dry the finnan haddie. Prepare in a large baking pan. Cover with onion, chopped parsley, chopped pepper, paprika, salt and pepper. Dot with pieces of butter. Cover with milk and bake in medium oven for one hour, basting with milk. Serve quickly.

Serves six.

Salmon Cutlet

1 pound can of salmon

1 cup canned peas

2 eggs

2 cups mashed potatoes

2 cups white sauce

2 teaspoons salt

Speck pepper

Bread crumbs

Mash salmon with fork, removing spine and bones. Beat one egg, add potatoes and seasoning. Mix well with salmon and form into cutlets.

Add one tablespoon water to second egg. Crumb and egg. Fry in deep fat. Serve with hot peas in white sauce. Garnish with parsley.

Broiled Halibut Steak

Lay halibut in salt water for one-half hour. Then soak in a bath of salad oil and lemon juice for another half hour. Dry and broil for fifteen minutes. Turn twice, being careful not to break the flesh. Spread with parsley butter, garnish and serve.

Baked Halibut

Place spices in a bread pan: allspice, bay leaf, whole pepper, cloves, etc. Rub lemon juice in fish and allow to stand for an hour or more. Sprinkle with salt and pepper and bake in bread pan for fifteen minutes in a hot oven. Dot with two tablespoons of butter. Serve with tomato sauce.

Baked Halibut in Tomato Sauce

Boil the halibut and break into small pieces. Make one cup of white sauce, adding one can of tomatoes, strained. Make the white sauce very smooth and stir while adding tomato juice. Place the halibut in a greased baking dish, cover with the sauce, season and cover with cracker crumbs. Dot with pepper and bake for twenty minutes until brown.

Sweet-Sour Fish

4 pound pike, trout or other fish	1 cup fish stock
½ cup vinegar	Tablespoon seeded raisins
½ cup brown sugar	½ teaspoon onion juice

Clean, salt and slice the fish and allow to stand several hours. Boil the fish until the flesh drops away from the bone. Drain, reserving the liquid, and bone the fish. Mix and cook the other ingredients. Pour hot over the fish.

Serve cool.

Mustard Sauce

Melt three tablespoons butter, add one teaspoon hot water, and three teaspoons prepared mustard. Serve while hot over fish.

Horseradish Sauce

Mix one-quarter cup grated horseradish with one tablespoon strong vinegar; add one tablespoon sugar and a pinch of salt and pepper. Beat one-quarter cup of cream and mix with other ingredients. Serve cold with baked ham, cold meat, tongue, etc.

Tartar Sauce

1 cup mayonnaise dressing
1 tablespoon chopped pickle
1 tablespoon chopped green olives
½ teaspoon chopped onion
1 tablespoon chopped capers
1½ tablespoons tarragon vinegar

Stir all ingredients together until well mixed. Chill and serve with cold fish, fried oysters, filet of sole, etc.

Parsley Butter

1 teaspoon fine chopped parsley
1 tablespoon butter
1 teaspoon lemon juice
Salt and pepper

Cream the butter, add seasoning, lemon juice and chopped parsley. Spread this paste over hot broiled steak, lamb chops or broiled fish.

Egg Sauce

Chop six hard cooked eggs and mix with one cup cream. Heat in a double boiler, add one tablespoon butter, pinch of salt and a little paprika. Cook for ten minutes. Remove from flame, add a little chopped parsley and serve hot over asparagus, brussels sprouts or fish.

Cold Gingersnap Sauce for Fish

4 gingersnaps
1/2 cup brown sugar
1/2 cup vinegar
1 lemon, sliced

1/2 cup raisins
1 cup soup stock or fish stock

Cook all the ingredients together until they are smooth. Pour over the fish hot and allow to cool. Serve cold.

Brown Sauce

2 tablespoons flour
2 tablespoons butter
1 cup hot water or soup stock

1/2 teaspoon salt
Pepper

Brown the flour in the butter. Add the hot liquid, season and cook for five minutes. Use to cover hot meats, dumplings, vegetables, etc.

Mushroom Sauce

Drain one can of mushrooms and cut into pieces. Use the mushroom liquor in making the brown sauce. Mix with the sauce and serve hot over meat.

Caper Sauce for Fish

Add one-half cup drained capers to the brown sauce and serve on fish.

Creole Sauce

4 tablespoons canned tomatoes
2 tablespoons chopped onions
2 tablespoons chopped green peppers
2 tablespoons chopped red peppers

2 tablespoons chopped parsley
2 tablespoons chopped mushrooms
Salt
Paprika
2 cups brown sauce
2 tablespoons butter

Simmer the onion in butter, add the peppers, tomato and mushrooms. Pour on the brown sauce and season very highly. Cook for fifteen minutes and serve hot over steak.

Tomato Sauce

½ can tomatoes
2 tablespoons butter
2 tablespoons flour
2 tablespoons chopped
onion

2 tablespoons chopped
peppers
½ teaspoon salt
1 teaspoon sugar
Bay leaf

Cook the tomatoes for fifteen minutes. Add onion, pepper and bay leaf. Strain.
Brown the flour in the butter, add the tomato liquid gradually and cook until it thickens. Season. Serve with meat, spaghetti, etc.

Sweet-Sour Sauce

2 tablespoons vinegar
2 tablespoons sugar
2 tablespoons butter

2 tablespoons flour
Salt and pepper
1 cup soup stock

Melt the sugar in a spider, brown the flour in the butter and then add soup stock gradually. Stir in the vinegar and seasoning. Serve hot over vegetables.

Hollandaise Sauce

4 egg yolks
1 cup butter
Juice of one lemon

¼ teaspoon salt
Pepper
½ cup water

Cream the butter and add egg yolks one at a time. Stir well, add the juice of lemon and seasoning. Just before serving, stir in the hot water and cook until thick in a double boiler.

Shrimp and Pea Patties

1 cup of shrimps
1 cup of canned peas
1½ cups milk
4 tablespoons butter

2 tablespoons flour
½ teaspoon salt
Paprika

Drain the peas. Melt the butter and add the flour and the seasoning. Stir constantly while adding the milk very slowly. Add the peas and then the shrimps, broken into small pieces. Be sure the shrimps are heated through. Then fill patty shells which have previously been warmed in the oven. Serve immediately and garnish with parsley.

Shrimps a la Creole

1 quart boiled shrimps	Cloves
1/2 can small peas	Bay leaf
1/4 can tomatoes	Salt and pepper
1/2 can small mushrooms	Paprika
1 onion	
2 tablespoons catsup or	
tomato chili	

Dice the shrimps.

Stew all the other ingredients in a casserole for one-half to
three-quarters of an hour then add the boiled shrimps and
serve out of the casserole very hot, on rounds of white bread
toast. Garnish with parsley.

Salmon and Crabmeat au Gratin

1 small can salmon	4 tablespoons flour
1 large can crabmeat	1/2 teaspoon pepper
1 1/2 cups milk	5 tablespoons butter
1 teaspoon salt	1/4 cup grated cheese

Mix flour, milk, butter and seasoning. Cover bottom of buttered baking dish with thin layer of this sauce. Add alternate layers crabmeat and salmon and sauce until dish is full.
Dot with butter, sprinkle on cheese and bake at 500 F. for
fifteen minutes or until cheese is brown.

Serves six.

Panroasted Oysters

1 pint oysters	1/2 cup tomato catsup or
1 1/2 tablespoons flour	canned tomato
1/2 teaspoon salt	Cayenne pepper
2 tablespoons butter	Worcestershire sauce
1 cup milk	

Drain the oysters. Melt the butter or fat, add seasoning and
tomato catsup. Make a paste of the flour with cold water, mix
with milk, and bring to a boil. Mix the milk and flour with
the tomato liquid. Stir slowly.

Turn off fire. Drop in oysters and let stand until edges curl.
Serve on hot rounds of toast.

Chop peaches and pineapple, add sugar, let stand one hour. Cook slowly 45 minutes then add nut meats and cook 10 minutes longer, turn into sterilized jars or glasses and seal cold, cover with paraffin. When fresh pineapple is in season it is most preferable.

Chili Sauce

½ bushel tomatoes
½ peck onions
6 green peppers
4 red peppers
6 bunches celery
10 cups vinegar
4 tablespoons ground mus-tard

6 cups sugar
1¼ cups salt
2 hands full whole cloves
2 5c boxes cinnamon
2 tablespoons ground red pepper

Tie cinnamon and cloves in cheese cloth bag. **Boil all together** for six hours.

Pepper Relish

12 green peppers
12 red peppers

12 large onions
1 stock of large celery.

Chop fine green peppers and also the red peppers, onions, celery. Then pour over boiling water and let stand five minutes and drain. Remove seeds from peppers.

2c mixed spice, tie in a sack
4 tablespoons salt

2 cups sugar
3 cups vinegar

Boil vinegar and spice, salt, sugar, green peppers, red peppers, onions, celery. Boil all together about 5 minutes and then put in jars and seal.

Pepper Relish

6 green peppers
6 red peppers
7 small onions

1½ pints of vinegar
1½ teaspoons salt
2 cupfuls of sugar

Grind peppers and onions and pour boiling water over them. Let stand fifteen minutes, then strain; add sugar, salt and vinegar. Boil twenty minutes and seal. You will find this a very appetizing dish when meat and potatoes are served.

Peach Conserve

15 peaches   3½ cups sugar
1 pint canned pineapple   1 cup almonds

Chop peaches and pineapple; add sugar and let stand one
hour. Cook slowly 45 minutes; then add blanched almonds
and cook ten minutes longer. Turn into sterilized glasses and
when cold cover with melted paraffin.

Cranberry and Apple Sauce

1 cup cranberries   ¾ cup sugar (more if
1 cup apple (diced)   sweeter sauce is desired)
1 cup water

Place the apple in the pot, the cranberries over the apples, and
the water (the water should not reach to more than half the
depth of the fruit). Cover closely and place on moderate
flame. After the berries have commenced to pop open, stir
sugar into sauce, and then stir mixture occasionally until berries
are all mashed and sauce is thick. This is delightful served
with meat or vegetables. The apples take away the extreme
tartness of the berries and the berries give the apples piquancy.
More or less of either fruit may be used.

Grape Conserve

2 quarts stemmed grapes   3 oranges
1½ pounds of raisins   ½ pound nuts

The grapes should not be over-ripe. Wash grapes and separate pulp from the skins. Cook pulp until soft and pass
through a sieve. Remove pulp and juice from oranges and
add to the grape skins, pulp and raisins. Measure and add
equal amount of sugar. Simmer until ready to jell. Add nuts
in broken pieces.

Cranberry Jelly

Cook until soft two quarts of cranberries, after being picked over and washed, and one and one-half pints of water. The berries will burst as soon as soft and should not be cooked longer than necessary to soften them. Strain juice through a jelly bag. Measure the juice and heat it to the boiling point. Add one cup sugar to two cups of juice; stir until sugar is dissolved. Boil for five minutes, skim and pour into moulds.

Green Grape Jelly

1 peck green grapes (not ripe)
1 slice candied pineapple
Boil till it jells.

Half and half (50-50) liquid and sugar
1 small can white corn syrup

Fruit Conserve

24 peaches
24 blue plums
2 lbs. red grapes

8 large tart apples
Juice and pulp of 2 oranges
Juice and pulp of 1 lemon

Peel peaches and apples and cut into 12 to 14 pieces. Stone plums and cut in quarters. Seed grapes and cut in half. Mix all together and add 2 cups of sugar to 1 cup of fruit. Cook until fruit looks clear and thick, about a half hour.

Apple Catsup

4½ lbs. chopped apples
2½ lbs. sugar
1 pint vinegar
Boil till thick.

1 tablespoon cinnamon, cloves and salt

Canned Peppers with Tomatoes

1 bushel red and green pep-   ½ bushel tomatoes
  pers, sweet

Scald tomatoes and cut up in small pieces. Put in granite pan
and cook tomatoes for 15 minutes, then add peppers that have
been washed and dried and cut lengthwise and seeds removed.
Add salt to suit taste and cook till done, then seal in jars
while hot. Cook up half amount at a time if pan is not large
enough. String beans are very nice done this same way.

Tomato Marmalade

Select four quarts of firm ripe tomatoes. Peel and slice thin.
Wash six lemons, slice and remove seeds, leaving the peel on.
Put in sauce pan with the tomatoes and lemons, one cup seeded
raisins and four pounds sugar. Cook slowly from one to one
and one-half hours until mixture is thick like marmalade. Put
in sterilized glasses and cover with paraffin.

Strawberry and Pineapple Jam

1 pineapple   4 cups sugar
1 quart strawberries

Pare and cut pineapple into small pieces. Add sugar and let
stand until thoroughly dissolved, about 4 hours. Cook until
tender, about 45 minutes, using low flame. Add strawberries
which have been washed and hulled, and cook 15 minutes
after berries have started to boil. Turn into sterilized glasses
and when cool cover with melted paraffin. Or turn into small
sterilized jars, ½ pint size and seal at once.
This recipe makes about 6 jelly glasses.

Stewed Green Cucumbers

3 medium or 2 large cucumbers
1 tablespoon butter

1 tablespoon flour
3 tablespoons sugar
3 tablespoons vinegar

Peel cucumbers; cut lengthwise in half or quarters; remove seeds. Cook in boiling salt water until tender. Drain. In a frying pan melt butter, add flour, then cucumbers. Add sugar and vinegar. Cook for ten minutes longer.

Peach, Cherry and Raspberry Marmalade

Two boxes red raspberries, one box sour cherries, washed and stoned, and same weight of peaches, chopped into small pieces. Weigh all together and use same amount sugar as fruit. Cook together slowly until thick. Fill glasses while hot and cover with paraffin after jelly has cooled.

Pear Honey

Peel and core ripe pears. Grind in a meat chopper. Measure pulp and add an equal amount of granulated sugar. Boil up quickly. Seal in sterilized jars.

Tomato and Apple Relish

12 tomatoes
12 apples
4 onions
3 pints vinegar

2 pounds sugar
1 teaspoon cinnamon
1 teaspoon cloves

Cook about three hours, or until very thick; then seal.

Pepper Relish

5 dozen sweet peppers
(green and red)
4 dozen onions
3 large stalks celery

½ gallon cider vinegar
2 pounds light brown sugar
4 tablespoons celery seed

Grind all ingredients. Put vinegar and sugar in a kettle. Let it come to a boil. Then drop in other ingredients and cook one hour. Put in jars and seal.

Cranberry Fancy

Boil one quart cranberries with sufficient cold water to cover. When nearly tender add one heaping cup of sugar and boil a few minutes longer. Strain and let cool. Serve sprinkled with nut meats and grated cocoanut.

Orange Marmalade

4 oranges
1 lemon

11 cups water
4 pounds sugar

Grind oranges and lemons, mix together, add water and let stand 24 hours, then boil for one hour with cover off. Let stand again 24 hours. Add sugar and boil until it jells, or about one hour. Makes ten glasses.

Corn Relish

12 ears sweet corn (cut from
cob)
1 head cabbage (chopped
fine)
4 red peppers (chopped fine)
Boil 20 minutes and seal.

1 tablespoon mustard
1 teaspoon celery salt
2 tablespoons salt
1 cup sugar
2 quarts vinegar (weak)

Green Pickles and Onions

25 pickles, size of dill pickles. Soak in water over night. Next morning slice pickles and 12 onions. Pour $\frac{1}{2}$ cup salt over this and let stand 1 hour. Then squeeze out of salt and add 1 quart vinegar, 2 cups sugar, 2 teaspoons mustard seed, 1 teaspoon ginger, 1 teaspoon tumeric. Let this mixture come to a boil and boil 3 minutes, then put in jars.

Bread and Butter Pickles

6 large cucumbers sliced thin
  (do not peel)
6 large onions sliced thin
1 quart vinegar
2 cups granulated sugar
2 teaspoons mustard seed

2 teaspoons celery seed
1 teaspoon ginger
2 teaspoons tumeric powder
$\frac{1}{2}$ teaspoon pepper
2 teaspoons salt

Let come to boil; add cucumbers and onions. Boil all 5 minutes, then seal. Makes 6 pints.

Dill Pickles

Wash and scrub clean 10 pounds small cucumbers; soak over night in cold salt water. Next morning wipe and pack in sterilized quart jars with dill between. Take 3 quarts water, 1 quart white vinegar, 1 level cup salt, few bay leaves; boil up and fill jars to overflowing. Place some dill on top and a pinch of alum, and seal while hot. Put away in dark, cool place. Will stay crisp and delicious for a year.

Crisp Dill Pickles

Wash and let stand over night in clear water. In the morning boil 1 cup salt, 1 quart vinegar, 3 quarts water, and pack pickles in fruit jars. Add the dill and pour the liquid over hot and seal.

Plum Conserve

Select one basket of blue plums. Cut into small pieces. Take three oranges, cut the skin into tiny dice, and pulp into pieces (grind). Add one-half cup chopped walnuts, and one-half cup chopped raisins.

Parboil orange peel in little water. Add to plums, oranges, nuts and raisins. Cook until plums are tender. Add an equal quantity of sugar and cook until it thickens.

Chile Sauce

30 tomatoes	2½ tablespoons salt
6 peppers (3 of each red and green)	1¼ cups of sugar
4 large onions	3 tablespoons of pickling spices tied in bag

Add 1 tablespoon of ground mustard and 1 teaspoon of cayenne pepper and 3 cups of vinegar. Let boil until thick.

Catsup

8 quarts tomatoes, chopped	1 quart vinegar
3 cups red peppers	3 teaspoons cloves
2 cups onions	3 teaspoons cinnamon
3 cups sugar	3 teaspoons ginger
¾ cup salt	2 teaspoons nutmeg
Boil 3 hours	

Bread and Butter Pickles

2 doz. medium cucumbers	1 teaspoon mustard seed
1 doz. medium onions	½ teaspoon tumeric
2 cups sugar	1 heaping teaspoon corn starch
1½ pint cider vinegar	
1 teaspoon celery seed	

Slice cucumbers (do not peel) and onions and soak in salt water about 2 hours. Mix corn starch and tumeric with sugar and add spices and vinegar. Drain cucumbers and onions. Pour vinegar and mixture over and cook till cucumbers are transparent. A little red pimento and stick of cinnamon in each jar adds to looks and flavor.

Preserved Pears

Pare and halve Bartlett pears and remove cores. Drop fruit as soon as peeled into cold water. Make a syrup by using sugar and water in proportion to a pint of sugar to a quart of water. Drop fruit into syrup as soon as it boils. Boil until tender. Fill the jars to overflowing and seal.

Grape Fruit Marmalade

For every grapefruit allow one sweet orange and a lemon. After cutting the grapefruit in half and removing the seeds and hard centers, slice it with the orange and lemon finely.

For every cup of fruit add three of water; let it stand for 24 hours, and then boil for 30 minutes.

After it has stood for another 24 hours, add a cup of sugar to every cup of fruit and then cook the marmalade for 45 minutes, or until the fruit becomes transparent.

Sliced Cucumber Pickles

3 dozen medium size cucumbers	2 teaspoons ground white pepper
1 dozen medium size onions	1 teaspoon celery seed
1 cup sugar	1 quart vinegar.
3 teaspoons mustard seed (whole)	

Peel and slice cucumbers, salt and let stand over night. Peel and slice onions, salt and let stand over night. In the morning wash and drain cucumbers and drain onions. Add sugar and seasonings; mix well. Heat vinegar; pour over all; let come to a boil and seal in fruit jars.

When opened these taste like fresh cucumbers.

Sweet Pickled Peaches

2 pounds brown sugar	½ ounce whole cloves
2 cups vinegar	4 quarts peaches (clingstone
1 ounce stick cinnamon	preferred)

Boil sugar, vinegar and spices 20 minutes. Dip peaches quickly in hot water; then rub off fuzz with a cloth. Place a few peaches at a time in the syrup and cook until tender Pack into sterilized jars. Adjust sterilized rubbers and fill each jar to overflowing with hot strained syrup. Put on covers and seal jars immediately.

Spiced Apples

Cut peeled apples into eights or quarters and cook till tender in a syrup of equal parts water, vinegar and sugar, to which has been added a few whole cloves, a few pieces of cinnamon and a little cayenne pepper. Remove the apples with skimmer, boil syrup until thick and pour over the fruit.
A fine relish. Serve cold.

Cucumber Mangoes

Soak in strong brine nine days as many large green cucumbers as you wish to use. Then lay them forty-eight hours in clear water. Cut a slit lengthwise in each, scoop out seeds, wipe dry, and fill with stoned raisins, lemon cut in long, thin strips, and 6 or 8 whole cloves. Tie up slit, pack cucumbers in stone jar, and cover with a boiling syrup made from the following: Add to 1 quart vinegar 5 pounds sugar, also mace, cinnamon and cloves to taste. Reheat syrup and pour boiling hot over cucumbers for nine successive mornings.

Pickled Peaches

1 gallon peeled peaches	2 dozen cloves
3 pounds sugar	6 sticks cinnamon
1 pint pure cider vinegar	

Boil vinegar, sugar, cinnamon and cloves 15 minutes, then pour liquor over peaches and let stand over night in stone jar covered with a plate. Next morning pour off liquor and heat to boiling point, then add the peaches to boiling liquor, and let cook slowly until tender. Seal in glass jars.

Spiced Figs

5 pounds figs	2 tablespoons stick cinna-
2 cups brown sugar	mon
1 cup granulated sugar	1 tablespoon whole cloves
2 cups vinegar	

Tie spices in piece cheesecloth. Boil sugar, vinegar and spices for five minutes. Wash figs and drop in syrup without peeling. Cook until tender but not broken, doing few at a time. Remove to sterilized crock as they are done and when all have been pickled pour boiling syrup over them. If not enough syrup to cover, an additional quantity should be made. Place bag of spices in crock with the figs.

Spanish Olive Oil Pickles

8 dozen medium sized cu-	½ cup white mustard seed
cumbers	1 cup tiny red chile pep-
1 quart onions	pers
1 cup olive oil	Vinegar
½ cup black mustard seed	

Wash, peel and slice onions and cucumbers, cover with brine made by adding one cup salt to four quarts boiling water. Let stand two hours and drain. Pour boiling water over peppers. Let stand ten minutes, drain and add to cucumber mixture. Mix oil and mustard seed and add to cucumbers. Add enough boiling vinegar to cover the pickles. Put in jars and seal while hot.

MEATS AND MEAT DISHES

MEAT SUPPLIES PROTEIN AND FAT

Meats

It requires fifteen minutes to warm a piece of meat thoroughly. Add this fifteen minutes to the following table:

Boiling

Boil all meat slowly over a low flame.
Beef requires one hour to the pound.
Corned beef requires half hour to the pound.
Ham requires twenty minutes to the pound.
Young chicken requires twenty minutes to the pound.
Tough chicken requires half an hour to the pound.

Roasting

Rare beef requires fifteen minutes to the pound.
Veal requires half an hour to the pound.
Pork requires half an hour to the pound.
Spring chicken requires half an hour.
Squabs require half to three-quarters of an hour.
Turkey requires twenty minutes to the pound.
Lamb requires twenty minutes to the pound.

Broiling

One inch steak requires eight minutes (rare); ten minutes (medium).
Two inch steak requires ten to fifteen minutes (rare); fifteen to twenty minutes (medium).
Lamb chops requires ten minutes.
Spring chicken requires twenty minutes to twenty-five minutes.

Broiled Steak

Trim the excess fat from the meat. Heat the oven for five minutes. Grease the broiling rack and place as near the flame as possible. Sear the steak for a minute, turn and sear the other side. Lower the rack an inch and cook the steak ten minutes for rare steak or fifteen minutes for medium to well done. Turn so as to broil evenly.

Spread with butter and season just before removing from the broiler.

Chops are prepared in the same fashion.

Pan Broiled Steak

Heat and grease the frying pan. Put in the steak and sear for a minute on one side, turn and sear on the other. Cook for five minutes (if steak is to be rare) turning often. Season with salt and pepper and a little butter.

Oven Baked Steak

Use a thick sirloin steak. Put in a pan and add 4 tablespoons catsup, salt and pepper, two tablespoons Worcestershire sauce and one tablespoon chopped onion. Dot with butter. Bake in a hot oven for fifteen minutes.

Swiss Steak

3 pounds of round steak   1 onion
3 tablespoons butter   Salt and pepper
½ cup flour

Have round steak cut one and one-half inches thick. Pound the flour into the meat, on both sides, with a potato masher. Season with salt and pepper. Melt the butter in a frying pan, add the onion, sliced; brown and put in the meat. Let brown on both sides.

Cover with boiling water, cover the pan and let simmer for two or more hours until meat is tender.

Roast of Beef

Dredge meat with flour. Season with salt and pepper.

Set in a roasting pan with two or three tablespoons of fat. Brown quickly in a hot oven; then reduce the flame and baste every fifteen minutes with the fat that drips off the roast. Allow fifteen minutes for each pound.

When meat is half done, turn, dredge with flour and baste repeatedly until the roast is done.

To make a gravy for the roast: Make a flour and water paste with two tablespoons of flour, add a little of the pan drippings. Remove the fat from the pan gravy and stir the flour paste in with the meat juices. Cook, add one teaspoon Worcestershire sauce, stir until smooth.

Fillet of Beef

Have the fillet skinned and larded. Place in the roasting pan in a hot oven for three-quarters to one hour, depending on the weight of the fillet. Baste several times with own drippings or add water if necessary.

Make a pan gravy as for roast beef and serve with potatoes and hot vegetables. A mushroom sauce is also very good with fillet of beef.

Pot Roast

3 pounds of beef (rump or top round)	Bay leaf
	Onion
1 pint hot water	Parsley
1 tablespoon flour	Celery salt and pepper
1 tablespoon drippings	Tomato

Sprinkle the meat with flour. Heat the drippings or fat in a tight covered kettle, brown the onion and add the meat browning on all sides. Add the bay leaf and pour on the boiling water. Let simmer two and a half to three hours or until meat is perfectly tender. Add hot water if necessary to prevent burning.

Lay slices of onion and tomato on top of roast half an hour before it is ready. Gravy may be thickened with flour.

Braised Beef

Have a three pound rump roast larded. Season with salt and pepper. Brown one sliced onion in fat, put in the rump and add one carrot sliced, one bay leaf, chopped parsley and brown all. Cover and let simmer for two and a half hours. Baste often adding soup stock or water. Remove the cover and brown the rump. Serve with horseradish sauce.

Chipped Beef and Cream

1 pound chipped dried beef   1 cup cream sauce

Chipped beef is very salty and should be soaked for half an hour before using. Drain the beef, add the cream sauce and cook for ten minutes in a double boiler. Serve on toast and with baked potato.

Boiled Smoked Tongue

Soak the tongue over night in cold water. Drain off this water and place tongue in fresh water to cover and cook in a large kettle.

Cook over a low flame for three hours.

Boiled Smoked Tongue

Soak the tongue over night in cold water. Drain off this water and cover with fresh water. Add bay leaves, whole pepper, cloves, and sliced onion to the water and cook slowly for three hours. Drain off the water. When sufficiently cool, remove the skin and roots. Serve with a brown sauce or a sweet-sour sauce.

Spiced Beef

Four to six pounds of beef from middle cut of shin.

Wash and trim well and pick off all fragments of bone. Cut meat into several pieces, cover with boiling water. Simmer till meat falls to pieces and the liquid reduced to half a pint. Remove the meat, season the liquid highly with salt, pepper, sage and thyme. Add it to meat and mix with fork until the meat is all broken.

Pack solid in a brick loaf bread or cake pan, put on ice and let it get firm and solid. When ready, cut in thick slices.

Delicious for sandwiches or luncheon dish, bordered with sliced tomatoes, beets and hard boiled eggs.

Birds

1 pound of round steak   Salt and pepper to taste
1/4 pound of bacon   4 slices of dry toast
1 small onion

Have steak cut thin. Cut in portions. Make filling by chopping bread, fried bacon, onion, salt and pepper together in chopping bowl.

Place filling in portions of steak, roll and tie together with string, or pin with toothpick. Roll in flour and brown in the bacon fat. Take out and put in casserole. Make gravy in pan and cover birds in casserole. Bake one hour in moderate oven. Can also be cooked in pan, if not wanted in casserole.

Filet Mignon

Tenderloin of beef is used for filet mignon. Cut the filets about an inch thick. Broil for three minutes under a high flame, turning once only. Serve on toast, placing each filet on a slice of orange or pineapple. Serve with mushroom sauce.

The tenderloin of beef is the most delicious and tender part of beef and therefore needs very little broiling.

Salisbury Steak (Meat Balls)

1 pound chopped beef	1 teaspoon onion, chopped
2 tablespoons butter	1 teaspoon salt
3 cups bread crumbs	Pepper

Mix all the ingredients except the butter and mold into round flat cakes. Melt the butter and sear the cakes first on one side, then on the other. Add a little boiling water, cover the pan and cook until tender.

Beef a la Mode

4 pounds top round of beef or rump	Pepper and salt
	5 carrots
2 tablespoons flour	1 cup boiling water
1 tablespoon fat	1 tablespoon vinegar

Rub the meat with the salt, pepper and flour. Put with the fat into a baking pan. Brown for half an hour, then add chopped carrots, and pour on a cup of boiling water. Simmer in a slow oven for three hours. Baste often. Pour vinegar over just before serving and thicken the self-gravy with a little flour.

Baked Corned Beef Hash

3 cups chopped cooked
   corned beef
6 good sized potatoes
1 onion
2 tablespoons bacon fat

1½ cups milk
Salt and pepper
1 tablespoon chopped
   pepper

Place the chopped corned beef in a greased casserole and add
chopped onion, pepper and place the sliced potato on top.
Arrange in layers seasoning throughout. Pour milk over all,
cover and bake in a hot oven until the potatoes are tender.
Brown for the last ten minutes with cover off of casserole.

New England Boiled Dinner

4 pounds corned beef
6 small carrots
6 onions
6 parsnips

6 potatoes
2 turnips
1 small cabbage (white)

If meat is salty boil up in water and drain. Cook the meat
covered with boiling water for three to five hours until tender.
When meat is about half cooked add the carrots, cabbage,
and turnips. One-half hour before ready add the onions,
parsnips and potatoes. Serve with meat in the center of
platter and each vegetable separate around the platter.

To Corn Beef:

Dissolve three-quarter tablespoon saltpeter in a little water.
Salt ten pounds brisket of beef, add pepper, garlic and one
cup of brown sugar. Put in an earthen jar, cover with an
old plate and weigh down the plate. Stand over night. Cover
with water and let pickle in the brine for ten days. Turn the
meat every three or four days.

Veal and Dumplings

2 cups cooked veal
4 tablespoons flour
3 tablespoons beef fat
1½ cups soup stock

1 teaspoon salt
Pepper
3 tablespoons chopped
   green pepper

Stir the flour, salt and pepper into the melted fat.
Add the soup stock and bring to a boil. Remove seeds and
spines from the pepper and chop. Add the diced cooked veal,

green pepper and seasoning; simmer for twenty minutes. Serve with egg dumplings.

Break the whites of three eggs into a cup, and add one-half teaspoon salt and enough milk to fill the cup. Mix with two tablespoons of butter and one cup flour in a spider and stir as the batter boils until it leaves the spider clean.

Cool the mixture and when cool stir in the yolks. Drop from a spoon into boiling salted water. Boil for five minutes.

Veal Mock Birds

1 pound veal steak	2 tablespoons fat drippings
2 cups hot water	Salt
1 teaspoon chopped onion	Mustard
1 tablespoon chopped pickle or pickle relish	Bay leaf

Have veal cut about one-quarter inch thick. Slice in four pieces and flatten the pieces. Season with salt and pepper. Spread on each piece some chopped onion, a little chopped raw bacon, mustard and a bit of bay leaf. Roll each slice and bind with a piece of string.

Roll each "bird" lightly in flour and brown in fat in a covered spider. Add boiling water and let simmer two and a half hours. Remove the strings and serve.

Roast Leg of Lamb

Bone the lamb, dredge with flour, sprinkle on salt and pepper. Roast in a roasting pan in a hot oven. When brown, baste every quarter hour and add water if necessary. Cook for two hours.

Serve with mint sauce or pour one glass current or gooseberry jelly over the meat just before serving.

Lamb Stew

Use shoulder or neck meat. Brown the meats, cut in pieces, and cover with boiling water. Add carrots, onion, celery and parsley all chopped. Season and cook for two hours. Potatoes cut in cubes may be added one-half hour before finished cooking.

Stuffed Breast of Veal

Have the butcher cut a pouch in a four pound breast of veal. Make a stuffing by grinding one-quarter pound salt pork, one cup bread crumbs, one-half teaspoon sage and salt and pepper. Stuff the pouch with this mixture and roast, averaging twenty minutes to the pound.

Crown Roast of Lamb

Have the butcher prepare the ribs for "crown roast." The center may be filled with bread stuffing, cooked vegetables, boiled chestnuts or mashed potatoes.

Cover the ends of the ribs with greased brown paper to prevent charring. Roast one and one-quarter hours or until tender in a hot oven.

Serve with fancy paper chop holders.

Liver and Onions

1 pound sliced calves liver	2 tablespoons bacon fat
2 tablespoons flour	Seasoning.

Dredge the liver with flour. Heat the bacon fat in a spider and sear the liver on both sides.

Keep in the spider while frying one large sliced onion. Let all simmer for ten minutes and serve.

Liver is most valuable when it is not cooked too thoroughly. Searing preserves the health giving properties.

Baked Calf's Liver

Season slices of liver with salt and pepper and sprinkle on flour. Spread melted fat over the slices and fry in a hot, greased spider. Add two slices of onion.

Cover the spider and bake for fifteen minutes in a hot oven; reduce the heat and bake slowly for an hour.

Boiled Sweetbreads

Soak one pound of sweetbreads in cold water for fifteen minutes, removing all membrane.

Cook for fifteen minutes in boiling salted water. Plunge into cold water to make firm. Break into pieces and serve on toast or in patties with white sauce.

Chicken, peas and mushrooms are often combined with sweetbreads.

Broiled Sweetbreads

Parboil sweetbreads, which have been washed and soaked. Split crosswise and sprinkle with salt and pepper. Broil for five minutes. Spread with butter and lemon juice. Garnish with parsley.

Scalloped Sweetbreads

2 pairs sweetbreads	2¾ cups top milk
1 cup mushrooms	½ cup bread crumbs
2 tablespoons beef fat	2 tablespoons butter
2 tablespoons flour	Salt and pepper

Soak the sweetbreads, cut in pieces, in cold water for fifteen minutes and then boil for ten minutes.

Peel and quarter the mushrooms. Simmer in the beef fat with the sweetbreads. Add the flour and seasoning and cook a moment longer. Pour on the top milk and cook five minutes. Turn into a greased casserole, sprinkle with bread crumbs and dot with butter; brown in a very hot oven for fifteen minutes.

Smothered Sausage:

1 cup sausage meat	1 egg
1 cup celery	1 quart mashed potatoes
2 tablespoons white sauce	

Simmer the sausage meat until tender. Slice the celery and add to the meat; cook until tender. Stir in the white sauce.

Season the mashed potatoes highly with salt and pepper and stir in the beaten egg. Place meat in center of a greased baking pan, surround and cover with mashed potato. Paint with a little egg and bake for twenty minutes in a hot oven until potatoes are browned.

Pour on the white sauce and serve.

Serves six.

Picnic Meat Roll

1¼ pounds forequarter of lamb	¼ teaspoon pepper
3 tablespoons onion	1 egg (raw)
3 tablespoons green pepper	1 cup crumbs
1 teaspoon salt	2 hard cooked eggs

To the finely chopped lamb, onions and green pepper, add remaining ingredients, excepting hard cooked eggs, and mix thoroughly. Turn out on to slightly floured board. Place eggs in center of meat, shape into roll and dredge with flour. Put in roasting pan and bake in a moderate oven (350 degrees) forty-five minutes. Serve sprinkled with chopped parsley.

Potatoes and Pork Chops

Put into a baking dish layers of raw potatoes, sliced one-quarter inch thick, seasoned with salt and dotted with pieces of butter. Fill the dish to within two inches of the top. Put on a layer of pork chops and sufficient milk to barely cover. Bake in oven about one and three-quarter hours.

Ham and Sweet Potatoes, Southern Style

1 slice inch thick ham	1/3 cup brown sugar
6 sweet potatoes	

Wash and trim the ham. Place in a hot skillet, brown on both sides thoroughly. Place in a covered dish in a slow oven and bake for one and one-half hours.

Boil the sweet potatoes until tender. When peeled and quartered, cook slowly in the skillet using the ham drippings. Sprinkle with sugar. Simmer slowly and turn often until very well browned.

Serve the ham surrounded by the potatoes.

Scalloped Ham

2 thick slices ham	3 carrots
4 large potatoes	1 pint milk
1 onion	Parsley

Chop onion, parsley, and carrots fine. Cut potatoes in slices and line baking dish with potatoes. Season with salt and pepper and place layer of vegetables on potatoes. Cover with one of the slices of ham, which has been trimmed, and cut in two or three pieces. Cover with another layer of potatoes and vegetables followed by pieces of ham until dish is filled. Have piece of ham on the top of the dish, pour over the milk and bake slowly in a moderate oven for one and one-half hours.

Pork Chops

Heat the frying pan, sprinkle the pork chops with pepper and salt and fry slowly in their own fat. Cook until tender and brown, and drain off the fat.

Pork Chops with Fried Apples

When chops are fried tender, fry apple slices one-half inch thick in the pork fat. Serve around the plate of chops.

Tenderloin of Pork

Flatten the tenderloins and roll in flour. Fry brown in butter and a little chopped onion; cover well and simmer until tender.
One-half cup sour cream may be used for basting.

Broiled Spareribs.

Broil the ribs on a greased broiler for ten minutes. Turn often to prevent burning. Serve with creamed potatoes.
Serve spareribs boiled, with spinach or cabbage.

Spareribs and Sourkraut

Boil the sourkraut and bake in a casserole with the spareribs. Bake until the kraut is browned.

Baked Virginia Ham

Soak the ham over night. Put it into a large kettle with three cups of cider, one cup molasses, one teaspoon ground cloves and enough water to cover.

Simmer for eight hours for a ham of about ten pounds. Let stand for twenty-four hours. Remove the outer skin of the ham and cover with brown sugar. Stick whole cloves into the ham. Bake for one-half hour in a very hot oven basting every five minutes with cider.
Serve either hot or cold.

Plain Meat Loaf

1 pound chopped beef	½ teaspoon chopped onion
½ cup bread crumbs	Salt and pepper
½ cup water or milk	½ teaspoon chopped green pepper

Mix all the ingredients together. Use only enough liquid to bind the meat and crumbs. Mold into a roll. Place in a bread pan, lay strips of bacon over the meat and bake in a hot oven about one-half hour.

Beef Stew

3½ pounds of beef	½ cup sliced onion
1 tablespoon beef drippings	½ cup sliced carrots
2 potatoes	½ cup tomatoes
¼ cup flour	Salt and pepper

Cut the meat into small pieces and dredge with flour. Brown on all sides in the melted fat in a spider. Cover the meat and onions with water and simmer for two to three hours on a low flame.

Half an hour before serving, remove any bones or fat and add the vegetables. Cook one half hour longer and serve with its own gravy thickened with flour if necessary.

Meat Pie

Cut left over steak or any cooked meat into pieces. Cover with boiling water and add half an onion. Cook on a low flame for one hour.

Thicken with a paste of flour and milk and season with salt and pepper.

Parboil potatoes for ten minutes in salted water. Cut into small cubes and put all into a greased baking dish. Cover with a baking powder biscuit dough and bake in a hot oven (450 degrees F.) for thirty minutes. Cut a large cross in the baking powder biscuit dough to let the gasses escape.

Rice and Meat Casserole

2 cups cooked meat or left over steak	1 tablespoon minced onion
	Salt and pepper
1 cup cooked rice	2 tablespoons bread crumbs
1 egg	1 tablespoon butter
¾ cup soup stock	

Chop the meat fine and mix with onion, salt and pepper. Beat the egg and add with the hot soup stock or equal amount hot water.

Grease a casserole, lay a layer of cooked rice on the bottom, then a layer of meat. Cover with the bread crumbs and dot with butter.

Bake for fifteen minutes in a moderate oven and serve covered with a thick tomato sauce.

Beef en Casserole

2½ pounds round steak	Sliced onion
1 tablespoon flour	Sliced carrot
2 tablespoons beef fat	Bay leaves
1 cup tomatoes	Salt and pepper

Flour the meat and season with salt and pepper. Heat the fat in a frying pan and brown the meat on both sides.

Mix the other ingredients in a casserole, add the meat, cover and simmer until tender. Will require about two and a half to three quarters hours to cook.

Mulligan Stew

1 soup bone
1 pound stew beef
3 large onions
6 carrots
6 sticks of celery

2 parsnips
1 can tomato soup
2 tablespoons of salt
½ teaspoon of pepper

Put on soup bone and meat, cooking slowly for two hours in six quarts of water, add vegetables after cooking meat one hour. Just before the mulligan is taken off the fire add the tomato soup stirring slowly for three minutes. Potatoes may be cooked in mulligan if desired.

Chop Suey

1 pound of round steak
1 stalk of celery
3 large green sweet peppers

3 to 4 onions
1 can tomatoes

Cut up steak in small pieces, fry in butter until brown. Cut up celery and add to meat and tomatoes. Cut the pepper and onions in small pieces and cook all together until done. Add salt and pepper to suit taste. Serve with rice or mashed potatoes.

Casserole of Meat and Rice

2 or 3 cups ground meat
1 level teaspoonful salt
1 small onion
1½ cups tomato sauce
2/3 cup of rice

3 cups boiling water
1 tablespoon butter
Cracker crumbs
Season with salt and pepper

Cook rice with salt in three cups of boiling water until tender. Line a casserole, or other baking dish, with a layer of cooked rice, a layer of the ground meat, which has been mixed with the ground onion, and one-half of the tomato sauce, then a layer of rice and another layer of meat and so on until rice and meat are all used. Then pour remainig one-half of tomato sauce on top, sprinkle with cracker crumbs, dot with butter and bake in a moderate oven one-half hour. Serve hot.

English Pot-Pie.

Parboil one dozen oysters in their own liquor. Slice one-half pound cooked ham and two pounds cooked veal into small pieces. Grease a baking-dish and lay the veal, oysters, boiled potatoes and slices of tomatoes in layers in the dish. Pour over some of the oyster liquor and about a cup of soup stock. Dot each layer with butter and cover with a pie-crust. Pierce the crust to allow the steam to escape and bake in a very hot oven (450 degrees F.) for fifteen minutes.

Serve in the baking dish.

Goulash

1 cup cooked beef	½ teaspoon Worcestershire
½ cup cooked veal	sauce
2 onions	¼ teaspoon paprika
2 tablespoons chili sauce	½ cup beef stock
2 tablespoons catsup	3 tablespoons butter

Fry the onion, sliced, in a frying pan, with the melted butter. Pour the stock, chili sauce, catsup, Worcestershire and seasoning into a double boiler. Add the browned onions and simmer for ten minutes.

Cut the meat in cubes and turn into the double boiler. Cook for five more minutes and serve.

Kidney Stew

1 large beef kidney	1 onion
1 tablespoon flour	Pepper and salt
1 tablespoon butter	

Wash the kidney and cook slowly in salt water until tender. Use just enough water to cover but change the water three or four times. Retain the last water.

Slice the onion thin and fry in the butter to a light brown, add the flour. Add the water and a little Worcestershire sauce. Add the kidney cut into pieces and cook together for ten minutes.

Hamburger Steak with Spaghetti

1 pound ground round steak	1 quart can of tomatoes
3 large onions	1 pound spaghetti
1/2 cup beef fat	1/2 pound grated cheese
2 tablespoons olive oil	1 cup chopped olives
6 green peppers	2 tablespoons chopped parsley

Peel and chop the onions and brown with the chopped meat in the fat and olive oil. Add the chopped peppers, tomato, parsley, salt and pepper. Simmer for two hours. Add olives during last half hour of cooking.

Cook long enough to evaporate the juice of the tomatoes and leave a soft paste.

Cook the spaghetti in boiling salted water. Cook until tender and drain.
Put the spaghetti on a platter, pour the meat and tomato sauce over it and cover with grated cheese. Place in the oven and allow the cheese to melt in. Serve.

Jellied Meat Loaf

(Chicken, veal, beef or ham)	1/2 cup cold water
2 cups chopped meat	1 teaspoon chopped onion
2 cups soup stock	Chopped celery, green or red pepper chopped, chopped parsley
2 tablespoons granulated gelatine	

Soften gelatine in cold water for five minutes. Boil soup stock and add to gelatine. Chill.

When gelatine mixture starts to stiffen, add the chopped meat and chopped onions, pepper and parsley.

Chill a loaf mold, turn in the mixture and allow to become perfectly stiff by chilling. Remove from mold, slice and serve. Thinned gravy may be used in place of the soup stock.

Chili Con Carne

1 pound of beef, cut into small pieces	1 tablespoon butter
3 dried sweet peppers	1 onion
1 cup red kidney beans	1 cup water
½ cup canned tomato	½ teaspoon paprika
	Salt and pepper

Melt the butter in a frying pan, fry the meat, sliced onion and peppers until browned. Add the water, tomato, and seasoning and cook until the meat is tender. Drain the canned kidney beans and add to the meat. Thicken with flour and serve. Dry kidney beans may be used. Soak for several hours in cold water. Cook until tender with one-half teaspoon soda, drain and add to the meat.

Beef Loaf

2 pounds ground beef	1 cup of dry bread crumbs or 12 large crackers
½ pound ground pork	
1 onion, grated	1 cup of canned tomatoes
1 tablespoon salt	Small amount of dry celery tops
1 teaspoon pepper	
1 tablespoon melted butter	
1 cup of thick cream sauce or 2 eggs	

Mix all together into a loaf with few strips of bacon or pieces of suet on top.

Place in a heavy baking pan, quite hot at first. Finish baking in a slow oven, 45 minutes to one hour.

To make thick cream sauce use three tablespoons flour, one cup liquid and two tablespoons butter. Cook until thick, then add to meat.

Mock Fried Chicken

3 pounds lamb chops	½ cup milk
3 cups cracker crumbs	2 teaspoons salt
½ cup butter or substitute	Pepper, paprika to taste
3 eggs	

Sear lamb chops. Mix eggs, milk, salt, pepper and paprika. Dip lamb chops in the above mixture, roll in cracker crumbs. Finish cooking in melted fat, cook for about one-half hour.

Baked Beans and Pork Chops

Soak about one pound of beans or more over night with a little baking soda added to water. Boil in salted water until done; put in baking dish, add small bottle of catsup, three tablespoons sugar; mix well. Put all in baking dish and place pork chops on top of beans and bake.

Pigs Feet Southern Style

2 fresh pig's feet; boil until tender. Make batter:

1 egg	Salt
½ cup flour	Milk to mix as in pancakes
½ teaspoon baking powder	

Have grease to frying point; dip pig's feet in batter and fry until brown. Serve while hot.

Chili Con Carne

1 lb. ground round steak   ¼ cup butter

Let meat brown in butter, then add a cup of water and let simmer half an hour. Then add one quart can of tomatoes and one can red kidney beans, 1 teaspoon of Chili Powder or more to taste, and add salt and boil ½ hour.

Stuffed Spare-Ribs and Mashed Potatoes

2 portions spare-ribs of 2 lbs. each	½ lb. prunes (parboiled and pitted)
5 large cooking apples	Salt and pepper

Rub salt on inside of ribs. Place apples that have been pared and sliced on ribs, then place as many prunes on as the ribs will hold. Place top rib on and tie or skewer together. Place a little butter in roaster. Sear ribs on both sides until brown. Continue roasting in a moderate oven, basting every 20 minutes until done. Thicken gravy after removing roast. Serve with mashed potatoes.

Veal and Ham Pie

1½ lbs. veal
2 hard-boiled eggs
½ lb. ham
1 tablespoon flour
1 teaspoon powdered herbs
Salt, pepper and mace to taste

1 tablespoon chopped parsley
Pastry or biscuit dough
Stock

Cut veal and ham into thin slices. Trimmings from roast may be used. Mix the flour, salt, pepper, mace, powdered herbs; roll each piece of veal in this seasoning and lay in deep casserole, alternately, layers of veal, ham, and eggs cut in slices. Pile this in center of the dish; add one cup of water and parsley. Cover with dough and bake in hot oven for 1¼ hours. When thoroughly baked, add a little well-seasoned stock and serve.

Baked Ham with Apples

2 lbs. ham, sliced
6 medium sliced apples
½ cup water

1½ cups brown sugar
10 whole cloves

Have ham sliced 1 inch thick. Wipe with a damp cheese cloth and trim off a portion of the fat. Then rub in as much of the brown sugar as it will take. Place in a pan, sprinkle with the cloves. Pare and cut the apples ⅛ inch slices. Place over and around the ham. Sprinkle the remaining sugar over the apples. Add the water, cover and bake in moderate oven 45 minutes or until ham is tender.

Ham Roll

1 lb. smoked ham, ground
2 lbs. fresh pork, ground
3 eggs

½ cup sweet milk
½ cup soft bread crumbs

Soak bread crumbs in the milk. Bake in loaf. Pour 1 cup tomatoes run through colander over loaf and bake 1 or 1½ hours. Serve with horseradish sauce.

Beef Stew

1 pound hamburger steak	1 teaspoon mustard
½ cup diced bacon	Dash of pepper
1 green pepper	6 potatoes (diced)
1 large onion	Salt
1 tablespoon vinegar	2 cups boiling water

Sear meat, with bacon, chopped pepper, vinegar, pepper and mustard, in frying-pan. Add potatoes, salt to taste, and water. Cover frying-pan, and let simmer till potatoes are cooked (about one hour).

Left-Over Dish

Chopped ham	Green peppers
Noodles	White sauce
Hard boiled eggs	Cheese

Butter a casserole dish. A layer of ham, then noodles, eggs, green peppers, chopped finely with ham; layer of eggs; then thin white sauce flavored with cheese. Continue until dish is filled; put a layer of buttered bread crumbs on top; bake in a hot oven until brown, about fifteen to twenty minutes.

Apples Stuffed with Sausage Meat

Scoop out the center of six good sized apples, leaving a thick shell and pulp from the core.

Chop this and mix with one cup of minced cooked sausage meat.

Refill the apples with mixture and bake in a medium hot oven until tender. Serve with baked or fried potatoes for luncheon or supper, or as a garnish for roast pork or chicken.

Baked Ham, Virginia Style

Mix a tablespoon of mustard and two tablespoons brown sugar with a little water to make a paste. Spread over a thick slice of ham, put in a baking dish, pour in enough milk and water to come to top of ham; bake until done. Baste with the liquid

Beef Loaf

2 pounds ground beef	1 large can tomatoes
1 large onion, chopped fine	Salt, pepper
1 cup corn flakes	

Mix all together; shape. Bake in slow oven one and one-half hours.

Pork Chops and Potatoes

4 pork chops	Butter
7 large potatoes	Milk
Flour	

Pare and slice potatoes and let stand in cold water about one-half hour. Use casserole and make a layer of potatoes and sprinkle with salt, bits of butter, and sprinkle flour over top; make another layer of potatoes and repeat until casserole is filled with enough space left for pork chops. Place pork chops on the top of these layers and sprinkle with flour, salt and milk enough to cover. A little garlic may be used for flavoring. Put in oven and let bake one and one-half hours with cover on casserole until almost done, and let stand in oven without cover.

Italian Veal or Pork Chops

6 good sizes veal or pork chops	½ teaspoon salt
	2 tablespoons shortening
2 cups canned mushrooms	1 teaspoon corn syrup
2 tablespoons vinegar	1 tablespoon corn starch
1½ cups water	½ cup canned tomato
2 cloves	½ tablespoon lemon juice
Few grains mace	

Broil the chops. In the meantime, cook the mushrooms for five minutes in the vinegar and water with the cloves, mace and the salt. Put the mushrooms in a sauce pan with the shortening and syrup and cook for five minutes. Add the corn starch, the tomato, lemon juice and the salt and a little pepper to taste. Place the broiled chops on a platter and pour the sauce over them. Serve with boiled rice.

Kidney Bean Stew

½ pound bacon, cut in cubes. Fry till brown with two green peppers "done to a turn." Add one can tomatoes, one can red kidney beans. Simmer over slow fire one-half hour.

Serve with one-half cup grated cheese poured over stew just before placing on table.

Ham Loaf

1 pound ham, 1 pound beef ground together
2 eggs
1 cup bread crumbs
¼ cup onions chopped fine

½ teaspoon salt
Pepper to taste
1 medium size can of tomatoes

Beat the eggs well, mix in the bread crumbs and onions and then put this mixture with the ground meat; add salt and pepper. Mix well, and form into a loaf. Bake in a moderate oven about two hours. Use a shallow pan and one large enough to add the can of tomatoes. About one-half hour before the loaf is finished, add the can of tomatoes. When loaf is done, thicken the tomato juice with a flour-water mixture to make tomato gravy.

Meat Loaf

1 lb. round steak
1 lb. pork shoulder
1 onion
3 or 4 salted crackers

1 egg
Salt and pepper to taste
½ teaspoon ground cloves

Grind steak, pork, onion and crackers. Add unbeaten egg, salt, pepper and cloves. Mix well; shape into loaf; put in casserole. Bake in slow oven 1½ hours.

The Virtue of Good Soaking

If only the housewife learns the value of soaking various articles of food before preparing them for the table, how much better would be the results of her culinary arts. For instance, though she may soak bacon for twelve hours before boiling it, it is very seldom that she will subject poultry to the same treatment. Yet the oldest boiling fowl if duly soaked in cold water, will prove, when cooked, almost as tender as a young chicken and lose none of its flavor in the process. It is well to use for boiling the water in which the fowl has been soaked. The bird may, however, be steamed above the water instead of being actually boiled in it. This will increase the tenderness.

White Sauce

1½ tablespoons flour   ¼ teaspoon salt
1 cup milk, scalded   Pepper
2 tablespoons butter

Melt the butter and remove from the flame before it browns. Add the flour and cook until it bubbles. Pour on half the hot scalded milk and boil, adding the rest of the milk, salt and pepper.

Use more flour if a thicker sauce is desired.

Egg Sauce

Beat two yolks and add ¼ cup of white sauce. Stir well, then add the rest of the sauce and cook over a low flame until the sauce thickens. Use hot over vegetables.

White Sauce (for croquettes)

1/3 cup flour   ¼ teaspoon salt
2½ tablespoons butter   1 cup milk

Melt the butter and remove from the flame before it browns. Add the flour and cook until it bubles. Pour on half the hot milk and then the rest of the milk, salt and pepper. Keep stirring to prevent lumps.

Mint Sauce for Lamb

1/3 cup chopped fresh   1 tablespoon powdered
   mint   sugar
                              ½ cup vinegar

Dissolve the sugar in the vinegar. If the vinegar is strong, dilute with water. Pour over the mint into a saucepan and let stand over a very small flme for half an hour. Serve hot. Cold mint sauce may be made by bringing the mint leaves to a boil and then allow the whole sauce to cool before using.

Menus

Relish—Celery Hearts
Soup—Creamed Asparagus Soup
Salad—Combination Fruit Salad
Meat—Jellied Chicken
Vegetables—Baked Stuffed Tomatoes
        Fresh Green String Beans
        Baked Irish Potato
Whole Wheat Bread and Butter
Dessert—Fresh Peaches with Cream

Hamburg Cakes   Mashed Potatoes
          Creamed Carrots
    Fruit Dessert   Tea

          Chicken Consomme
Creamed Chicken   Dumplings
       French Fried Potatoes
Lettuce Salad   Thousand Island Dressing
      Green Peas   Celery
    Coffee   Cocoanut Cake
      Consomme   Bread Sticks
Jellied Chicken Loaf   Au Gratin Potatoes
      Green Beans   Carrots and Peas
Lettuce Salad   Thousand Island Dressing
    Fruit Sherbet   Sponge Cake
         Coffee

Cream of Barley Soup
Cold Slaw Salad

Broiled Lamb Chops   French Fried Potatoes
Steamed Young Peas and Carrot Cubes
Hot Rolls

Chilled Berries   Iced Tea
Olives   Celery

Roast Chicken   Mashed Potatoes
Stewed Sweet Peas

Fruit Sherbet   Cake
Coffee

Baked Ham   Potatoes au Gratin
Buttered Beans
Cabbage Salad
Apple Pie

Swiss Steak   Mashed Potatoes
Scalloped Corn   Boiled Asparagus
Celery and Cabbage Salad

Devils Food Cake   Coffee or Tea
Roast Veal
Riced Potatoes
Buttered Lima Beans
Beet Salad
Pineapple Sherbet
Bread and Butter
Coffee

Baked Fish with Lemon Cream Sauce
Potato Salad
Vegetable Salad
Green Apple Pie with American Cheese
Iced Tea
Chicken and Mushrooms on Toast
Brussel Sprouts
Gingerbread and Cream
Tea or Milk

Dinner Menu

Grapefruit Cocktail
Entree of Baked Halibut with Lemon Butter Sauce
Olives   Radishes
Roast Breast of Veal, Apple Dressing
Potato Dumplings   Peas
Stuffed Tomato Salad
Parker House Rolls
Lemon Sherbet   Sunshine Cake
Coffee

Menu

Cream of Tomato Soup   Soup Sticks
Veal Cutlets
Rice
Rolls   Butter
Cucumber Salad   Wafers
Snow Pudding, Custard Sauce
Cakes   Coffee

Dinner Menu

Cucumber Ring   Mayonnaise
Brown and White Sandwiches
Clear Soup
Celery, Olives, Radishes and Nuts
Toast Rings
Broiled Chicken Breasts and Mushrooms   Thin Cream Gravy
Carrot Ring and Peas
Rice Timbale on Pineapple Ring
Rolls
Grapefruit and Avacada Pear Salad   French Dressing
Cheese Straws
Raspberry Ice and Vanilla Mousse   Sponge Drops
Coffee

Luncheon Menu

Macaroni and Cheese   Head Lettuce Salad
Bread   Butter
Chocolate Drop Cookies   Pineapple Ice
Iced Tea

Hallowe'en Festivities

Chicken Almond Sandwiches
Cream Cheese and Pineapple
Sandwiches
Individual Pumpkin Pies
Whipped Cream
Cider

Piquant Sandwiches
Orange-Pecan Salad   Gingerbread
Coffee

Curried Eggs on Toast
Baking-Powder Biscuits
Cider Ice   Sponge Cake
Coffee   Salted Nuts

Creamed Shrimps with Eggs
Bread and Butter Strips
Spook Salad   Cakes
Coffee

Thanksgiving Dinners

Cream of Tomato Soup
Roast Turkey   Southern Giblet Gravy
Potato Croquettes
Brussels Sprouts
Cauliflower with Hollandaise Sauce
Cranberry Jelly
Romaine Salad   French Dressing
Individual Pumpkin Pies
Whipped Cream   Cider Ice
Nuts   Raisins

Halves of Grapefruit
Roast Duck   Apple Stuffing
Baked Sweet Potatoes
Creamed Turnips   Cole-Slaw
Baked Squash   Cider
Indian Pudding   Foamy Sauce
Nuts   Coffee

Fruit Cocktail
Chicken Fricassee   Riced Potatoes
Celery   Buttered Onions
Squash Pie

Breakfast

Orange Juice
Omelet
Melba Toast
Coffee or Milk

Lunch

Macaroni   Waldorf Salad
Baked Custard
Cookies

Dinner

Oyster Stew
Roast Leg of Lamb
Creamed Potatoes   Spinach
Watercress Salad
Skillet Cake

Breakfast

Sliced Oranges
Dry Cereal
Poached Eggs on Toast   Coffee

Luncheon

Cream of Pea Soup
Potato Cakes
Lettuce and Grapefruit Salad
Canned Peaches

Dinner

Tomato Soup
Baked Halibut
String Beans   Mashed Potatoes   Creamed Lettuce
Prune Whip

Breakfast

Apple Sauce
Oatmeal   Cream
Creamed Dried Beef
Toast   Coffee or Milk

Luncheon

Salmon Loaf
Popovers   Grape Jelly
Tea

Dinner

Onion Soup
Stuffed Cabbage   Carrots and Peas
Lettuce and Egg Salad
Tapioca Pudding

Hot Weather Sunday Meals

Dinner

Orange Cocktail
Pressed Chicken   Creamed Potatoes en Casserole
Fresh String-Bean Salad
Chocolate Cornstarch Pudding

Supper

Cucumber Salad with Salmon Dressing
Brown Bread and Butter Sandwiches
Iced Tea   Cinnamon Cake

Dinner

Cream of Lettuce Soup
Sliced Cold Lamb   Asparagus
New Potatoes with Butter Sauce
Peach Ice Cream   Sponge Cake

Supper

Stuffed Tomato Salad   Graham Bread
Cream Cheese Sandwiches
Blueberry Cake   **Iced Fruit Punch**

Cold Weather Sunday Meals

Dinner

Vegetable Soup
Lamb Chops   Sautéd Bananas
Buttered Carrots
Orange Bavarian Cream

Supper

Lobster and Mushroom en Casserole
Brown Bread and Lettuce Sandwiches
Nut Cake   Tea

Dinner

Cream of Tomato Soup
Chicken en Casserole   Steamed Rice
Scalloped Onions
Baked Apple and Cream

Supper

Curried Eggs in Chafing Dish   Hot Biscuits
Fruit Salad

Dinner Menu

Fruit Salad with Crackers

Split Pea Soup

Baked Trout with Tomato Sauce

Creamed Mashed Potatoes and Butter Peas

Lettuce with Thousand Island Dressing

Coffee   Chocolate Cake

Menus

Rice Soup
Roast Beef   Mashed Potatoes
Whole Cereal Bread
Carrots and Green Beans
Cabbage Salad   Apple Pie
Coffee

Breakfast

Sliced Oranges
Farina
Scrambled Eggs on Toast
Cocoa

Lunch

Creamed Salmon on Toast
Mexican Salad
Baked Custard
Milk

Dinner

Meat Cakes
Boiled Potatoes
Combination Salad, French Dressing
Sliced Pineapple

Dinner

Tomato Soup
Roast Veal with Brown Gravy
Mashed Potatoes
Creamed Cauliflower
Lettuce, Orange and Tomato Salad
Custard Pie

Dinner

Fresh Fruit Cocktail
Broiled Lamb Chops   Creamed Peas
French Fried Potatoes   Tomato and Chopped Celery Salad
French Dressing
Rye Bread Toast
Peach Custard with Cream

Dinner

Veal Stew   Buttered Cabbage
Fresh Fruit Salad
Whole Wheat Biscuits   Jelly
Sour Cream Pie
Coffee

Dinner

Cream of Celery Soup
Meat Loaf, Tomato Sauce
Baked Potatoes
Corn on Cob   Buns
Lemon Pie
Cereal Coffee

Supper

Roast Beef, Browned Potatoes   Scalloped Cabbage
Lettuce with Mayonnaise
Apple Dumplings
Iced Tea

Supper

Broiled Halibut
Mashed Potatoes   Macaroni
Tomato Salad
Coffee

Supper

Lamb Chops   Green Beans
Head Lettuce   Thousand Island Dressing
Chocolate Soufflé
Tea

Supper

Pineapple Fruit Salad
Virginia Baked Ham   Sauerkraut
Mashed Potatoes   Tomato Salad
Apple Pie
Coffee

Luncheon

Fruit Cocktail
Celery Hearts   Olives
Creamed Chicken
Mashed Potatoes
Peas   Parker House Rolls
Angel Food Cake   Pineapple Whip
Coffee

Dinner

Roast Pork
Candied Sweet Potatoes
Baked Tomatoes and Onions   Apple Salad
Indian Pudding
Coffee

Sunday Dinner Menu

Fruit Cocktail
Lettuce and Tomato Salad
Fried Spring Chicken
Candied Sweet Potatoes
Peas and Diced New Carrots   Mashed Yellow Turnips
Custard Pie
Coffee or Iced Tea

Dinner

Olives   Celery
Mock Turtle Soup
Roast Chicken   Sage Dressing
Mashed Potatoes   Corn on Cob
Combination Salad, Dressing
Pineapple Jello, Whipped Cream
Peach Cake   Coffee

Cold Weather Breakfasts

I

Hot Baked Apples with Cream
Omelet, Spanish
Corn Meal Muffins   Coffee

II

Orange Juice
Sausage and Fried Apples
Popovers   Jam   Coffee

III

Prunes
Whole Wheat Cereal   Ham Toast
Coffee

IV

Orange Sections
Oatmeal   Coffee

V

Sliced Bananas with Cream
Bacon and Eggs
Butter Rolls   Coffee

VI

Sliced Canned Peaches
Creamed Dried Beef on Toast
Coffee

VII

Stewed Dried Apricots and Dates
Scrambled Eggs on Toast
Farina   Coffee

Menu for the Week

SUNDAY

Breakfast
Cantaloupe
Oatmeal Cooked in Milk   **Top Milk**
Corn Fritters   Bacon
Coffee
Luncheon or Supper
Fried Tomatoes with Milk Gravy
Muffins and Butter   Baked **Custard**
Hot or Iced Tea
Dinner
Braised Steak
Mashed Potatoes   "Lady" **Cabbage**
Bread and Butter
Beet Salad   Peach Shortcake
Hot or Iced Coffee
Cheese   **Nuts**

MONDAY

Breakfast
Pears
Flakes   **Top Milk**
Plain Omelet   Rolls and **Butter**
Coffee
Luncheon or Supper
Cream of Tomato Soup with Crackers
Toasted Egg Salad Sandwiches
Stewed Blueberries   Nut Cookies
Tea
Dinner
Broiled Veal Chops
Creamed Potatoes   Corn on the **Cob**
Bread and Butter
Fruit Betty   Hard Sauce
Hot Coffee or Tea

TUESDAY

Breakfast

Prunes

Farina   Top Milk

Shirred Eggs

Corn Muffins and Butter   Coffee

Luncheon or Supper

Potatoes and Egg Salad

Boiled Dressing

Graham Rolls and Butter   Caramel Bread Pudding

Coffee or Tea

Dinner

Nut Loaf   Peanut Cream Sauce

Cauliflower and Brussels Sprouts

Bread and Butter   Cucumber Salad

Blueberry Mold   Cream

Coffee or Iced Tea

WEDNESDAY

Breakfast

Apricots   Nut Loaf (Browned)

Coffee (adults)   Milk (children)

Luncheon or Supper

Creamed Salmon

Lettuce Dressed at the Table

Coffee Cake   Coffee or Tea

Dinner

Brown Fricassee of Chicken

Mashed Potatoes   String Beans

Bread and Butter

Cole-Slaw

Charlotte Russe   Coffee or Tea

THURSDAY

Breakfast

Baked New Apples
Hominy   Top Milk
Boiled Eggs
Toast and Butter
Coffee (adults)   Milk (children)

Luncheon or Supper

Stewed Fresh Lima Beans
Sliced Tomatoes with French Dressing
Raisin Bread and Butter
Iced Cocoa

Dinner

Chicken Stew with Dumplings
Fried Egg Plant
Lettuce and Pepper Salad
Sponge Cup Cakes (left overs) with Rich Cocoa Sauce
Hot or Iced Coffee

FRIDAY

Breakfast

Peaches
Frizzled Dried Beef with Potatoes
Rolls   Butter
Coffee

Luncheon or Supper

Macaroni in Cheese Sauce
Rye Bread and Butter
Grapes
Hot or Iced Tea

Dinner

Beefsteak Pie   Buttered Carrots
Bread and Butter
Sliced Tomatoes
Old-fashioned Baked Apple Sauce with Cream
Cake   Coffee or Tea

SATURDAY
Breakfast
Sliced Bananas in Cream
Flakes   Top Milk
Waffles   Honey
Toast and Butter
Coffee

Luncheon or Supper
Tomato and Cheese Stew
Crackers and Butter   Warm Gingerbread
Hot or Iced Tea

Dinner
Baked Stuffed Fish
Potatoes en Casserole   Stewed Onions
Bread and Butter
Combination Salad   Uncooked Fruit Pie
Coffee or Tea
Nuts

DINNER
Grapefruit Cocktail
Panned Chicken
Corn Fritters   String Beans
Glaced Sweet Potatoes
Hearts of Lettuce   Russian Dressing
Pumpkin Pie   Cheese
Demi Tasse

AN AUTOMOBILE LUNCH
Cold Sliced Ham with Parker House Rolls
Brown Bread Sandwiches with Celery and Olive Filling
Potato Salad   Dill Pickles
Chocolate Cake   Coffee

Baked Ham   Cider Sauce
Baked Sweet Potatoes
Creamed Green Beans   Head Lettuce Salad
Peach Cobbler

Split Pea Soup
Baked Stuffed Fish   Parsley Potatoes
Boiled Onions
Sliced Buttered Beets   Molded Cucumber Salad
Cake and Coffee

———

Vegetable Soup
Veal Cutlets   Horseradish
Mashed Potatoes
Dressed Celery   Creamed Lima Beans
Cherry Pie

BREAKFAST

Sliced Oranges   Ready-to-serve Cereal
Creamed Beef on Toast
Coffee or Milk

LUNCHEON

Baked Macaroni with Cheese
Whole Wheat Bread   Butter
Peach Cobbler with Milk
Milk

DINNER

Baked Ham
Glazed Sweet Potatoes   Creamed Cabbage
Sliced Tomatoes on Lettuce
Butter Scotch Pie   Coffee

———

Relishes
Mock Turtle Soup
Filet Mignon on Toast with Mushrooms
Cottage Fried Potatoes
Combination Salad with Thousand Island Dressing
Strawberry Ice Cream   Waffles
Coffee

Oyster Cocktail   Clear Soup
Olives   Celery   Radishes
Broiled Sirloin Steak (2 inches thick)
Mashed Potatoes   Stewed Tomatoes
Baking Powder Biscuit   Honey
Lettuce and Tomato Salad, Garnished with Hard-boiled Egg
Mayonnaise
Salted Crackers   Cheese

Campers Breakfast

Melt one tablespoon butter in a frying-pan. Warm one can baked beans in the pan. Break three eggs into it and scramble.

Poultry

The food value of poultry is its protein content. Its properties are those of other meats but poultry is more easily digested than meat.

Stewed Chicken

Have a four to five pound fowl dressed and drawn and cut up as for fried chicken. Rather tough birds may be stewed and found very good. Put the cut-up chicken into a kettle, cover with boiling water and add salt. Cook slowly until the chicken is tender.

Serve with dumplings or with rice.

Fricassed Chicken

Prepare as for stewed chicken but when tender remove from the liquid, dip in flour and saute in fat until brown.

Time Table for Poultry

Turkey   15 minutes to the pound
Goose   20 minutes to the pound
Chicken 15 minutes to the pound
Capon   15 minutes to the pound
Duck   15 minutes to the pound
Squab   15 minutes each

Chicken a la Maryland

Clean and joint a young chicken. Dip in flour mixed with beaten egg and bread crumbs. Season with salt and pepper.
Place in a greased dripping pan and bake in a hot oven for fifteen minutes. Baste with one-half cup melted butter.
Serve on a platter. Pour two cups hot white sauce over the chicken and garnish with sprigs of parsley.

Roast Chicken

Stuff the chicken with dressing, allowing some space for the expansion of the bread, etc., for the stuffing. Insert some stuffing through the slit in the neck. Sew up the slit in the neck and in the body with white heavy cotton thread.

Truss the bird by drawing the thighs close to the body and tying or fastening with a skewer. Draw the wings in close and tie them also. Fasten the neck skin down to the wings and tie down the ends of the drumsticks so they will not burn off. The whole bird may be tied together with string to keep all parts close in to the body.

Place the stuffed, trussed chicken in a covered roaster. Sprinkle with flour, salt and pepper and roast, removing cover of roaster for last fifteen minutes so that chicken will brown. Remove the chicken when tender and make chicken gravy from juices drawn.

Chicken a la King

2 cups diced chicken meat
1 can mushrooms or 1½ cups fresh mushrooms
5 tablespoons salad oil
2 tablespoons chopped pimentos
5 tablespoons chopped green peppers
1 tablespoon capers
½ teaspoon salt
3 cups rich cream
2 tablespoons flour
1 tablespoon fat
Yolks of two eggs

Cook the mushrooms for five minutes in the oil. Add the chicken, capers, peppers and pimentos, salt and paprika.

Make a white sauce of the fat, flour and cream. Beat the egg yolks and pour the one into the other. Add the chicken mixture, heat thoroughly and serve on toast.

Casseroled Duck

1 roasting duck
3 cups beef soup-stock
1 pound white onions
1 teaspoon Worcestershire sauce
½ cup brown sugar
1 teaspoon salt
½ teaspoon celery salt
1 small bottle pimento olives
1 lemon, juice
Pepper

Slice the onions thin and brown with the sugar in a saucepan. Stew until onions are brown and dry.

Split duck down the back, place flat in a large baking dish. Pour over the soup-stock, the olives halved, the olive brine and the other ingredients and seasoning.

Bake in a moderate oven for two and one-half hours. When done, the flesh should drop from the bone. Remove the biggest bones and serve in the casserole.

Chicken may be prepared in the same manner.

Chicken Pie with Rice

Split three small broilers into fourths. Fry until about half done. Stir one tablespoon butter into one and one-half cups hot cooked rice. Add salt and pepper to taste. Beat five eggs and stir into butter and rice. Put chickens into a baking dish, pour over the rice and egg. Bake in a moderate oven for about twenty minutes. The rice should brown lightly.

Jellied Chicken

1 cup chopped white meat of chicken
1 cup heavy cream
½ cup hot chicken broth
1½ tablespoons gelatine, granulated
¼ cup cold water
1½ cups milk
Salt and pepper
3 egg yolks

Soak the gelatine in cold water, add the hot chicken broth and stir until the gelatine entirely dissolves.

Beat yolks, add the milk and cook to a custard in a double boiler. Add to the chicken broth, turn in the minced chicken and season.

Cool and add the cream whipped fairly stiff. Grease a ring mold. Chill over night in the ice-box. Serve at luncheon, turning out of mold onto a round platter and fill the center with chilled cooked vegetable salad.

Chicken with Vegetable Dressing

Prepare fowl as for baking; boil whole for one hour with water half covering. Turn after forty-five minutes and immerse the part out of the water. Salt and pepper before starting to boil.

Prepare the stuffing with one quart bread crumbs moistened with broth from fowl, season and add two eggs, one grated potato, one carrot, one onion and small parsnip if desired. Leaves from small bunch of celery, some parsley, one-half each red and green pepper, half a dozen leaves of spinach, shredded mushroom, if desired (and a half pint of fresh oysters make it delicious, but may be omitted, if desired).

Mix vegetables into bread crumbs, add one heaping teaspoon baking powder, salt to season the vegetables, pepper to taste. Lift fowl from broth and fill with stuffing. Bake in moderate oven until tender and the vegetables are cooked.

Chicken Timbales with Stuffed Tomato Salad
Chicken Timbales

Chop raw breast of chicken and then pound until smooth enough to force through a fine strainer. To $1/2$ cup of the strained chicken gradually add two egg whites and beat until smooth. Then add gradually one cup of cream. Season to taste with salt and pepper. Turn into slightly buttered timbale cups, set in pan of hot water, cover with buttered paper and bake in moderate oven until delicately firm. Remove from molds, pour white sauce around each serving and sprinkle with paprika.

Sauted Chicken Livers and Mushrooms

12 chicken livers	3 tablespoons butter
1 cup mushrooms	Salt and pepper

Use only the tops of the mushrooms which have been peeled and washed. Saute the mushrooms in butter.

Parboil the chicken livers and add them to the sauted mushrooms. Season and serve on toast with the butter in which the mushrooms cooked.

Chicken Croquettes

1¾ cups c h o p p e d cold cooked chicken	1 teaspoon lemon juice
$1/2$ teaspoon celery salt	1 teaspoon finely chopped parsley
Few grains cayenne	1 cup thick white sauce

Mix ingredients in order given. Cool. Shape and fry as croquettes.

Brochette of Chicken Livers

12 chicken livers   6 slices bacon
6 metal or wood skewers

Cut each strip of bacon into four pieces. Put a piece of bacon, a piece of parboiled liver alternately onto the skewer until it is filled. Fry in bacon fat and simmer for ten minutes; turn the skewers frequently so the whole will brown evenly.

Drain the fat and serve on the skewers on toast.

Pate de Foies Gras

2 dozen chicken livers   1 teaspoon chopped onion
1 truffle   1 teaspoon minced parsley
2 tablespoons butter   Pepper and salt

Parboil the chicken livers, drain and cool. When cold, put through the food chopper twice.

Brown the onion and parsley in the butter, remove from the fire.

Add the chopped truffle and the riced chicken livers. Stir smooth and keep in a crockery dish in the ice-box.

The truffle may be omitted if difficult to obtain.

Serve on toast as an appetizer.

Chicken and Rice

3 small broilers   5 eggs
1½ cups cooked rice   Salt and pepper
1 tablespoon butter

Split the chicken in quarters and fry until half done. Heat the rice and stir in the butter and seasoning. Add the beaten eggs and stir in well. Put the chickens in a baking dish, cover with the rice and egg mixture and bake in a moderate oven for twenty minutes to half an hour.

Casseroled Chicken

1 roasting chicken   1 teaspoon salt
3 cups soup-stock   ½ teaspoon celery salt
½ cup brown sugar   1 teaspoon Worcestershire
1 pound white onions   sauce
1 cup chopped stuffed   Juice of one lemon
   green olives

Slice the onions thin and simmer dry and brown in brown sugar. Split the chicken down the back and lay in a large casserole covered with the rest of the ingredients and the sugar and onions.

Bake in a moderate oven for 2½ hours. Remove the biggest bones and serve in the casserole.

Fried Spring Chicken

1½ pound spring chicken

Dress, clean and cut the chicken in half through the back and breast bones. Dip each half in bread crumbs, then in beaten egg seasoned with salt and pepper, then once more in the bread crumbs. Fry in butter until well browned and tender. Use enough fat or butter so that the chicken will not burn.

The chicken may be fried in deep fat. Dredge first with flour, season with salt and pepper and fry to a rich brown.

Rub fat into the chicken, roll in bread crumbs and bake in a pan in a hot oven for half an hour.

Stuffing Squabs

The delicate flavor of squabs may be brought out by adding a few tablespoons of orange juice to the stuffing.

If squabs are broiled or roasted add two tablespoons of orange juice and the grated rind of the orange to the gravy.

Baked Squabs

6 squabs   2 large tomatoes
6 boiled potatoes   1 large onion, chopped
½ chopped green pepper   Salt and pepper

Let the squabs stand for half an hour in salty water, after they have been dressed and washed.

Chop all the other ingredients together and mix well, season to taste. Stuff the squabs with this dressing and arrange them in a baking pan with a slice of bacon over each.

Roast in a moderate oven.

Pigeon Pie

6 pigeons   1 tablespoon butter
6 strips bacon   2 cups soup-stock
1 tablespoon flour   3 onions, quartered

Have the pigeons cleaned and place in a glass baking dish or casserole with a strip of bacon on each bird. Bake for five minutes in a very hot oven.

Brown the flour in the butter in a saucepan, add the soup stock, salt and pepper and bring to boiling point. Add the onions and set the pigeons in this gravy. Simmer for one hour and then replace the pigeons and the gravy in the baking dish, cover with a baking powder or pie dough, with incisions for the steam to escape. Bake in the hot oven for another fifteen minutes and serve in the baking dish.

Roast Turkey

Dress and clean the turkey. Stuff as desired. Truss the legs and rub salt over the whole bird.

Cream one-half cup butter with one-fourth cup flour and spread over the breast and legs of the turkey. Place in a covered roaster and roast in a very hot oven for ten minutes to keep in the juices. Reduce the flame and roast for three to four hours.

Test the turkey by pressing the breast meat with the finger. If the meat is soft, the turkey is done. Do not pierce with a fork.

Serve with the stuffing left in and with cranberry sauce.

For left-over Pieces of Turkey

Turkey a la Creole

Make a sauce of one sliced onion and two chopped green peppers browned in one tablespoon fat. Add one can tomato soup and one tablespoon flour. Stir all together and season with salt and add one teaspoon sugar.

Slice the turkey and arrange the slices overlapping at the edge in a baking pan. Dot with butter and heat through. Transfer the sliced turkey to a platter and pour over the creole sauce.

Turkey Hash with Rice

2 cups diced turkey meat
1 cup raw rice
1 tablespoon fat
1 chopped green pepper
1 minced onion
1 small tart apple, chopped

½ cup strained tomato juice
2 cups soup-stock
2 egg yolks
2 tablespoons grated cheese
Salt and pepper

Heat the fat, and brown the chopped pepper, and minced onion in it. Add the chopped apple, the rice, soup-stock, tomato juice and seasoning. Stir in the diced turkey meat and turn all into a casserole.

Bake in the covered casserole for three-quarters hour in a hot oven. Cover the top of the hash with beaten egg yolks and grated cheese; reheat until the cheese melts and serve with hot gravy.

Roast Goose

Singe and wash the goose, clean well. Dress, clean and wash the goose and rinse the inside with a hot solution of one teaspoon soda to one quart of water.

Dry and rub in salt both inside and out. Rub with lemon or onion as desired.

Stuff and truss the goose and bake, allowing twenty minutes to the pound.

Roast Duck

Draw, clean, singe and rinse the duck.

Fill the cavity with whole, pared apples. Do not use these apples for serving as they are employed to stuff out the duck and to take in the strong flavor of duck.

Dredge with flour and tie bacon or salt pork over the breast. Roast in a covered roaster, on a rack, for twenty minutes in a very hot oven (500 degrees F.) and then reduce the heat to 400 degrees F. for the remainder of the time. Remove the pork or bacon when reducing the heat. Allow fifteen minutes to the pound.

Baked Rabbit

1 rabbit	1 teaspoon sage
3 tablespoons fat	4 cups thin white sauce
1/3 cup flour	1 teaspoon salt
3 strips bacon	

Dress and clean the rabbit and cut into pieces for serving. Mix the flour, sage and salt; roll the rabbit pieces in this mixture. Saute in the fat until brown all over.

Put the rabbit pieces into a casserole and lay bacon strips over them. Pour on the white sauce. Bake for two or more hours in a moderate oven. The meat must be tender.

Rabbit Stew

Dress and clean the rabbit and disjoint into pieces suitable for serving. Put in a kettle with six small onions, a bay leaf, half a cup of chopped celery and season with two teaspoons salt.

Cook slowly for two hours with water to cover.

Add three potatoes which have been pared and quartered. Thicken with three tablespoons flour made into a paste with a little cold water.

When the gravy thickens, add parsley chopped fine and serve.

Bread Stuffing

Use very stale bread crumbs for sutffing. Put four cups of coarse bread crumbs into a bowl and pour on one cup boiling water. Let absorb for half an hour. Squeeze out any excess water, leaving moist but not soppy breadcrumbs. Beat one egg and add together with half a cup of melted fat.

Mix together one cup chopped celery, one chopped onion and minced parsley. Combine this with the bread-crumb mixture and stuff poultry. This amount will fill a six-pound bird.

Celery Stuffing

½ bunch celery	½ teaspoon pepper
2 eggs	1 quart stale bread crumbs
2 tablespoons salt	

Chop the celery. Mix the celery with the salt and pepper and add the slightly beaten eggs.

Melt the fat or butter and add the bread crumbs. Combine the two mixtures and use to stuff chickens preferably.

Oyster Stuffing for Turkey

1 pint oysters   ¼ cup butter or fat
2 cups dry bread crumbs   Salt and pepper

Mix all the ingredients together and add to the melted butter.

Chestnut Stuffing

1 quart large chestnuts   Onion juice
2 tablespoons butter   Chopped parsley
1 egg   Turkey liver, chopped
2 cups bread crumbs   2 tablespoons cream

Shell and blanch the chestnuts and cook in boiling water until
tender. While hot, press through a ricer or chop fine.
Add the other ingredients and mix all well together.

Apple Stuffing

5 sour apples   ½ teaspoon salt
1 cup bread crumbs   Pepper

Peel, core and quarter the apples and stew until half done.
Mix with the rest of the ingredients and stuff into the bird
and roast.

Creme de Volaille

1 boiled c h i c k e n meat,   White sauce made of 1 ta-
   ground   blespoon butter, 1 table-
2 raw eggs   spoon flour; ½ pint milk
1 small onion, salt and pep-
   per

Cook sauce, mix with the above ingredients and place in buttered mold; steam for 2½ hours. Serve on platter with creamed
peas all around it.

Escalloped Chicken for Luncheon

Cook chicken until it falls away from the bones; cut in small
pieces. Two pints chicken, two pints broth, one pint cracker
crumbs, three eggs, well beaten. Mix all together and put in
pan. Bake about thirty minutes or until nicely browned. Serve
with a ring of sweet green pepper on each portion. Will serve
sixteen.

Oven Fried Chicken

Take a 3 pound young chicken, cut up as for frying. Salt and roll in flour, put 1/2 cup of melted butter in baking pan. Place chicken in pan and cover with sweet milk; sprinkle with pepper. Bake until tender, turning so it will brown on all pieces. You will find this a change and delicious.

 *Salads*

SALADS AND SALAD DRESSINGS

Chicken Salad

2 cups diced cold chicken
1 cup cut celery

1 cup oil mayonnaise

Have all the ingredients chilling in the ice-box. Mix the dressing well into the chicken and celery and serve on lettuce leaves.

Garnish with radishes, ripe and green olives.

Chicken Salad

1 cup white grapes seeded
2 cups chicken, diced
1 cup celery cut in small pieces

½ cup mayonnaise
3 tablespoons lemon juice
½ teaspoon salt

Combine celery and grapes. Mix mayonnaise, salt and lemon juice. Chill for an hour. Just before serving, combine the mixture.

Crab Meat Salad

1 pound crab meat
4 hard cooked eggs
½ cup almonds
1 green pepper

Lettuce
Salt to taste
Pepper
Dash paprika

Bone crab meat cut in good sized pieces. Cut whites of eggs in cubes. Blanch and chop almonds. Mix crab meat, eggs and nuts with a good mayonnaise. Add salt. Serve on lettuce. Garnish with green pepper strips, riced yolk of eggs and paprika.

Fig Salad

One canful finely cut figs mixed with one package cream cheese previously thinned with sweet cream. Pour over shredded lettuce and top with a spoonful of salad dressing.

Fruit Salad

2 oranges	2 eggs
2 bananas	Speck mustard, salt, pepper
1 grapefruit	3 tablespoons vinegar
1/2 pound white grapes	1 cup whipped cream
1/3 cup shelled nuts	

Skin the fruit, seed the grapes and cut the fruit in pieces. Beat the eggs, add the vinegar and seasoning and cook until thickened in a double boiler. Stir smooth. Cool and beat in the whipped cream. Chopped marshmallows may be added here. Pour over the fruit which has been arranged on lettuce leaves. Garnish with nuts and chill before serving.

Frozen Fruit Salad

2/3 cup heavy cream. Beat until stiff and gradually beat in
1/3 cup mayonnaise dressing.
1 teaspoon gelatine soaked in
3 tablespoons pineapple juice and dissolved over hot water.
1 teaspoon powdered sugar
2 tablespoons lemon juice and
1 tablespoon maraschino syrup. Fold in.
1/2 cup canned apricots
1/2 cup bananas
3/4 cup pineapple
1/2 cup maraschino cherries, all cut in small pieces. Freeze like ice cream and serve on salad leaves.

Pimento Salad for Sandwiches

1/2 pound boiled ham	Small can pimento
1/4 pound walnut meats	

Grind all together and mix with mayonnaise.

Stuffed Tomatoes

Pare medium sized tomatoes, scoop out centers and chill. Fill with chopped celery and hard cooked egg moistened with mayonnaise. Decorate top with cream cheese rosettes and nuts.

Peach Pecan Salad

Select ripe, juicy peaches. Peel off the skin, cut in medium pieces, blend with a small amount of mayonnaise. Place a crisp lettuce leaf on individual salad plates, and then a generous serving of salad. Sprinkle with salted pecans, and serve chilled.

Perfection Salad

1 can sliced pineapple cut fine

1 cup pecan meats

1 cup sweet pickle diced

1 small can pimento chopped fine

Dissolve one package mint jello in one pint boiling water and when cool add pineapple, pecans, pickles and pimentoes. Put into molds and when solid, serve on lettuce leaf with any good salad dressing mixed half and half with whipped cream.

Pineapple Gelatine Salad

1 cup pineapple juice

3 slices pineapple

1 package gelatine

1 cup water

1 tablespoon lemon juice

½ can pimento

1 cucumber

Dissolve the gelatine in boiling water.

Slice the cucumber fine and salt. Drain off the water before using.

Add the pineapple and lemon juice to the gelatine and chill. When the gelatine begins to set, add the pineapple cut into cubes, the chopped pimento and the cucumber slices.

Turn into a large mold or a ring or use small individual molds. Chill until the gelatine is very firm. Serve with a cream mayonnaise dressing.

Serves six.

Pineapple and Cream Cheese Salad

6 slices canned pineapple   Chopped walnut meats
1 cake cream cheese   French dressing

Put one slice of pineapple on each salad plate resting pineapple on lettuce leaf. Roll the cream cheese into balls and roll in chopped nuts.

Place one ball in the center of the pineapple slice and pour french dressing over it. Must be served cold.

Carrot and Pineapple Salad

1 cup grated carrots   Juice of ½ orange
1 cup minced pineapple   1 pkg. lemon gelatine

Pour one pint boiling water over gelatine and when cool put in carrots and pineapple (drained), also orange juice. Mix and put in individual molds. This makes six or seven. When firm serve on lettuce with a boiled dressing made fluffy with whipped cream.

Jellied Cucumber Salad

1 tablespoon gelatine   1 bay leaf
2½ cups water   1 blade mace
1 cup vinegar   1 teaspoon chopped green
3 cups diced cucumber   pepper

Dissolve the gelatine in hot water. Simmer the spices with the vinegar and the hot water. Strain and add the dissolved gelatine.

Place the cucumbers in a mold and distribute the chopped green pepper for color; pour on the liquid and allow the gelatine to set. Set on ice and serve very cold as a separate course.

Waldorf Salad

2 cups celery, cut small   ½ cup walnut meats
2 apples   ½ cup mayonnaise

Wash and scrape the celery and keep crisp in a wet towel on the ice. Peel the apples and cut into small pieces.

Mix the ingredients into the mayonnaise. Serve cold on lettuce and garnish with chips of red apple peel.

Chiffonade Salad

2 green peppers
Watercress

3 small tomatoes
2 medium size beets

Chop the tops of the watercress leaves; chop the peppers; cut the tomatoes into quarters and chop the beets. Keep each vegetable separate and arrange on a bed of shredded lettuce. Serve with mayonnaise and sprinkle one chopped egg over the dressing.

Lima Bean and Asparagus Salad

Drain one can of asparagus. Open the can at the bottom so that the tender tips will not be broken when the stalks are slipped out.

Take equal amount of sliced cucumbers, sliced tomato and cold canned lima beans.

Arrange on lettuce leaves and garnish with green pepper rings.

Chill and just before serving, add french dressing.

Kidney Bean Salad

1 can kidney beans
10 sweet slices pickles

1 stalk celery cut fine
1 cup mayonnaise

Mix ingredients. Make about four hours before using.

Old Fashioned Potato Salad

1 cucumber
3 hard cooked eggs
6 tablespoons of mayon-
naise
1 tablespoon lemon juice or
vinegar

2 cups diced boiled potatoes
1/2 medium sized onion
2 tablespoons minced green
pepper
1/2 head lettuce

Dice potatoes and marinate with vinegar, salt and pepper. Mix mayonnaise with lemon juice or vinegar. Let potatoes chill, drain, then mix with minced onion, diced cucumber and six tablespoons mayonnaise mixture. Arrange in a bowl on a nest of lettuce, garnish with sliced boiled eggs and spoonful of mayonnaise with chopped green pepper.

German Potato Salad

1 quart cold boiled potatoes
1 large onion
3 slices of chopped bacon fried crisp. Salt and pepper to taste.
3 tablespoons vinegar
1 teaspoon sugar

Cut potatoes in cubes or slices, add chopped onion, crisp bacon, bacon grease, vinegar and sugar. Mix this well and add one egg well beaten. Last add one teaspoon hot water to keep moist.

Potato Salad

1 small head lettuce shredded
1 tomato
1 medium sized onion
½ small cucumber

2 cups cooked cubed potatoes
½ pound bacon squares
Salt

Place shredded lettuce, tomato, onion, cucumber into a bowl and add the salt. Fry out the bacon squares until crisp, then add potatoes and stir until heated through, but do not fry. Add to the vegetables. Take one-quarter cup cider vinegar and one teaspoon sugar and mix well. Pour this over the salad.

Hot Potato Salad

6 potatoes, diced
6 slices of bacon
2 hard cooked eggs
½ teaspoon salt
⅛ teaspoon pepper
6 tablespoons of bacon fat

3 tablespoons vinegar
3 tablespoons onion in long thin slices
Mayonnaise
(Onion may be left out)

Cook potatoes until tender. Cook bacon over a very low flame, until crisp. Remove from pan, break into small pieces and add to hot potato cubes. Cut up hard cooked eggs into small pieces, and add eggs and seasoning. Cut green pepper and onion. Combine fat and vinegar. Pour over potato mixture. Then add mayonnaise. Serve hot or cold.

Potato Salad

6 cold boiled potatoes
½ grated onion
2 hard cooked eggs
2 tablespoons vinegar

1 cup milk
2 tablespoons butter
Salt and pepper
½ teaspoon mustard

Slice the potatoes, add the white of eggs chopped and then the onion. Mash the egg yolks and mix with mustard, salt and pepper. When dry ingredients are mixed well add the vinegar. Scald the milk and pour into the egg mixture, add the butter and then pour all over the potato mixture.
Cool and serve with additional boiled mayonnaise if the salad seems dry.

Molded Egg Salad

6 eggs   2 packages lemon gelatine

Boil, and stuff eggs, cutting them lengthwise, removing yellows, and season as desired with mayonnaise, salt, pepper, paprika, a chopped pickle or relish. Put back together and place in loaf cake pan. Pour gelatine over eggs and when congealed, turn out on lettuce leaves, fill hole with salad dressing. This is very attractive served at the table by the hostess.

Cinnamon Apple Salad

8-10 apples
2 cups sugar
1 cup water

Red coloring
2-3 sticks of cinnamon

Make a thin syrup of sugar, water, cinnamon and coloring. Core and pare apples. Cook in syrup until tender but be careful and do not break. Allow to cool. Serve on lettuce leaf with salad dressing. The center may be filled with cream cheese and nuts. This is a very delicious salad. It may be used as a dessert if whipped cream is used instead of salad dressing.

Butterfly Salad

Cut slices of canned pineapple in two. Place two halves with the curved sides together on a lettuce leaf. These are the two wings. Make the body of the butterfly with a stoned date, the feelers of candied orange peel, the spots on the wings of rings of stuffed olives or maraschino cherries. Pass the mayonnaise or place it beneath the butterfly.

Spook Salad

Lettuce	Mayonnaise
Celery	Peaches
Apples	Cloves
Red grapes	Pimento

Make a nest of shredded lettuce. On this place a salad of celery, grapes, and apples, allowing for each serving about two tablespoons of chopped celery and chopped apple and six grapes, cut in halves, and blended with mayonnaise. On this salad place a half peach, with the rounded side up. Insert two whole cloves for the eyes, one (with the large end down) for the nose, and a narrow strip of pimento for the mouth. This strip may be placed at different angles to give different expressions. This salad is particularly good for Hallowe'en parties.

May Morning Salad

1 bunch water cress	2 large oranges
1 bunch fresh onions	1 bunch radishes

Wash and clean cress, onions and radishes. Arrange water cress on a salad plate, place in center finely chopped onions, then diced orange and garnish with radish roses. Serve with French dressing.

Candlestick Salad

6 slices canned pineapple	1 green pepper
3 bananas	2 tablespoons lemon juice
6 maraschino cherries	

Cut each banana in half crosswise and roll in the lemon juice. (The lemon juice prevents discoloration of the bananas.) Fit a banana half into the hole of each pineapple slice and decorate the top with a cherry to imitate the flame. Cut the pepper in thin strips and place a curved strip at the side of the banana to represent the handle of the candlestick. Arrange on shredded lettuce on individual plates and serve with French dressing.

Fruit Salad

6 oranges   **1 cup nuts**
1 large can pineapple
1 box marshmallows, cut in
   small cubes

Veal Salad

(Mock Chicken Salad)

Two pounds of veal. Cook until tender, adding one bay leaf,
one-half onion and salt to taste. When done and cold, cut up
to small pieces, then add one-half can small peas, a stalk celery
cut up, and grate a half onion. Mix with mayonnaise dressing
and serve with head lettuce.

Celery Salad

For this salad the celery must be very young. Clean it well
and cut it into small bits. Serve with a French dressing and
some hard-boiled eggs cut in halves.

Canned Kidney Bean and Vegetable Salad

1 medium size can kidney   1 red pimento
   beans   ½ cup diced celery
1 hard-boiled egg   ½ cup black walnut meats
6 small sweet pickles

Chop pickles and nuts. Mix all ingredients. Marinate in the
following dressing for one hour, then serve with mayonnaise.
Dressing: Beat together 2 tablespoons vinegar, ½ teaspoon
salt, 4 tablespoons salad oil.

Green String Bean Salad

1 cup cooked green beans   1 teaspoon salt
¼ cup cut celery   ¼ teaspoon paprika
¼ cup pimento, cut fine   ½ cup salad dressing
1 hard cooked egg, diced   6 pieces of lettuce

Mix thoroughly the beans, celery, pimento, egg, salt and
paprika. Add the salad dressing and serve on a piece of crisp
lettuce.

Frozen Cheese Ring

1 can pineapple
1 bottle maraschino cherries
1 can pimentos
1 large green pepper

1 cup walnuts
2 cakes cream cheese
1 cup mayonnaise
½ pint whipping cream

Chop the fruits and nuts. Cream all together. Dissolve two tablespoons gelatine in a little cold water. Add half glass boiling water. When the gelatine starts to stiffen, add the first mixture, pour into a mould and chill in the ice box.

Tuna Fish Salad

½ lb. can tuna fish, minced
½ teaspoon salt
1 small onion, cut fine
2 pieces celery, cut fine

4 green olives, cut in pieces
1 hard-boiled egg, cut up in fine pieces

Mix ingredients and add 1 or 2 tablespoons of sour cream. Mix well together and serve on hearts of head lettuce which have been washed, dried and chilled. Serve on slice of tomato.

Combination Salad

1 cupful of chopped chicken
1 cupful celery, 1 cupful apples
2 oranges

2 hard-boiled eggs
2 tablespoonsful of chopped nuts

Let stand ½ hour, then mix with 2 chopped red peppers with mayonnaise dressing. Serve on lettuce.

Pea Salad

Drain can of peas
1 cup of peas
4 tablespoons chopped sweet pickle
4 tablespoons chopped onions

4 tablespoons chopped cheese
4 tablespoons chopped hard boiled eggs

Mix with mayonnaise dressing and whipped cream. Salt to taste.

Frozen Walnut and Cheese Salad

¼ pound cheese; put through food chopper with
¼ cup walnut meats, and
1 chopped pimento. Fold in
½ cup cream beaten until stiff,
2 teaspoons lemon juice,
2 tablespoons green peppers, chopped, and
2 tablespoons celery, chopped. Season with a little salt.

Put into small round mold, previously chilled. Pack in ice and salt for four hours. Slice and serve on lettuce with thousand island dressing.

Beet Salad

Drain one large can of beets or an equal amount of fresh-cooked beets—chop in small pieces. Add one small onion, finely chopped; one tablespoon vinegar; two tablespoons of sugar, and one tablespoon mustard.
Serve as a salad or a relish.

Shrimp Salad

1 can shrimp
2 tart apples, diced
8 stuffed olives, sliced

1 green pepper, chopped
2 hard cooked eggs, sliced

Break shrimp into pieces, mix with other ingredients and stir in enough mayonnaise to bind. Serve cold on lettuce leaves. The apples are a valuable addition to the flavor of the salad.

Stuffed Tomato Salad

Wash perfectly formed tomatoes, cut in shape of baskets, removing seeds and pulp. Mix a little of the pulp with cold cooked peas, well seasoned French dressing and refill the baskets.

Twenty Four Hour Salad

1 large can sliced pineapple (diced)
½ pound marshmallows (quartered)
½ pound almonds, blanched and chopped
1 bottle red maraschino cherries

Dressing:
4 beaten egg yolks—add ¼ cup sweet cream
Pinch of salt
Juice of 1 lemon
1 tablespoon sugar

Mix this together and let come to a boil in a double boiler. Boil until thick and smooth; let cool and add one cup whipped cream. Now mix this dressing with fruit and set in cool place for 24 hours. Serve on lettuce.

Pineapple Supreme Salad

Arrange tender lettuce leaves on salad plate—on these place a slice of pineapple; in middle of slice put a ball of cottage cheese a little larger than a walnut. Over this put a tablespoon of mayonnaise and sprinkle with a little paprika.

Tuna Fish or Salmon Salad

1 small can tuna fish or ½ can salmon
Dressing:
½ cup sugar
½ cup water

Small stalk celery

½ cup vinegar and butter size of walnut

Bring to a boil and add one egg yolk, one and one-half heaping teaspoons flour, one teaspoon dry mustard. When thick enough, partly cool and add one-fourth teaspoon salt and one stiffly beaten egg white.

To serve, arrange the fish and celery on lettuce; thin the dressing with very rich milk or cream; pour over the salad and garnish with hard cooked eggs cut in thin slices.

Pineapple and Date Salad

Thoroughly drain one cup crushed pineapple. Discard pits from one cup dates and cut in pieces. Mix with pineapple and arrange on lettuce. Serve with French dressing.

Hot Cabbage Salad

½ medium size head cab-
  bage
1 stalk celery

1 green pepper
1 small onion

Cut all fine and put in cold water to crisp; then drain.
Dice two slices of bacon; fry brown; remove from grease and add to cabbage mixture. Put one tablespoon of flour in grease, add one-half cup water and one-half cup of vinegar, one tablespoon of sugar, salt and pepper to taste; cook to thick gravy and mix in cabbage mixture while hot, and serve.

Fruit Salad Dressing

4 eggs
4 tablespoons sugar
2 tablespoons flour

½ cup lemon juice.
1 cup pineapple juice

Beat eggs; add sugar. Mix flour with pineapple juice; add lemon juice. Cook in double boiler until thick. When cold and ready to serve, thin with cream to as thick as wanted. Arrange fruit on lettuce and pour dressing over all when ready to serve.

Salad Dressing for Vegetables

1 teaspoon salt
1 teaspoon mustard
3 teaspoons sugar
Few grains pepper

1 teaspoon cornstarch
3 teaspoons butter
Yolks 2 eggs

Mix well, then add three-fourths cup hot milk. Put on stove and stir constantly while adding one-fourth cup hot vinegar.

Cream Cheese Dressing

½ cup French dressing   ½ cup cream cheese
⅛ teaspoon onion juice

Mash the cream cheese and blend gradually with French dressing. Season with onion juice.

Mayonnaise

2 tablespoons sugar   ½ teaspoon mustard (dry)
1 tablespoon flour   1/3 cup vinegar and water
1 egg

Boil until it thickens.

Uncooked Mayonnaise

1½ to 2 cups olive or salad   2½ teaspoons dry mustard
oil   2 tablespoons lemon juice
1 teaspoon sugar   2 egg yolks
1 teaspoon salt

Beat the egg yolks thoroughly, add salt, sugar and mustard Add the lemon juice and then very gradually beat in the oil. Keep very cold.

Boiled Mayonnaise Dressing

2 egg yolks   ½ cup milk
Juice of one lemon   2 tablespoons sugar
½ cup cream   2 tablespoons dry mustard
1 tablespoon flour   ½ teaspoon salt

Heat the cream in a double boiler, add the flour, sugar, mustard and salt. Stir smooth and pour in the milk.
Beat egg yolks and add lemon juice; turn into the mixture, cook for three minutes. Whipped cream may be added before serving.

Cooked Mayonnaise Dressing

4 tablespoons butter   1 tablespoon sugar
2 tablespoons flour   1 teaspoon salt
1 cup milk   1 teaspoon mustard
2 eggs   ¼ cup vinegar

Melt the butter in a double boiler and add the flour, stirring until smooth. Pour on the milk and cook until rather thick. Beat the eggs in a bowl and add the dry ingredients that remain. Pour on the hot mixture slowly, beating constantly. Return to the double boiler and cook until thick. Add vinegar when mass has thickened and stir in well.

Cool and then keep in ice-box. Thin with cream when needed.

French Dressing

Salad oil	Pepper
Lemon juice (or vinegar)	Dry mustard
Salt	Worcestershire sauce

Put a lump of ice in the mixing bowl. Pour the oil slowly over the ice. Use one-half to three-quarters cup of oil for salad to serve six or eight people. Add two tablespoons lemon juice, salt, pepper, paprika and dry mustard stirring all the while. Add Worcestershire sauce to taste.

Beat all the ingredients thoroughly with a fork and pour over the chilled salad.

Add one-quarter pound Roquefort cheese grated and stirred in well for Roquefort dressing.

One tablespoon English Chutney sauce mixed with the French dressing makes a palatable addition.

Italian Dressing

½ cup olive oil	Pepper and salt
1 clove garlic	6 drops tabasco sauce
1 tablespoon catsup	1 teaspoon minced parsley
1 tablespoon tarragon vinegar	

Rub the bowl with garlic and place a cube of ice in it. Mix all the ingredients except the oil. When well blended, slowly stir in the oil. Remove the ice and if possible put the salad into the bowl and serve the salad from this bowl.

Fruit Salad Dressing

2 tablespoons lemon juice
2 tablespoons orange or
  grapefruit juice
½ teaspoon powdered
  sugar
¼ cup olive oil

Mix all the ingredients thoroughly, chill and stir well just before serving.

Thousand Island Dressing

1½ cups mayonnaise
1 teaspoon chili sauce
1 teaspoon tomato-catsup
1 tablespoon chopped red
  pepper
1 tablespoon green pepper
  chopped

Stir the catsup and peppers into the mayonnaise. Serve ice cold on head lettuce.

Sour Cream Dressing

½ cup sour cream
1 egg
½ cup sweet milk
1½ teaspoons butter
½ teaspoon salt
1 teaspoon dry mustard
1 teaspoon sugar
1/3 cup vinegar
1 tablespoon flour

Beat the egg and add the milk. Mix all the dry ingredients and beat into the egg and milk mixture. Cook in a double boiler but do not let the water in the boiler boil. Keep on a very low flame.

Heat the vinegar and add, then the butter; stir smooth. Cool and add the sour cream. Chill and pour over salad.

Russian Dressing

12 tablespoons mayonnaise
3 tablespoons whipped
  cream
1 tablespoon taragon vin-
  egar
6 tablespoons chili sauce
½ tablespoon chopped
  capers
1 tablespoon prepared mustard

Stir all the ingredients into the mayonnaise.

Chill and serve over lettuce, cold asparagus and similar fresh salads.

Hot Dressing for Cole-Slaw

1 egg	½ teaspoon sugar
1 teaspoon salt	1 teaspoon butter
1 teaspoon dry mustard	¼ cup vinegar

Beat the egg and add the remaining ingredients. Heat in a saucepan until the mixture thickens. Stir well and while still hot pour over the cole-slaw.
Cool and later chill on the ice.

Imperial Dressing

1 cup sugar	½ cup vinegar
6 tablespoons catsup	Pinch of salt
2 tablespoons Worcester-shire sauce	

Let boil slowly until it is "sirrupy."
Keeps very well.

Thousand Island Dressing

2 cups oil	3 hard boiled eggs
3 egg yolks	2 pimentos
½ cup vinegar	½ green pepper
½ bottle chile sauce	¼ teaspoon paprika
1 bunch chives or onions	½ teaspoon salt

Mix oil, yolks of eggs and vinegar; add slowly chile sauce until well mixed; then chop together (very fine) chives or onions, hard boiled eggs, pimentos and green pepper, salt and paprika and add.
Can use onions in place of chives—more pimentos and green pepper; also few olives and little Worcestershire sauce. Can omit boiled eggs. This will make about one quart of dressing.

Dressing

2 egg yolks	Juice of 1 lemon
1 tablespoon sugar	¼ teaspoon mustard
¼ cup cream	

Cook over gas flame until thick, then cool. Whip bottle of whipping cream until stiff; then add the above dressing. Be sure to drain off all juice of fruit, then add to the whipped cream and set aside in a cool place.

Soups

Soup

The juices of meat are drawn out by soaking the meat in cold water for a length of time. These juices are cooked in the water with vegetables to form soup stock. Celery leaves, onion leaves, meat trimmings, marrow bones and pan gravies may be saved from the regular meals and made into soup stock.

Cook all the ingredients together in a large kettle and keep for future use. In summer, the stock should be boiled daily to prevent its souring.

Soup Stock

2 pounds beef brisket
2 quarts cold water
2 teaspoons salt
A few dried onion peels
½ cup tomato, raw, stewed
  or canned

1 small onion
1 carrot
½ cup celery, diced
Sprig parsley

Wash, wipe and then salt the meat. Let stand one hour in the soup kettle without water. Pour on the cold water and let stand another hour. Cook over a low flame for three or more hours.

Add vegetables and more water if much is cooked off. Cook for one more hour. Strain the soup, cool and allow fat to rise to the top. Skim off this fat, add salt and pepper and a little chopped parsley just before reheating to serve.

Bouillon

Three pound beef bone

Two pound veal bone

Chicken bones

4 pounds lean beef meat

4 quarts cold water

1 onion sliced

1 carrot

1/2 cup diced celery

A few dried onion peels

1 sliced potato

1/4 cup corn

Bay leaf

Let meat and bones stand for one hour in the cold water to draw the juices.

Boil slowly in the soup kettle for four or more hours. Add the vegetables and boil for one additional hour.

Strain and season. Allow to cool and remove cake of fat from top. Reheat and serve in bouillon cups.

Chicken Soup

4 pound chicken

Extra chicken feet

4 quarts cold water

1 onion

1/2 cup diced celery root

Tablespoon salt

Pepper

Scald and skin the chicken legs and the wing tips of the chicken. Singe and unjoint the chicken, rub with salt and soak several hours in water.

Drain this water, put on the range in cold fresh water and bring to a boil. Skim the top at this time for a clear soup. Boil slowly for three hours and add the vegetables and boil for one hour longer.

Take the chicken out when it has cooked thoroughly, so that the flesh falls away from the bones. Use with a cream sauce for chicken with rice, with dumplings or cold for chicken salad.

Serve the soup hot with a slice of lemon in each soup plate.

Cold Chicken Bouillon

Soak a tablespoon of crystallized gelatine in cold water. Add one-quarter cup boiling water to dissolve the gelatine. Add two cups of hot chicken soup and beat in well.

Cool and serve in bouillon cups with one slice lemon and a sprinkling of chopped parsley on top of each cup.

For cold beef bouillon, use two cups hot beef soup in place of chicken soup.

Beef Consomme

2 pounds lean beef	1 carrot
2 pounds marrow bone	½ cup diced celery
2 pounds chicken	1 tablespoon salt
2 pounds veal bone	Pepper
6 quarts cold water	¼ teaspoon celery salt
1 onion	

Chop beef into pieces and with marrow from bones, brown in a hot spider. Place in soup kettle.

Clean chicken and cut in pieces and place in kettle.

Add cold water and let come to a boil. Skim the liquid if a clear soup is desired.

Turn down flame and allow to cook slowly for five hours. Stew the vegetables in a little fat and when half tender, add to the liquid and boil for one additional hour.

Strain the soup and season. Allow to cool and remove the cake of fat that forms on the top.

Remove the chicken from the soup as soon as it has boiled tender. Use this chicken for salad.

Russian Borsht

6 beets	2 green apples
6 cups cold water	2 pounds flank steak
3 big onions	Citric salt (size of a pea)

Grind the raw, scraped beets in a meat grinder. Cook with the flank steak, onions and a little salt until meat and beets are tender.

Cook the apples and add when beets are nearly tender.

Add the citric acid and boil twenty minutes. Serve hot or boil down and serve as Cold Borsht.

Chicken Gumbo

Use chicken soup. Add chopped chicken from the soup to the clear liquid. Boil with one-half cup rice, cut okra, chopped onion and three stalks of cut celery.

Boil slowly for one hour, season with salt, pepper and celery salt and serve.

Barley Soup

½ cup barley
1 quart water
2 quarts strong soup stock
Pepper

1 teaspoon salt
½ cup diced carrots
½ cup chopped celery

Salt the water and bring to boiling point. Drop in the barley and allow to boil with the carrots and celery for about two hours or until the water has evaporated.

Add the soup stock to the barley and vegetables and bring to a boil. Serve hot with crackers or croutons.

Mulligatawny Soup

3 pounds chicken
4 quarts water
¼ cup butter
2 teaspoons flour
4 tablespoons diced celery
4 tablespoons chopped
   green pepper

4 tablespoons diced carrot
4 tablespoons chopped onion
½ teaspoon celery salt
½ teaspoon table salt
Pepper
Mace

Brown the chicken and the vegetables except the seasoning, in butter. Add the flour and a little curry powder if available. Add the water (cold) and allow to simmer until the chicken is soft and falls away from the bones.

Strain the liquid and press the softened vegetables through a sieve. Cut the chicken meat into small pieces. Add the chopped chicken to the soup when it is strained and serve hot.

Vegetable Soup (Without Soupmeat)

4 tablespoons butter
2 quarts water
½ cup diced carrots
½ cup sliced onion
½ cup peas
½ cup green beans
½ cup sliced cabbage
   (white)
1 cup diced potato

1 cup tomatoes
¼ cup corn (from the cob
   or drained canned corn)
½ cup diced celery or
   celery root
1 teaspoon salt
1 teaspoon sugar
Pepper

Use any vegetables that are available, preferably fresh vegetables. Proportion should be half vegetables and half water.

Wash vegetables, scrape carrots and potatoes and cut all fine. Melt butter in a spider and add all the vegetables except the corn, potatoes and tomatoes. Stir continually and stew for about fifteen minutes.

Add the water, boiling hot, then the potatoes, tomatoes and corn. Boil one hour or over or until all the vegetables are tender. Season with salt, pepper and celery salt to taste. Serve hot.

Potato Soup

3 potatoes	Parsley
1 quart water	1 tablespoon flour
½ teaspoon salt	2 tablespoons butter
Pepper	1 tablespoon chopped onion
Chopped celery	

Simmer the onion and celery in the butter and add the flour. Add the potato and let simmer with one cup of water for one hour. Add more water and cook until potatoes are soft. Serve hot with a dot of butter in each plate and season well.

Lentil Soup

2 cups of lentils	Onion
1 ham bone or	1 stalk celery
1 pound smoked sausage	Pepper
1 tablespoon flour	Very little salt

Wash lentils and soak over night in cold water. Drain and boil with the ham bone or the sausage in three quarts of water. Boil for four to four and a half hours. Add the celery and cook until all is tender.

Brown the onion in the flour with a little butter.

Add this to the soup and keep hot. Remove the ham bone or the sausage and skim the fat from the top of the soup. Serve very thick, with a piece of sausage sliced in each plate and a piece of rye bread toasted crisp.

Use salt sparingly since both ham and sausage contain a good deal of salt.

Yellow Pea Soup

Beef soup bone   Soup greens
1 cup yellow dried peas   Salt

Enough cold water to cover. Cook until tender. Serve with toasted bread cubes.

Tomato Soup

Boil one can of tomatoes in a pint of water with one stalk celery, chopped, one slice of onion and one tablespoon sugar. Boil for fifteen minutes.

Brown two tablespoons flour in an equal amount of butter and add to the strained tomato liquid. Serve hot as a clear bouillon.

One tablespoon hot dissolved gelatine may be added, the liquid chilled and served jellied.

String Bean Soup

Wash and cut in small pieces one quart green or wax beans with enough water for soup. Boil till nearly done, then add three or four raw potatoes diced. When tender add a cup of thick sour cream and a tablespoon of butter. Salt and pepper to taste. Boil up once and serve hot.

Vegetable Soup

8 medium size carrots   1 pound peas
3 medium size potatoes   1 quart milk

Cut carrots and potatoes in small pieces. Cover vegetables with water and boil until tender. Add milk and season to taste.

Onion Soup With Cheese

4 medium sized onions   1 cup water
3 tablespoons slightly   2 cups milk, scalded
  browned flour   1¼ teaspoon salt
3 tablespoons butter

Slice onions, add water and cook slowly till tender. Rub through sieve, saving the water. If the water cooks away, add enough to make a cupful. Melt butter, add browned flour and stir in hot milk gradually. Cook until mixture thickens slightly. Add onion pulp and one cup of the water. Season with salt. Serve with grated Parmesan cheese.

Lentil or Split Pea Soup

2 cups lentils or split peas.
Soak in cold water over night.
½ cup celery.

Wash and put in kettle with one and one-quarter pounds smoked pork butts and let come slowly to a boil and let simmer for three and one-half to four hours. Fry one small onion cut fine in one and one-half tablespoons butter. Add one tablespoon flour and one tablespoon sugar. Add this gradually to boiling soup.

Vegetable Soup

2 pounds soup bone with
marrow
2 stalks celery
4 carrots
2 turnips
2 onions
3 tomatoes
½ bunch parsley
Parsnips when in season

One tablespoon of flour beaten up in pint of water and poured into the soup after it has commenced to boil. Pepper and salt to taste. Cook three hours.

Navy Bean Soup

1 small ham hock
½ pound navy beans
2 small potatoes
1 small piece garlic

Soak beans over night. Pour off water and use enough fresh water to cover. Take ham hock and let boil with beans till beans are nearly done, then cut up potatoes into small cubes and add garlic. Cook until potatoes are done.

Cream or Potato Soup

2 cups potatoes cut fine
1 small onion cut fine
½ cup celery cut fine
2 cups water

2 cups milk
Lump butter
Chopped parsley
Salt and pepper to taste

Cook potatoes, onion and celery in water until soft. Add boiling milk and butter. Sprinkle with parsley and serve. Left over mashed potatoes may be used and added when onion and celery are done.

Celery Soup

2 cups celery
2/3 cup potatoes
2 tablespoons flour
4 cups milk

1 teaspoon salt
2 teaspoons butter
1 onion

Cut celery, potatoes and onion into small pieces, cook until tender. Use water the vegetables were cooked in. Make a cream sauce of milk, flour and butter and add to soup. Add one-half cup of cream.

Cream of Tomato Soup

1 quart tomatoes
¼ teaspoon soda
4 tablespoons butter
4 tablespoons flour

1 quart milk
1 tablespoon salt
½ teaspoon pepper

Stew tomatoes slowly one-half hour. Melt butter, stir in flour and cook over slow fire adding milk slowly. Add seasoning. Strain tomatoes, add soda, stir into sauce.

Cream of Potato Soup

3 good sized potatoes
1 quart of milk
1 small chopped onion
3 tablespoons butter
3 tablespoons flour

1 tablespoon chopped
    parsley
1 tablespoon salt
Celery salt
Pepper

Prepare the soup in a double boiler.

Use boiled potatoes or cook the potatoes until soft. Scald the milk in a double boiler and add the potatoes; press through a sieve and replace in double boiler.

Brown the flour and onion in the melted butter. Add a little of the hot liquid to make a thin paste. Pour back into the double boiler and cook for about ten minutes. Serve fairly thick and very hot. Sprinkle with parsley.

Cream of Tomato Soup

½ can of tomatoes
¼ teaspoon baking soda
1 quart milk
1 teaspoon chopped onion
2 tablespoons butter

2 tablespoons flour
1 teaspoon salt
1 teaspoon sugar
Pepper

Brown the flour and onion in the butter; add the scalded milk and seasoning.

Strain the tomatoes and place over flame. Add the soda and when gas bubbles have all burst, combine the two liquids.

Stir well and serve very hot. One tablespoon of whipped cream topped with a little paprika may be dropped on each bowl of soup just before serving.

Cream of Corn Soup

1 can of corn
1 quart milk
2 cups water
2 tablespoons butter

2 tablespoons flour
1 slice of onion
Salt and pepper

Press the corn through a strainer and boil with the water for fifteen minutes. Scald the milk, adding the slice of onion; when hot, remove the onion.

Brown the flour in the butter and then add the scalded milk. Cook until thickened and add to the corn, heat all thoroughly and stir together. Further season if necessary.

Cream of Spinach Soup

2 quarts spinach   1 pint white sauce
1 quart chicken soup

Pick over the spinach carefully and wash in cold water. Cook very slowly in a thick aluminum kettle without water. When some water has drawn, allow the spinach to boil for about a quarter of an hour or until tender.

Allow the moisture to boil off, but do not drain, since the small amount of remaining water contains some of the best properties of the spinach. Grind the spinach through a meat grinder or press through a strainer. Add the soup, when hot, add the white sauce and stir well to mix. Season and serve hot sprinkled with chopped parsley.

Cream of Celery Soup

Break three stalks of celery into pieces and mash. Scald three cups of milk with a slice of onion; remove the onion. Cook the celery with the milk for fifteen minutes.

Brown two tablespoons of flour in two tablespoons of butter. Gradually add the celery liquid to the browned flour and stir in one cup of cream to make a smooth thick soup.

Season well and serve sprinkled with chopped parsley.

Cream of Mushroom Soup

½ pound mushrooms   2 tablespoons butter
1 quart chicken soup   2 tablespoons flour
1 cup cream   Salt and pepper

Simmer the mushrooms, chopped or sliced, in one tablespoon of butter for ten minutes.

Brown the flour in the other tablespoon of butter and stir in a little hot soup. Then add the mushrooms and the rest of the soup.

Heat and add the cream and season quite highly to bring out flavor of mushrooms.

Fresh mushrooms make a more tasty soup than canned mushrooms, but canned mushrooms may be used.

Oyster Stew

1 pint oysters	1 teaspoon salt
2 cups milk	Pepper
1 tablespoon butter	

Scald the milk. Heat the oysters in a saucepan with the butter until the edges of the oysters curl. Do not cook oysters hard or they will be tough. Pour on the hot milk, stir, heat through thoroughly and serve. Season well and drop a dot of butter in the plate just before serving.

Bisque of Lobster

2 pounds of lobster	2 tablespoons butter
2 cups water	2 tablespoons flour
1 quart milk	

Crack bones of lobster and remove the meat. Cook the small claws and lobster bones for twenty minutes in two cups of cold water. Brown the flour in the butter. Drain the bones and cook with the browned flour.

Cut the tail meat of the lobster in small pieces and add the scalded milk. Combine the two liquids; add the body and claw meat cut fine. Season and serve sprinkled with paprika.

Clam Chowder

1 quart of clams	1 tablespoon butter
4 cups milk	1 sliced onion
6 crackers	Pepper and salt

4 cups potatoes cut in cubes

Drain the clams and remove any pieces of shell. If canned clams are used retain the liquor and use in place of water. Cut the clams into good sized pieces.

Do not cook clams over two or three minutes, as this makes them tough and indigestable.

Fry the onion brown, add water or clam liquor enough to cover the potatoes. Cook until the potatoes are tender, turn into a kettle, add the milk, butter, pepper, salt and a little celery salt. Cook until potatoes are thoroughly done and add clams and the soda crackers just before serving.

Season very well and serve as hot as possible.

Corn Chowder

1 can corn	2 cups water
2 onions	2 cups milk
4 potatoes, cut in cubes	2 tablespoons butter

Brown the flour and the onion in the butter in a spider. Add the water and potatoes and cook until the potatoes become tender.

Add the corn and the milk, scalded, and cook for five minutes. Season highly with salt and pepper.

Croutons

Cut stale bread into small cubes and brown in the oven. Croutons may be browned and buttered by cooking in a spider or may be fried in deep fat.

Soup Crisps

Cut stale bread into long strips, spread with butter and brown in the oven.

Toast for Soup

Cut white or rye bread very thin and dry brown in the oven.

Egg Drops

Beat one egg, add a pinch of salt and two tablespoons water. Stir into a smooth paste with three tablespoons flour.
Pour in drops off the end of a spoon and cook for three or four minutes just before serving the soup.

Cracker Balls

½ cup cracker crumbs   2 tablespoons butter
1 egg   ¼ teaspoon salt
1 tablespoon soup

Stir the egg and butter together. Stir in the soup and season.
Mold into little balls and let stand on a plate to expand. Drop
into the boiling soup fifteen minutes before serving.
Nuts may be added to the paste before molding.

Baking Powder Dumplings

2 teaspoons baking powder   1/3 cup milk
1 cup flour   ¼ teaspoon salt

Sift the flour, salt and baking powder. Stir into the milk and
smooth into a batter. Spoon into the boiling soup and let boil
covered for five minutes before serving the soup.

Tomato Soup With Dumplings

2 cups flour   1 dessert spoon lard
2 teaspoons baking powder   Pinch salt

Mix above, then add one cup milk and one egg well beaten.
Drop into one quart boiling tomatoes to which has been added
one tablespoon butter. If onion flavor is desired, one chopped
onion may be cooked with tomatoes before dropping dumplings. Cook above twenty minutes. Pour on platter and
garnish with parsley.

Marrow Balls

Cream two tablespoons marrow fat extracted from marrow
bones. Cream the marrow and mix with two beaten eggs,
add one-half teaspoon salt and enough cracker meal or matzos
meal to make a soft dough. Let the dough stand for several
hours.
Test the dough by making a small ball and dropping it into
boiling water. If the ball crumbles and falls apart, more meal
should be stirred into the dough. Make into small balls and
boil in the soup for fifteen minutes before serving. Serve three
or four balls to each plate of soup.

Noodles

Beat up one egg slightly, add one-quarter teaspoon salt and stir in enough flour to make a stiff dough. Knead thoroughly and set aside to stand half an hour.

Roll the dough out very thin and spread on a cloth to dry for an hour or more, depending on the weather.

Cut into long strips about four inches wide, stack one on top of the other and cut crosswise as fine as possible with a very sharp knife. Separate the strands and dry on a cloth. When completely dry, put into tight jars or a covered casserole and keep for subsequent use.

In using noodles, drop them into the soup about five minutes before serving.

The dough may be made into a long loaf, allowed to harden and then grated into small crumbs. Drop these into soup about ten minutes before serving.

Perfect Dumplings

1¼ cup flour   1 teaspoon sugar
3 teaspoons baking powder   1 well beaten egg
1 teaspoon salt   1 cup milk

Sift together dry ingredients. Add milk to well beaten egg, and add to dry ingredients, blending or folding the mixture but not stirring or mixing. When combined thoroughly, drop by spoonsful in boiling stew and steam fifteen minutes, keeping the stew boiling continuously. Makes about one dozen dumplings.

Farina Balls

½ cup farina   2 eggs
1 cup milk   Salt and pepper
1 tablespoon butter

Heat the milk and butter in a bouble boiler, add the farina and stir as for breakfast farina. Cool and stir in the beaten eggs. Season and then roll into small balls. Drop into the boiling soup, let boil for about ten minutes and serve. Chopped nuts and chopped parsley may be mixed before forming into balls.

Vegetables

Time Table for Boiling or Steaming Vegetables

Artichokes	30 to 45 minutes
Asparagus	15 to 30 minutes
Beans, young string	30 to 45 minutes
Beans, old string	60 minutes
Beets, young	45 to 60 minutes
Beets, old or large	2 to 3 hours
Brussels Sprouts	15 to 30 minutes
Cabbage	15 to 20 minutes
Carrots	25 to 45 minutes
Cauliflower	25 minutes
Celery	20 to 30 minutes
Sweet Corn	10 to 15 minutes
Onions	30 to 45 minutes
Parsnips	15 to 30 minutes
Peas, fresh green	15 to 20 minutes
Potatoes, sweet or yams	30 to 35 minutes
Potatoes, Irish	35 to 45 minutes
Spinach	30 minutes
Squash (summer)	30 to 40 minutes
Squash (winter)	60 minutes
Tomatoes	15 to 20 minutes

Drain vegetables after cooking, season, add butter and serve at once.

To skin beets: cover with cold water after cooking and slip off the skins. Reheat or chill as desired.

Vegetables are valued for their salts, vitamines, water and for the ruffage which they supply to the body. Fresh vegetables are always to be preferred to canned vegetables and should be used whenever available at a reasonable price.

Wash vegetables very carefully to remove any soil, scrape whenever possible. Much of the health giving property of the vegetable is wasted if the outer layer is removed by deep paring.

In boiling or steaming vegetables, conserve all the cooking water. Boil only in enough water to cover and use the vegetable water for soup, gravy or sauce to cover vegetables.
Use plenty of salt in cooking vegetables, one teaspoon to one quart of water, for this brings out the water in the vegetables and adds to the palatability of the food.

If the saucepan is left uncovered during the boiling, the vegetables will retain their color. A pinch of bicarbonate of soda in the water when cooking green vegetables tends to preserve the fresh coloring.

Artichokes

Boil the artichokes until the leaves pull out easily. Boil in salted water and when cooked, stand on the tips to drain out excess water.

Cut the bottoms so the artichokes stand firmly and serve hot with melted butter or Hollandaise sauce.
May be served cold with vinaigrette sauce. The "choke" should be removed and some of the dressing poured in in place of the smallest leaves and the fuzzy parts.

Asparagus

Cut the tough part off the bottom of the asparagus. Wash and remove side scales. Reform in a bunch and tie together.

Stand on end in boiling salted water so that tips remain out of the water for the first ten minutes. Cook the bunch lying on its side for five more minutes or until tender and drain. Cut the string, serve on toast covered with browned butter, white sauce, cream sauce or bread crumbs browned in butter.

Canned Asparagus

Open the can from the bottom and slide out the stalks so as not to injure the delicate tips. Drain and run cold water over the asparagus. Replace them in the can, pour on boiling water to cover and heat in a pan of water on the stove or heat in the can in the oven. Serve with browned butter, Hollandaise sauce or white sauce.

String Beans

Remove the strings from the beans and wash in cold water. Cut on the slant into pieces an inch long.
Cook in boiling water until tender. Add salt a short time before the beans are tender. Drain and serve with butter, salt and pepper or with a brown sauce.

String Beans With Tomato

Melt two tablespoons butter and add two tablespoons flour and a cup of strained tomato juice. Make a smooth sauce of this and pour over the cooked string beans. Simmer for fifteen minutes and serve hot.

Boiled Beets

Wash but do not cut the beets. Cook in boiling water until perfectly tender. Beets take a very long time to cook.
When thoroughly cooked, drain and pour on cold water. This will loosen the skins so they may be rubbed off. Serve young beets with melted butter, salt and pepper.

Pickled Beets

Boil old beets or very large beets until tender, slice and place in a crock covered with two cups vinegar, salt and pepper. Add a little caraway seed, raw sliced onion and clove. Serve as a relish or a salad.

Fried Beets

Wash five large beets and boil them until soft. Then peel them and chop them up fine. Cut up three slices bacon in small pieces, and fry until crisp. Add the chopped beets and fry. Put the beets to one side and add two tablespoons vinegar and bring to a boil, then add one tablespoon sugar and mix. Sprinkle one tablespoon (level) flour over the beets and season to taste.

Makes a very delicious dish to serve with a beef roast.

Brussel Sprouts

Remove the wilted leaves from the outside of the sprouts. Soak in cold water and then cook in boiling salted water for about twenty minutes. Drain and serve with melted butter, salt and pepper; with brown sauce; or with white sauce.

Add a pinch of bicarbonate of soda to the water in which the sprouts are to be cooked. This will keep them green.

Boiled Cabbage

Chop a quart of cabbage and add to browned flour and onion. Melt two tablespoons butter and let steam for ten minutes under cover.

Pour on a quart of boiling water and let boil for an hour or more until tender. Thicken with a little flour, boil a few minutes longer to cook the flour and serve hot, with ham or pork.

Boiled Whole Cabbage

Wash the cabbage in cold water and remove wilted leaves. Cut into quarters and cover with boiling salted water. Boil until tender. Add a strip of bacon while the cabbage is boiling for flavor.

Drain, sprinkle with salt and pepper and heat with two tablespoons of butter. Serve hot

Red cabbage may be prepared in the same way but the water must be changed four times to destroy the strong taste.

Cabbage au Gratin

Pour a cream sauce over the boiled cabbage and put into a baking dish. Sprinkle with grated cheese and bake in the oven until browned.

Swiss Chard

Prepare just like spinach.

Carrots

Scrape the carrots, wash them and cut into slices or dice. Cook until tender in boiling salted water. Serve with melted butter, salt and pepper.

Carrots and Peas

Wash, scrape and dice the carrots. Cook in salted water until tender. Drain canned or cooked fresh peas and mix with the carrots. Sprinkle with about two tablespoons flour, add two tablespoons butter, season and add one-half cup soup stock. Boil a little longer and serve.

Carrots and peas may also be served with a cream sauce.

Puree of Carrots

Cook as above. Press the carrots through a coarse mesh sieve. Add butter and seasoning.

Braised Celery

Wash and scrape clean the stalks of celery; cook in two cups of hot soup-stock until the celery is tender. Add a little melted butter and serve.

Use only the outside stalks reserving the tender stalks and the hearts for table use fresh.

Boiled Broccoli

Broccoli is an Italian green cauliflower.

To prepare: remove the outer leaves, boil for three-quarters of an hour in salted water with a pinch of bicarbonate of soda. Boil only until tender and use great care in removing from the hot water since the vegetable breaks apart easily.

Drain and serve with a Hollandaise sauce.

Fried Eggplant

1 eggplant   ½ teaspoon salt
3 ripe tomatoes   Cornflakes
1 egg

Serve six.

Peel and slice the eggplant. Beat the egg and add salt. Dip the eggplant slices into the egg and then into cornflakes.

Fry in hot fat until tender and cooked through.

Cut tomato into thick slices. Dip in cornflakes.

Brown until tender in a greased spider.

Serve hot, placing the fried tomato on the fried eggplant.

Creamed Lettuce

Remove any wilted leaves. Use four heads of lettuce. Open the heads and wash the leaves. Boil the lettuce for about fifteen minutes in as little water as possible.

Press through a coarse mesh sieve and mix with one cup of cream. Serve hot seasoned with salt and pepper.

Baked Mushrooms

12 large mushrooms	2/3 cup cream
Salt and pepper	Toast
2 tablespoons butter	

Wash the mushrooms, remove stems, peel caps and place in buttered dripping pan, cap side up. Sprinkle with salt and pepper, dot over with butter and add cream. Bake ten minutes in hot oven. Arrange on dry toast and pour over remaining cream and serve hot.

Creamed Onions

Cook two cups of small white onions for about one-half hour in boiling water. Drain and add cream sauce. Put into a double boiler and cook for five more minutes.
Season and serve.

Baked Onions

6 large Spanish onions.
Bake the onions in their peels for one hour. Remove from the fire, peel and return to the dish. Pour over them two cups beef-stock, salt and pepper and bake for ten more minutes, basting a few times with the stock.

French Fried Onions

Peel large white onions and cut across the grain. Separate the rings and put them in a frying basket. Dip the basket in hot deep fat. Shake constantly and fry to a light brown. Drain on brown paper and serve with steak.

Stuffed Onions

Parboil large onions for ten minutes. Remove part of the center leaving the root for the onion to stand on. Fill the cavity with the chopped onion just taken out, chopped cooked meat and bread crumbs in equal amounts.

Season and moisten with cream or melted butter. Arrange in a greased baking dish, pour one cup soup-stock over all and bake in a moderate oven three-quarters to an hour.

Stuffed Green Peppers

Take six green peppers, cut off top, remove all seeds and wash well. Mix together one-half pound pork and one-half pound veal ground together, three heaping tablespoons cooked rice, one onion cut fine, salt and pepper. Then fill the peppers and pour over them one can tomatoes, strained. Add a few pieces of butter and simmer slowly one hour.

Stuffed Green Peppers

6 medium sized peppers (green)	1 cup canned tomatoes
	1 small onion
2 eggs	12 soda crackers
2 slices smoked ham	

Parboil the ham. Drain and keep the liquor. Cut off the stem and remove the seeds of the peppers. Wash them and cut in half lengthwise. Chop the ham and break up the soda crackers into very small bits. All may be ground through a meat grinder.

Mix the meat and crackers with the tomatoes and add the beaten eggs. Fill the empty peppers with this mixture and arrange in a low baking dish. Surround by the liquor in which the ham was parboiled. Bake for twenty minutes in a hot oven (450 degrees F.).

Hubbard Squash With Bacon

1 squash	1 cup cream
6 slices bacon	½ cup crumbs

Quarter the squash and remove the seeds. Cook until tender, peel and cut up the pulp. Press it through a potato ricer until you can fill three cups with the pulp. Add cream, salt and a little pepper. Mix well, place in a greased baking dish and sprinkle with bread crumbs.

Parboil the bacon and lay over the squash. Bake in a very hot oven, 500 degrees, for fifteen minutes.

Candied Parsnips

Wash and scrape the parsnips. Boil in salty water until tender. Cut lengthwise and place in a baking dish or fireproof dish. Cover with brown sugar and dot with butter. Put in a very hot oven and brown for about ten minutes.

Serve in the baking dish.

Baked Spinach

2 cups cooked spinach	2 tablespoons grated cheese
2 egg yolks	$\frac{1}{2}$ teaspoon salt
2 egg whites	Paprika

Cook the spinach, drain and chop fine. Add the grated cheese and then the beaten yolks. Season. When cool, add the stiffly beaten egg whites.

Turn into a buttered ring mold and bake for twenty minutes in a pan of water.

Baked Squash

Split the squash in two crosswise. Remove the seeds and place in a drip pan shell side up. Bake for two hours or until soft. Remove the pulp from the shell, mash to remove any lumps and season with pepper and salt. Mix in one teaspoon butter.

Summer Squash

Cut summer squash into quarters and remove the seeds and pulp. Cook in salted boiling water for half an hour.

Drain and mash the soft squash through a coarse sieve. Add butter and season.

Cream may be used instead of butter. Use about two table-spoons of cream.

Winter Squash

Cut the squash into quarters and remove seeds and pulp. Boil just as for summer squash. Prepare in same manner but boil twice as long.

Boiled Spinach

Wash spinach carefully several times to remove any grit. Put the spinach in a kettle with as little water as possible. Add one teaspoon salt and a pinch of bicarbonate of soda. Boil until the spinach is reduced to a pulp.

Drain off any water and use in soup, gravy, etc. Run cold water over the spinach, and drain again. Press the pulp through a course sieve. Mix in a tablespoon of butter, season and garnish with sliced hard boiled eggs.

Creamed Spinach

Add one-half cup of cream to the boiled spinach.

Spinach Ring

½ peck spinach.	2 tablespoons flour
3 eggs	½ cup milk
2 tablespoons butter	Salt and pepper

Cook the spinach for half an hour with as little water as possible. Drain and chop fine.

Heat the butter and brown the flour; then add the milk. Stir in the beaten yolks and stir until smooth and fairly thick. Add the spinach and seasoning.

Cool. Then add the stiffly beaten whites and pour into a greased ring mold. Stand the ring in a pan of hot water and bake in a moderate oven for fifteen minutes or until the mixture is set.

Loosen edges and turn onto a platter. Fill center with creamed mushrooms, chicken a la king; or serve with other cooked vegetables in the center as a course.

Spinach Souffle

Boil spinach, drain well and press through a coarse mesh sieve until about a cup of spinach pulp is left.

Heat one tablespoon butter in a saucepan, season and stir in the spinach. Stir in yolks of three eggs, one at a time.

Remove from the flame and when cool beat in one-quarter cup whipped cream. Beat the whites of the eggs stiff and fold in the spinach. Grease a souffle dish, turn in the spinach and bake in a moderate oven (325 degrees F.) for one hour. Serve immediately so that the puffy souffle will not fall.

Stuffed Baked Tomatoes

½ pound green beans
4 smooth tomatoes
2 tablespoons butter
½ teaspoon salt

½ teaspoon sugar
Few grains nutmeg
1 sweet green pepper

Cut beans in small pieces and cook in boiling water for twenty minutes. Let the water cook away and add pepper cut in shreds, butter, salt, sugar and nutmeg. Cut a slice from the top of each tomato and scoop out the seeds. Fill with the bean mixture and place on a buttered shallow pan. Bake thirty minutes in a moderately hot oven.

Skillet Tomatoes on Toast

Place one can of solid pack tomatoes (or fresh tomatoes sliced) in skillet with small amount of bacon grease; chop tomatoes fairly well, bring to boiling point; add salt and pepper, sugar and sufficient flour to thicken; simmer until flour is thoroughly cooked. Add about three crackers rolled if there is much juice on tomatoes. Serve on dry white toast, garnish with long strips of **crisp** bacon, fried **very slowly** over low fire.

Tomatoes and Okra au Gratin

1 cup okra, cooked	½ cup bread crumbs
6 tomatoes	1 tablespoon butter
1 cup grated cheese	
1 cup chopped left-over meat	

Grease a baking dish and cover the bottom with some of the cooked okra. Slice the tomatoes and place a layer over the okra, season and sprinkle with cheese, bread crumbs, and some of the onion. Alternate layers until all the ingredients are used. Finish with a layer of bread crumbs and cheese. Bake for half an hour in a moderate oven.

Turnips in Sugar

Scrape and dice the turnips; boil in salted water until they are tender.

Make a thick sauce of two tablespoons of flour in two tablespoons butter; add a cup of milk, three tablespoons of sugar, and season. When thick, add to the turnips and simmer for about ten minutes.

Puree of Turnips

Press the turnips through a coarse mesh sieve. Add butter and seasoning. Reheat before serving.

Corn Oysters

Take one-half dozen ears of sweet corn; with a sharp knife split each row of corn in the center of each kernel lengthwise. Scrape out all the pulp, add one egg well beaten, a little salt, one tablespoonful of milk, flour enough to make a stiff batter. Drop into hot lard and fry a delicate brown.

Beans

Wash beans carefully and cut in uniform lengths. Heat a tablespoon lard (this is proportion to use for about a half gallon beans after they have been cut). Slice an onion in this hot grease and allow to cook for a few minutes. Add beans and a cup of hot water. Allow to simmer for two hours or until tender. Then thicken this with a level tablespoon corn-starch dissolved in two tablespoons water. Season with salt and pepper. (If desired seasonings can be added at first.)

Hot Slaw

Cook one head of cabbage, cut fine, until tender in salt water; pour off water; let dry; add a lump of butter; mix well.
Make a mayonnaise dressing:
Two tablespoons of flour, two tablespoons of sugar, one tea-spoon of mustard, one egg, one-half teacup of vinegar, one cup sour cream. Mix all together and add to cabbage.

For Dried Fruits

An over-night soaking is essential for haricots and butter-beans. Dried fruits, such as prunes and figs, also make a far more delicate dish if soaked for twelve hours in water to which the sugar has already been added.
A baked apple which prior to its cooking has been soaked in cold water for a couple of hours is more succulent than the ordinary rather dried up dish. It plumps out to a large size, and when the skin is broken, the inside is found to be full instead of half empty.
Lettuce and radishes should not be served without having been soaked for at least an hour in slightly salted water to bring out the crispness. If either be left over for a second meal the soaking should be repeated for ten minutes. This will enhance the crispness without producing a sodden effect.

Chestnut Balls

Boil, hull, and blanch enough Spanish or Italian chestnuts to measure a cupful when mashed smooth, or run through the ricer.

Put into the double boiler:

1 cup sweet milk	½ cup ground bread
1 tablespoonful butter	crumbs
½ teaspoonful grated onion	Salt and pepper to taste

Stir until thick; remove from fire and add the chestnuts. When cold, form into balls the size of a walnut; dip in egg, then in cracker crumbs, and fry in deep fat.

Spanish Fried Rice

½ cup boiled rice	2 medium sized onions
1 tablespoon butter	Season with salt, red pepper,
2 tablespoons of ham fat or	paprika and clove of garlic
bacon	if desired
1 large can tomatoes	

Put butter and fat into a fry pan; when hot add the dry rice. Fry until a golden brown, stirring often to prevent burning. Heat tomatoes and onions to boiling point, add the fried rice and seasoning and cook one hour or until rice is tender. If too thick when cooking, a little water may be added.

To Cook Rice

Use enameled pan; deep pan is preferable, and one that you can cover closely. Put the rice into the pan and wash it thoroughly, changing the water until it is perfectly clear. Drain off the water and measure the rice in proportion of one and a half cups of water to every cup of rice used. Cover tightly and cook over a high flame until it comes to a boil, and then continue cooking five minutes longer. Reduce the flame gradually every five minutes until the rice has absorbed all the water. Set the rice on the back of the stove, where it is warm, for about fifteen minutes. The oriental cook covers the rice in the pan with a clean cloth wet with hot water when the rice is not sufficiently cooked after the water has all been absorbed. If this is done, great care must be taken that the cloth be perfectly clean. Cover the pan tightly and let stand in a warm place 15 minutes.

Red Cabbage—Slaw

Cut a medium sized red cabbage fine. Let stand over night in 3 tablespoons of salt and water to moisten. In the morning wash once in colander. Boil 2½ cups water, 2 cups vinegar, ½ cup sugar, with a cloth sack of mixed spices together. Pour over the cabbage. This needs no cover.

Corn Custard

Put a cupful of canned or fresh corn through the meat chopper, add four egg yolks (beaten), one and one-half cupfuls of hot milk, a teaspoonful of grated onion; salt, pepper, and a bit of sugar to taste; a tablespoonful or more of minced pimento; and last, the stiffly beaten whites of the eggs. Pour into a well buttered baking dish, place the dish in a pan of hot water, and bake slowly until set.

Carrot Fritters

To two bunches fresh carrots that have been cleaned, cut in pieces, boiled in salt water until tender and mashed, add 3 eggs and ½ cup of cracker meal, a pinch of salt and a dash of pepper. Mix well and fry as fritters in hot bacon drippings.

Savory Carrots

Scrape and cut lengthwise eight carrots; pour enough hot water over them to cover; add one-half teaspoon salt, three tomatoes, skinned and cut up, two medium onions cut fine, and boil about one-half hour, watching carefully to let water boil down till almost dry, then add a tablespoon of butter and pepper to taste.

Egg Plant Fritters

1 cup cooked egg plant	1 teaspoon salt
1 cup flour	3 teaspoons baking powder
½ cup sweet milk	2 eggs, well beaten

Cook egg plant until well done. Drain and wash. Add eggs, milk, salt and the sifted flour and baking powder. Beat all lightly and fry in fat drippings. Serve hot.

Red Cabbage Cooked with Apples

Cut two-pound head of red cabbage as for cold slaw. Put in kettle; cover with water; add two medium sour apples which have been pared and sliced; one heaping tablespoon of lard, sugar and vinegar to suit taste. Cook slowly about one hour or a little longer. Cabbage should be a deep red when cooked.

Bavarian Cabbage

Very good to serve with roast pork or pork chops.
Shave a small cabbage as for slaw. Cut up 1 large onion and fry it in 1½ tablespoons butter; then add cabbage and let it steam in this for a few minutes. Add water gradually. Add vinegar to taste. Then salt, caraway seed and sugar to taste. When done, thicken with flour which has been browned.

Eggplant Pancakes

1 medium sized eggplant	5 tablespoons flour
2 eggs	1 teaspoon salt

Bake eggplant until tender. Peel and remove seeds. Mash pulp to which add the well beaten eggs, flour and salt. Mix all the ingredients. Drop by spoonfuls on a hot buttered pan. Turn and brown on both sides.

STARCHY VEGETABLES AND POTATOES

Baked Beans

1 quart dried beans	1/3 pound salt pork
1½ teaspoon salt	4 tablespoons dark corn
1 medium sized onion	syrup

Wash beans thoroughly and soak over night. In morning use the same water to cook beans. Boil one hour counting from time the water starts to boil, put in bean pot, add onion, syrup and salt. Place one piece of pork in center of beans and put remainder, cut in slices, on top, bake in a slow oven (about 250 degrees).

Boston Baked Beans

1 quart navy beans   4 tablespoons brown sugar
1 cup water   ½ teaspoon baking soda
½ pound salt pork   ¼ teaspoon mustard
2 tablespoons molasses

Select and wash the beans, soak over night in cold water. Drain and cover with fresh water, cook slowly until tender. When the beans are easily pierced with a fork, they are tender.

Drain again and blanch with cold water. Scald the pork, scrape the rind until white, cut the pork in half inch strips and bury the pork in the beans in a pot, leaving only the rind of pork exposed.

Mix the sugar, molasses and mustard in a cup of boiling water. Pour over the beans and add enough water to cover them. Cover the pot and bake six to seven hours in a slow oven (350 degrees F.), removing the lid for the last hour to crisp the pork.

Baked Lima Beans

Wash one pound dry lima beans and let soak in tepid water for about two hours. When the beans wrinkle, drain and cover with fresh warm water. Bring to a boil, reduce the flame and let simmer for about one hour.
Season with pepper and salt and a little paprika.
Make a brown gravy of flour, fat and some of the bean water. Turn the beans into a greased casserole and pour the gravy over; bake for half an hour in a slow oven.

Creamed Lima Beans

Soak one cup of dried limas over night in enough cold water to cover. Drain and cook until soft in hot salted water.
Drain and add three-quarters cup cream, stir through and season with salt, pepper and paprika.
Serves six.

Casserole of Kidney Beans

Serves six generously.

1 pint kidney beans	meat
2 chopped carrots	1 tablespoon sugar (brown
2 slices onions	or white)
1 cup canned tomatoes	1½ teaspoons salt
1 cup chopped left-over	Speck of pepper

Soak the kidney beans and then cook in salted water until tender. Drain and add the carrots and onions.

Warm the tomatoes, season and add the sugar. Spread the chopped meat on the bottom of a greased casserole, season and pour over the beans and other vegetables. Dot with butter, cover and bake in a hot oven until the vegetables are tender. Uncover for a short time to allow to brown.

Lima Beans and Marshmallows

1 pound dry lima beans	4 strips bacon
3 tablespoons brown sugar	Salt and pepper
3 tablespoons butter	1 dozen marshmallows

Soak the limas in cold water for five or six hours. Drain off this water and add boiling water to cover. Cook on a low flame for half an hour or until tender.

Melt the butter and add the sugar, then the seasoning. Turn the tender beans into a greased casserole, pour over the butter and seasoning. Lay the strips of bacon on the top. Bake with the cover on for about one hour in a warm oven (350 degrees F.), add water if necessary. Remove the cover and put the marshmallows on top of the bacon. Brown under the broiler flame.

Serve in the casserole.

Mexican Beans

1 pound ground round steak	1 medium sized can tomato
1 large onion	soup
1 sweet green pepper	1 can kidney beans
2 tablespoons butter or	
shortening	

Heat the butter or shortening. Add finely chopped onions and let simmer until brown. Add meat and finely chopped peppers. Stir until the meat becomes juicy. Take from fire and add seasoning to taste. Place in greased baking dish. Pour a can of tomato soup and a can of kidney beans over it. Dot with butter. Place in hot oven about a half an hour, or, until done.

Boiled Sweet Corn

Remove the husks and silk from the corn. Cover with boiling water and cook for ten to twenty minutes. More cobs require longer time. Drain the water and serve with butter and salt.

Canned Corn

Sprinkle one tablespoon flour over a can of corn, add one tablespoon of butter and one-half cup milk. Stir and cook until thoroughly heated through. Season and serve hot.

Corn Pudding

1 can corn
2 eggs
Pepper and salt

2 tablespoons butter
2 tablespoons sugar
1 pint milk

Beat the eggs slightly and mix all the other ingredients with it. Pour into a baking dish and bake in a moderate oven until a firm pudding is formed.

Corn Saute

Cut the tops of the kernels of twelve ears of corn. Cut along the center of the line of kernels. With the back of the knife, scrape out the pulp and avoid taking the kernel or the husk. Add salt and pepper and cook in a pan with two tablespoons butter or bacon fat. Simmer under cover for five minutes and cook uncovered for five more minutes until the corn is tender. A little chopped green pepper may be added.

Escalloped Corn

2 cans corn	1 cup of milk
1 large cup of cracker crumbs	¼ pound American cheese
	Butter, salt, pepper

Put layer of corn in bottom of baking dish. Then a generous sprinkling of grated cheese, dot with butter, season with pepper and salt. Last a layer of cracker crumbs, repeat over again and last pour over milk. Bake about forty minutes.

Baked Sweet Potatoes

Wash, peel and bake enough sweet potatoes to cover shallow glass baking dish. When thoroughly baked, remove from oven and cover with a layer of marshmallows. Put back in oven for a few minutes, and serve hot.

Baked Potatoes

Select smooth potatoes of uniform size. Wash and scrub off any dirt. Rub with sweet butter or olive oil before placing in oven to bake. Small potatoes take twenty-five minutes in a very hot oven, medium size require forty-five minutes and large Idaho potatoes an hour.

Baked Potatoes and Cheese

6 large potatoes (baked)	¼ pound pimento or
1/3 cup hot milk	American cheese, grated
2 teaspoons salt	⅛ teaspoon paprika

Cut potatoes in half lengthwise and scoop out the centers. Mash thoroughly. Add cheese to hot milk and beat with egg beater until smooth. Mix with the potatoes, add seasoning and whip out until light and creamy. Refill the potato shells and bake in a hot oven for ten minutes.

French Fried Potatoes

Wash, pare and cut potatoes in long strips one-quarter inch by one-quarter inch. Stand in cold water. Heat fat to 400 degrees F. Shake the potato slices dry in a towel and put a few at a time in the hot fat.

Fry for about five minutes or until crisp and brown.

Lyonnaise Potatoes

Cut cold boiled potatoes into slices, season with salt and pepper. Slice an onion and fry in two tablespoons butter or beef fat. Have the butter very hot and turn in the potatoes. Cook until the potatoes have taken in the fat and serve with chopped parsley.

Creamed New Potatoes

6 small new potatoes   ¼ cup cream
1 tablespoon butter   Salt and pepper
1 teaspoon lemon juice

Scrape the new potatoes and let stand for half an hour in cold water. Boil in the salted water until tender.

Put them in a sauce pan, with the cream, butter, lemon juice and seasoning. Shake well over the fire. Sprinkle with chopped parsley or caraway seed or both.

Potato Cakes

Season cold or hot potatoes highly and add enough beaten egg to moisten. Mold into cakes and roll in flour. Saute a golden brown.

Mashed Potatoes

6 hot cooked potatoes   1 teaspoon salt
6 tablespoons milk   Pepper
3 tablespoons butter

Rice or mash the potatoes thoroughly to free from any lumps. Add the hot milk, butter and then salt and pepper. Beat with a fork to make creamy and fluffy. Reheat and serve in a hot dish garnished with parsley and dotted with butter.

Potatoes O'Brien

6 medium-sized potatoes   Salt and pepper
Chopped pimentos

Wash, pare and dice potatoes. Shake dry in a towel. Fry in hot fat and drain on brown paper, sprinkle with salt. Just before they are done put the pimento chopped fine, a few drops of onion juice in a frying pan, add the potatoes and cook together. Keep shaking the potatoes so that they do not stick to the pan.

Puffed Potatoes

Cut the potatoes thicker than for chips. Drop at once into warmed fat. Bring the fat to a boil. Shake the slices while cooking. When they puff up and become brown, they are ready to serve.

Saratoga Chips

Pare the potatoes and slice them very fine. Soak in cold salty water for one hour. Shake in a towel to remove the moisture. Put into a frying-basket and fry in deep fat to a golden brown. Drain on brown paper and while drying, sprinkle with salt. Serve with broiled meats.

To freshen stale or moist chips, place in a hot oven a few minutes before serving.

Marshmallow Potato Balls

8 marhsmallows $\frac{1}{2}$ teaspoon salt
2 cups riced boiled sweet   Pepper
  potatoes   Cornflakes
1 egg

Rice the boiled and peeled sweet potatoes. Beat the egg and with seasoning stir into the riced potatoes. Roll the paste over the marshmallows into balls. Use one marshmallow to a ball.

Roll the balls into the cornflakes and fry in deep hot fat.
Brown and drain on brown paper.

Scalloped Potatoes

6 medium potatoes   1 tablespoon flour
1 tablespoon butter

Peel and slice the potatoes and soak in water for half an hour.
Drain and arrange the slices in a deep baking dish by layers.
Sprinkle each layer with flour, salt and pepper and dot with
butter before covering with the next layer. Pour milk over
the whole and sprinkle with grated cheese if desired. Bake
for an hour in a very hot oven (450 degrees F.).

Candied Sweet Potatoes

5 large cooked sweet pota-   3 tablespoons butter
    toes   ½ cup brown sugar

Slice the potatoes lengthwise and arrange in a flat baking dish.
Dot with butter. Sprinkle with sugar, cinnamon and a little
salt.
Put under the flame on the broiling rack and baste the syrup
over the potatoes. Serve in the baking dish.

Boiled Rice

1 cup rice   8 cups water

Boil the water and add one teaspoon salt. Drop the rice in
very slowly so that the water continues to boil. Boil rapidly
for half an hour.
Drain off the water in a colander. Run very cold water over
the rice for five minutes. Drain the water off, stand the
colander in a bowl in the oven and let the rice dry. Have
the oven door open. When dry and fluffy, turn into a dish,
add butter and serve.

Spanish Rice

½ cup rice (cooked)   1 cup soup-stock
1 tablespoon butter   1 teaspoon chopped onion
½ cup tomato juice

Wash and drain the rice and fry to a light brown in butter.
Add the tomato-juice and the chopped onion. Cook for ten
minutes. Then add soup-stock and season.

Simmer under cover until all the liquid is gone. To cook the rice thoroughly will take about three-quarters of an hour.

Spanish Rice, Casserole

2 cups of cooked rice
1½ cups canned tomatoes
2 tablespoons butter or
  olive oil
2 tablespoons chopped
  onion
2 tablespoons chopped
  green pepper

2 tablespoons chopped
  mushrooms
1 tablespoon capers
½ teaspoon salt
¼ teaspoon paprika

Cook onions, peppers, mushrooms, capers and seasoning in butter or oil until onions have browned. Add tomatoes and cook until some of moisture has cooked off. Mix with rice in greased casserole.

Cover with crumbs and a little cheese. Bake in a hot oven until thoroughly heated thru.

Spanish Rice Casserole

2 cups cooked rice
2 tablespoons butter
1 tablespoon chopped onion
2 tablespoons chopped
  green pepper

1½ cups canned tomatoes
1 tablespoon chopped
  mushroom
Bread crumbs
Salt and pepper

Melt the butter and brown the onion in it, add the green pepper, mushroom, tomato and seasoning. Cook until the moisture has nearly evaporated and leaves a thick paste.

Arrange in alternate layers in a greased casserole. Cover the top with crumbs. Bake in a hot oven until the mixture has heated through and the crumbs have browned.

Wild Rice Ring

Wash the wild rice, drain and place in a double boiler and steam for three-quarters hour until tender. Season and add three tablespoons butter.

Turn into a greased ring mold or melon mould and bake in a moderate oven in a pan of hot water. Bake about fifteen minutes. To turn out, loosen the edges and place upside down on a platter. Serve with wild game or poultry. Ordinary rice may be treated in the same manner.

Spaghetti Italienne

½ pound spaghetti	¼ cup olive oil
1 teaspoon salt	2 tablespoons chopped
Grated cheese	green peppers

Cabbage, Spaghetti and Cheese

4 cups shredded cabbage	4 tablespoons butter
2 cups cooked spaghetti	½ pound American cheese
2 cups milk	1 teaspoon salt
4 tablespoons flour	

Cook the spaghetti in boiling salted water until tender. Make a sauce of the flour, butter, milk, and salt. Shave up the cheese and add it to the hot sauce. Put the cabbage, spaghetti and sauce in a buttered baking dish in layers and cover the top with buttered bread crumbs. Cook for 20 to 30 minutes in a moderate oven.

Strawberry Fritters

Sift together one-half cup of flour, one-half teaspoon of baking powder, one-eighth teaspoon of salt. Add one egg beaten very light, two tablespoons of milk and, last, two teaspoons of melted buter. Drop 12 large strawberries in batter, coat well and, using a large spoon, drop into hot fat. Serve with sugar.

Sweet Potato Pudding

Grate four good sized sweet potatoes; add one pint milk, two eggs beaten light, two cups sugar, one-fourth pound of butter, one-fourth teaspoon cinnamon, one-fourth teaspoon nutmeg. Bake in moderate oven one-half hour. Before removing from oven cover top with marshmallow, and brown. Fine served hot or cold with whipped cream.

Sweet Potato Pone

Boil sweet potatoes, peel, mash and put through a sieve. To two cups of the potato add a half cup of cream or rich milk, a full teaspoon of butter, a little lemon flavoring and one beaten egg. This recipe calls for a quarter cup of sugar but may use less. Now beat all ingredients until they become light and creamy. Put in a buttered baking dish and bake until it is a golden brown on top.

Corn and Cheese Souffle

1 tablespoon butter
1 tablespoon chopped green
  pepper
½ cup flour
2 cups milk
1 cup chopped corn
1 cup grated cheese
3 eggs
½ teaspoon salt

Melt the butter and cook the peppers thoroughly in it. Make a sauce out of the flour, milk and cheese; add the corn, egg yolks and seasoning; cut and fold in the whites beaten stiffly; turn into a buttered baking dish and bake in a medium oven thirty minutes.

Spaghetti and Bacon

Cook one package spaghetti in boiling salted water for half an hour. Turn into colander and rinse with cold water. Cut six slices bacon in inch lengths. Cook over slow fire, turning frequently. Remove bacon and fry three medium sized sliced onions in the bacon drippings until light brown. Then add 2 cups tomatoes, a level teaspoonful salt and a sprinkling of cayenne pepper. Cook until onions are soft. Then add bacon and spaghetti. Cook over hot water until flavors are well blended.

Corn Pudding

2 eggs well beaten
1 cup milk
Salt and pepper to taste

Add to above 1 can golden bantam corn and 2 cups corn flakes. Mix all together well and place in dish ready to bake.

Top with butter and bake at 350 degrees until custard has set. Test it by cutting a knife into it, which should come out dry if done.

1 pint can of tomatoes	2 teaspoons sugar
2 medium sized onions, chopped	Chopped parsley

Cook spaghetti in salted water.

Cook onions and pepper in olive oil until half tender. Add canned tomatoes, parsley, salt and sugar. Cook very slowly until onions are tender.

Turn cooked spaghetti into a warmed dish, stir cheese into sauce, pour sauce over spaghetti and serve very hot. Serve additional dry grated cheese in a side dish.

Vegetable Pudding

6 large potatoes	1 quart milk
1 large onion	1 pound bacon
2 cans corn	1 tablespoon flour

Cut the bacon into small pieces and brown. Cut the onions fine and brown in part of the bacon fat. Put in a layer of potatoes, a little flour, a layer of corn, bacon and browned onion. Repeat until all the ingredients are used. Cover with milk and bake.

Succotash

Mix one cup boiled lima beans and one cup boiled corn; using left over corn from cob if available. Season with salt and pepper and heat in a little melted butter, add one-quarter cup milk and when thoroughly heated, serve. Chopped green pepper may be added for flavor and color.

Red Rice

4 tablespoons rice	5 slices bacon
1 small can tomatoes	Salt and pepper
4 small onions	

Place rice and tomatoes in cooking dish; add sliced onions and bacon cut into small pieces. Add 1 cup hot water. After mixture begins to cook, season and allow to steam for 1½ hours.

SPECIAL CANNING RECIPES

Canning Peaches
(Open Kettle Method)

To six cups of water add 4 cups of sugar, and bring to a boil. Select firm peaches, immerse in boiling water to steam off the skins—peel, cut into halves, removing pits, and dump into syrup. Boil until the peaches seem to be sufficiently cooked—not soft, but they must be thoroughly heated through.
Seal while hot.

Green Gage Plums
(Open Kettle Method)

To six cups water add 5 cups sugar, and bring to a boil. Wash the plums, prick with a fork and turn into the syrup. Cook until the plums are thoroughly heated through, and seal boiling hot.

If the plums are not quite ripe or unusually sour, more sugar will be required, but the above proportions will suit the taste of most people.

Corn on the Cob

Remove husks and silks, blanch (boil) on cob for five minutes. Pack into hot clean jars, adding 1 level teaspoon salt to each quart jar and fill with boiling water. Partly seal and process for 3 hours in a hot water bath, or for 60 minutes in a steam pressure cooker of 10 pounds. Remove from canner and seal immediately. When using 2 quart jars, process for 4 hours in hot water bath or for 90 minutes in a steam pressure cooker of 10 lbs. One 2 quart jar will hold 7 or 8 ears.

Carrots

Sort and grade for uniform size. Wash and scrub with a stiff vegetable brush. Scrape, if carrots are old. Boil for 15 minutes. Slice or pack whole into hot jars. Add 1 level teaspoon salt to each quart, fill with cooking water; partly seal and process for 2 hours in a hot-water bath or for 45 minutes in a steam-pressure cooker at 10 pounds. Remove from canner and seal immediately.

Green Peppers

Cut around the stem of each pepper, removing the stem and all seeds. Wash each pepper carefully, and cover with boiling water as many as will, when partially softened, fill a jar. Cover and simmer for about five minutes, then drain again. Press out any excess water, then squeeze the peppers, one by one, into sterilized jars, setting it, on a cloth, in the rack of a steam cooker. Fill jars and cooker with warm water, adjust the rubber and cover but not tightly, cover the cooker and "process" for about 10 minutes after water begins to boil. When the peppers seem tender (test with a fork) replace the cover, adding enough boiling water to completely fill the jars and cook for 10 minutes more, then remove the jars and tighten the covers.

Tomato Juice

Take good red sound tomatoes, set on to boil with a sliced onion, a dried bay-leaf and a sprig of dried thyme, not forgetting salt and pepper to taste. Simmer together until the tomatoes are soft. Drain off liquor and press tomatoes through a sieve with a wooden masher. Add the pulp to the juice, bottle while hot and seal well.

Green Tomato Mincemeat

Three pounds green tomatoes, 3 pounds apples, 2 pounds raisins, 5 pounds brown sugar, 1 tablespoon salt, 1 cup suet, 1 cup vinegar, 2 tablespoons cloves, 2 tablespoons cinnamon, 1 nutmeg, and orange peel if desired.

Chop tomatoes and let come to a boil. Drain. Chop apples, raisins and suet, add all ingredients to the tomatoes and cook until thick.

To Make Sauerkraut

It is best made in a keg kept for the purpose from year to year.

Take firm white cabbages and slice or shred very fine. This is best done with a machine, of course.

At the bottom of the barrel place a layer of coarse salt then one of cabbage, and so on, alternately, until the barrel is full,

ending up with a layer of salt on top. Press down each layer
with a large masher, adding fresh layers as soon as the juice
floats on the surface. Add a few peppercorns and a few
grains of coriander to each alternate layer. When the keg is
full, set in a cool place, cover with a cloth, then a plank or
wooden cover, placing heavy weights on top.

In a few days it will begin to ferment, during which time
the liquid must be drawn off and replaced by fresh until it
becomes quite clear. This should be done every day. Renew
the cloth, replace the cover and weights and let it stand for
a month, when it will be ready for use. Keep the cover perfectly clean and, when taking out some of the kraut, be sure
to allow as little air as possible to enter the barrel, closing
it again very carefully.

Vegetables for Soup

Take 1 quart diced carrots, 1 quart sliced green beans, 1
quart sliced wax beans, 1 quart diced onions, 1 quart diced
celery, 1 quart corn, cut from cob, 1 quart cauliflower, in
small pieces, 1 quart diced potatoes, 3 chopped green peppers,
2 quarts tomatoes, cut up, 1 cup Scotch barley. Wash, pare
and dice carrots, onions and potatoes, scald tomatoes, dip in
cold water, remove skins and slice. Cut beans in ¼ inch
pieces, scald peppers, remove stems and seeds and chop.

Mix all the vegetables in a large preserving kettle, add
boiling water to cover and boil for five minutes. Pack at
once, all boiling hot, into clean hot jars, adjusting the rubbers and placing a teaspoon of salt into each quart jar. Close
covers tightly. Process for one hour in pressure cooker, at
10 lbs. pressure, or for 3 hours in hot water bath . Remove
jars, invert to cool.

Pumpkin for Winter

Cut a sound pumpkin in half, remove seeds and coarse
threads and cut the halves into narrow strips. Pare these and
cut into short pieces, placing them in an enamelled pan, adding a cup of water. Cover and cook very slowly, stirring
often, for about five hours on a low heat, then press the pulp
through a sieve and put into hot sterilized jars. Set these

in a preserving kettle with their covers beside them, adding lukewarm water nearly to top.

Process for one hour, adding boiling water if jars are not quite full of the pumpkin pulp, then adjust rubbers and covers and process 15 minutes longer, then tighten covers and store in a cool place.

JELLIES

Apple or Crabapple Jelly

For crabapples, leave whole, but cut ordinary apples into quarters. Wipe, remove stem and blossom ends. Place in kettle, adding enough cold water to come nearly to top of apples. Cover and cook slowly until apples are soft, then mash and drain through a coarse sieve. Do NOT SQUEEZE, or your jelly will become cloudy. Place the fruit into the jelly bag and allow to drip, undisturbed. Boil it for 20 minutes then add ¾ the quantity of heated sugar, boil 5 minutes, skim, test and set in clean heated glasses. If you want a lighter colored jelly, pare the apples.

Blueberry Jelly

Take 3 quarts of fresh clean blueberries, put into a heavy pan and crush with a wooden potato masher. Heat slowly; when hot through, drain in a jelly bag, pressing out juice. Set this on the fire and heat, quickly, to boiling point. Allow to boil for six or seven minutes, then add 1 cup of sugar for every cup of juice, let boil for one or two minutes more, then pour into the glasses, which must be ready in a pan of hot water as the jelly will often "jell" in the saucepan and become difficult to pour.

Currant Jelly

If procurable, use equal proportions of red and white "cherry" currants. Pick fruit over but do not remove stems. Wash and drain well. Mash a few in bottom of preserving kettle, using a wooden potato masher (by the way, ALWAYS use wood for jam and jelly making). Continue crushing the berries until all are done. Cook slowly until the currants look white. Strain through a coarse strainer, then drip in a jelly bag. Measure juice, bring to the boiling point and boil 5 minutes, then add an equal measure of HEATED sugar, boil 3 minutes, skim well and test. Place in a sunny window and allow to stand there for 24 hours after pouring into the heated glasses.

Grape Jelly

Grapes should be picked over, washed and stemmed. Place in kettle, bring to the boiling point, boil for 30 minutes, after well mashing, then proceed as for currant jelly. Wild grapes make the best (and cheapest) jelly.

Mint Jelly

Wash mint and chop fine. To each cup of chopped mint add ¼ cup sugar and ¼ cup water, and let stand for several hours, or over-night. Bring to boiling point, then strain. Combine sugar and apple juice, using 2-3 cup sugar to 1 cup apple juice. Cook and test for jelly, and when the jellying point is obtained, add green vegetable coloring and 1 or 2 tablespoons of prepared mint juice for each quart of apple juice.

Spiced Grape Jelly

1 peck grapes	½ cup whole cloves
1 quart vinegar	½ cup stick cinnamom

6 pounds sugar

Put the grapes, spices and vinegar on to cook—until grapes are soft. Strain through jelly bag and boil 20 minutes. Then add the sugar, heated—and boil 5 minutes, or until the mixture will "jell." Turn into glasses.

Wild grapes are best, but the regular blue grapes will do.

PRESERVES

Apple Butter (Old Fashioned)

Boil 10 gallons of sweet apple cider until reduced to one-half, then add, a few at a time, three pecks of pared, quartered and cored apples of the cooking variety. Stir constantly with a wooden spoon and allow to cook for four or five hours, then add 10 pounds of sugar and 5 ounces of ground cinnamon, cooking again until the mixture is like marmalade.

Apple and Peach Jam

Three cups diced peaches, three cups diced apples, three cups sugar, one teaspoon salt, one orange put through food chopper, two tablespoons lemon juice, sprinkle with nutmeg or cinnamon.

Cook fruit rapidly with one cup of water until tender. Add sugar and cook until clear and transparent. Add lemon juice, salt and spice. This makes four glasses.

Blackberry Jam

Select slightly underripe fruit.
Weigh, wash and drain thoroughly. Mash slightly.
Boil rapidly two minutes (after boiling begins).
Add equal or three-fourths weight of sugar.
Boil two minutes as before.
Pour into sterilized glasses.
This will jelly and keeps well and tastes more like the fresh fruit than most jams.
Loganberries may be used instead of blackberries.

Cherry Conserve

Use the nearly transparent or "sour" cherries. Remove stones, taking care not to spoil the shape, and allow one pound of sugar to every pound of fruit and one cup of water to every pound of sugar. Melt the sugar in the water, boil and skim, then add the cherries, a few at a time, and boil very gently for about 15 minutes. Skim off the cherries onto plates and boil the syrup after straining back into the kettle any juice from the plates. When the syrup is thick pour over the cherries which you will have packed into warm, clean jars.

Pineapple Preserve

Peel, remove "eyes," weigh and cut up fine sound pines. To each pound of fruit allow a cupful of water. Place water and fruit in pan, cover and set on the fire, boiling gently until the slices of pineapple are clear and tender, then remove from water and set in a dish. Add to the water one pound of sugar for each pound of fruit, stir until sugar is dissolved, then add pineapple and boil gently until it is transparent throughout. When this is done remove fruit, cool and set in jars. Simmer syrup gently until it is thick and rich, and, when it is nearly cool, pour over the fruit. Next day seal jars. Pineapple done in this way is a beautiful and delicious preserve.

Peach Butter
Peel and stone peaches. Cook them in a very small amount of water until they are reduced to a pulp. Add 2-3 as much sugar as pulp, and cook the mixture until it is thick and clear, stirring it frequently. Pour it into clean, hot jars and seal them.

Plum Conserve
Five pounds plums, four and one-half pounds granulated sugar, five oranges, one pound nectar raisins, one-half pound English walnuts, one and one-half lemons.
Wash and pit the plums and run them through a food chopper. Put through the food chopper also the oranges (using the pulp and rind of three and only the pulp of the remaining two), all raisins, the pulp and rind of the lemons, and the sugar. The walnuts should be chopped coarse. Let the mixture stand over night and in the morning boil it slowly for 40 minutes, stirring frequently. Put into glasses and when cool, cover with paraffin. Makes 24 glasses.

Raspberry Bar-le-duc
One quart perfect raspberries, 3 cupfuls of sugar, 1 cupful currant juice and 1 cupful red raspberry juice.
Combine the fruit juices. Add the sugar and let boil until they are very thick and almost jelly. Then drop in the raspberries, a few at a time. Cook for 2 or 3 minutes and remove with a skimmer to small glasses. When all the berries are cooked, the syrup will be considerably thin, so boil it down until very thick again. Pour into the glasses containing the raspberries and seal as usual.

Strawberry Preserves

To four pounds of berries take three pounds of sugar. Pick over, wash and hull the berries. Add the sugar and heat gently until the sugar dissolves. Then cook rapidly until the fruit is plump and transparent and the syrup thick. Pack carefully in sterilized jars and seal.

All berries may be preserved in this manner, adding more sugar if you wish the preserves sweeter or if the berries are tart, but the above proportions will be found suitable for nearly every taste.

Strawberries, Preserved Whole

To every pound of fruit allow 1½ pounds sugar and 2 cups red currant juice. Choose berries large, not too ripe and of good color. Hull, lay in a platter and sprinkle over them half the quantity of sugar. Shake gently to coat the fruit on all sides and set platter in a cool place to stand for one day. Meantime take good sound red currants and press the juice through a sieve until you have 2 cups. Boil this with the remainder of the sugar until it forms a thin syrup and in this simmer the strawberries until the whole begins to "jell" when tested on a cold plate in the customary manner. Do not stir the fruit roughly. It will take about 20 minutes to cook the berries.

PICKLES

Watermelon Pickle

Four pounds watermelon rind, 2 quarts salt water, 2 quarts vinegar, 1 pint water, 4 pounds sugar, 2 tablespoons whole cloves, 2 tablespoons whole allspice, 12 inch pieces stick cinnamon.

Before weighing the watermelon rind trim off the green skin and pink flesh. Cut the rind in inch cubes and soak over night in the salt water (¼ cup salt to 2 quarts cold water). Drain, cover with fresh cold water, and boil until tender. Mix the vinegar, water and sugar, add the spices tied in a cheesecloth bag, and boil for 5 minutes. Add the drained watermelon rind and boil gently until it is clear. Remove the spice bag, pack the pickle in clean, hot jar and seal.

Mustard Pickle

1 quart small cucumbers or sliced large ones

1 quart sliced green tomatoes.

1 quart small white button onions

1 large cauliflower, cut small

4 sweet green peppers, sliced fine.

Make a brine of four quarts of cold water and two cupfuls of salt, pour over vegetables and allow to stand 24 hours. Cook on stove to scalding point, drain thoroughly in colander.

Sauce

½ pint flour

6 rounded teaspoons dry mustard

1 tablespoon celery seed

1 tablespoon tumeri

1 cup brown sugar

8 cupfuls vinegar.

Mix the flour, mustard, celery seed, tumeric and sugar together. Stir to a smooth paste with about a cup of vinegar. Then stir in the remaining vinegar. Boil until it thickens, stirring constantly. Add vegetables and let all come to boiling point. Place in jars and seal.

Spiced Cherries

9 pounds of fruit

4 pounds of sugar

1 pint of cider vinegar

½ ounce of cinnamon bark

½ ounce of whole cloves

Let the syrup come to a boil before putting in the fruit. Cook the fruit until the skins break. Then take out the fruit and boil the syrup down until thick. Pour over the fruit.

Pickled Beans

String and break 2 gallons of beans. Take ¾ cup vinegar, ¾ cup brown sugar and 1 cup salt. Put all together in a kettle, adding water to cover. Cook one-half hour and pack in jars while hot.

Before cooking, be sure to soak the beans in cold water 3 or 4 hours.

Thousand Island Pickles

Slice 1 dozen cucumbers, and arrange in alternate layers with sliced onions, salting each layer well. Let stand 3 hours, and then remove from the brine by squeezing the pickles.

Put in a preserving kettle 4 cups vinegar, 1 pound of brown sugar blended with 2 tablespoons tumeric. Add a little mustard seed and mix well. Add the pickles and bring to a boil. Seal in jars.

ON THE SUBJECT OF ENTERTAINING

Linens Come First

After the invitations are issued, the first concern of the perfect hostess is the matter of table linens. For the formal dinner or luncheon, of course, nothing has yet replaced the quiet elegance of pure white damask. However, just as correct these days are the pastel shades in damask, or an Italian or Spanish filet, for those who prefer them.

For the summer cottage, or for bridge tables, snappy colored covers are in order. A trip through the shops will provide no end of variety in these—quaint checkered gingham effects, Roman stripes, modernistic designs in hand blocked linens, hand embroidered sets, organdy—and runners and doilies galore. Any of these may be used for the informal meal, and are THE thing at impromptu luncheons, suppers or midnight snacks.

For the children, and novel occasions, there are charming sets of oilcloth, in Scotch plaid and chintz patterns, to say nothing of the great variety of paper sets suitable for all occasions.

The hostess who does a great deal of entertaining often goes in for filet or embroidered doilies under glass, which is very charming.

The Silver

Silver should be in harmony, as near as possible, with its surroundings. Since most of us cannot have several sets, it is best to buy a pattern suitable for all occasions, in open stock, adding more pieces as time goes on. Designers and manufacturers offer a wide variety, from which to choose. While the plain and simple lined solid service handed down for generations, is greatly prized by many, there are any number of "new" patterns carrying the charm of good taste, from which to choose.

Setting the Table

The proper arrangement of silver is often a problem to the hostess who is unaccustomed to entertaining.

First of all—knives to the right, forks to the left—except, of course, in the case of the oyster fork, which, since it is used with the right hand, must be placed on the right.

Spoons also must be placed on the right, and all silver should be arranged in the order to be used—the tool to be used first at the outside of the row. For instance, if the first course be soup, then the soup spoon must be at the extreme right of the row; if it be oysters, then the oyster fork. To the left the dinner fork first, and the salad fork next to the plate.

The fork or spoon to be used for dessert does not appear on the table, but is brought in with the dessert on the individual plate.

The water glass appears at the right, just at the tip of the knife.

The bread and butter plate at the left, just above the fork. With white damask and solid silver, crystal glassware is in order. The modern hostess oftens favors pastel linens with tinted glassware to harmonize, which makes a pretty table. Candlelight lends charm to any table. Many of the best dining rooms are not equipped with electricity, which insures the serving of every evening meal by candlelight. Several sets of candles in different colors will provide no end of variety to your color scheme.

The China

The china, like everything else, must match the character of the house. For the cottage or bungalow Early American patterns are charming. For the modern home choose Wedgewood, or any of the many inexpensive varieties that suit your personal taste. The home that runs to the modernistic may safely go in for china of like trend—black and white or other contrasting colors in chic designs.

Tips for Table Setting

Never decorate your table with ribbons.

Pickle jars, catsup bottles and tooth picks likewise have no place on the well dressed dinner table. Pickles and sauces, if you must have them, are served in glass dishes with small serving spoons—likewise jelly or marmalade.

Place folded napkin, at the left, or on the service plate. Fancy foldings are not in good taste.

While ash trays have no place on the strictly formal dinner table, the modern hostess provides them if she knows her guests will require them—ladies no longer retire to the drawing room while the gentlemen smoke.

Table Decoration

Suit the decorations to the type of entertainment, or character of the house, and remember that simplicity is always the keynote of good taste. A bowl of fruit flanked with plain candle sticks is better than an elaborate centerpiece. Flowers properly arranged, and in keeping with the color scheme are lovely, but should not be high. Keep table decorations low always, so that your guests will have no difficulty in looking at each other.

Do not go in for novelty decorations unless the occasion is novel—such as Halloween, Valentine or St. Patrick's Day.

Place cards may be placed just above the plate, or on the napkin.

Buffet Service

Buffet service is very popular, for it solves the problem of entertaining large groups.

Again the table arrangement is the first consideration. The cloth may be of damask, lace or embroidery—or runners if the hostess prefers. Careful arrangement of the centerpiece, be it flowers or fruit, are its main charm. Candlesticks come next—or a candelabra may be used for the center, with flowers on either side. Candles are not used, however, before four in the afternoon.

The coffee or tea tray, or the punch bowl, are placed at opposite ends of the table. Plates filled with sandwiches, tea cakes, etc., are arranged down each side, with the silver and china needed close by so that guests may serve themselves easily. Piles of napkins, too, must be where easily reached. Guests stand or sit at a buffet meal, as they wish. Bridge tables are often arranged for their convenience.

MENUS AND RECIPES FOR SPECIAL OCCASIONS

The following menus and recipes are reprinted with special permission of Good Housekeeping Institute—all recipes tried in the Institute's kitchens—and all measurements are level.

Bridge Luncheons

Sometimes the hostess who is entertaining at bridge decides on a luncheon rather than serving refreshments afterward. This is delightful to the guests, and sometimes easier for the hostess, especially if she serves at the card tables.

Cover each table with a luncheon cloth, place the napkins and arrange the necessary silver, glassware, etc., dispensing with both bread-and-butter plates and floral centerpieces. Plan your menu so that you can arrange the entire main course on the individual plates before bringing them to the table. If hot bread is served, butter it before placing it on the plates. Then after luncheon is over you need only remove the used dishes in a tray or tea wagon, fold up the luncheon cloths, and quickly arrange the necessary "tools" for playing bridge.

But what will you give them to eat?

Here are a few menus that may help, together with recipes:

BRIDGE MENUS

Tomato Juice Cocktail
Sweetbread and Almond Salad
Cheese Biscuits

Celery   Radishes

Orange Layer Cake
Iced Tea

Sweetbread and Almond Salad

3 pr. sweetbreads	Mayonnaise
1 cup blanched almonds	Radishes

Soak sweetbreads in cold water for one hour, changing the water two or three times. Then drain and plunge into boiling water to which one teaspoon vinegar has been added and cook for fifteen minutes. Next drain and place immediately into ice cold water to blanch. Let stand ten minutes. Wipe dry and chill. Dice sweetbreads and mix with almonds, and add just enough mayonnaise to bind. Serve on lettuce with a few drops of French dressing. Garnish with radish roses. Serves 6.

Jellied Shrimp Salad
Cheese Biscuits
Pickled Peaches   Crisp Celery
Honey Ice Cream Cake
Coffee

Jellied Shrimp Salad

1 quart canned tomatoes	2 tablespoons granulated
1¼ cups water	gelatin
1½ teaspoons salt	1½ cups shrimp
¼ teaspoon pepper	½ cup finely diced celery
4 cloves	¼ cup diced green pepper
1 bay-leaf	Boiled dressing
1 tablespoon sugar	Lettuce
1 teaspoon mustard	1 small onion, minced

Cook the tomatoes, one cup of water, the salt, pepper, cloves, bay-leaf, sugar, mustard and minced onion together for fifteen minutes. Strain and pour the mixture over the gelatin which has been softened in one-fourth cup of cold water. Cool until it begins to stiffen and add the shrimps, which have been cleaned, the viscera removed and cut in halves; then add the diced celery and the diced green pepper from which the skin has been removed by parboiling. Pour into wet individual molds and chill until hardened. When ready to serve, turn out on beds of lettuce, and garnish with boiled dressing, or mayonnaise. Serves 6.

Honey Ice Cream Cake

Cut slices of Sponge or Angel Food Cake three inches square and one-half inch thick, and arrange on individual dessert plates. Top each piece of cake with a square of chocolate or vanilla ice cream, and then garnish each with two tablespoons strained honey and one tablespoon salted pecans.

Chicken Timbales

Asparagus Tips with Hollandaise Sauce

Nut Graham Muffins   Currant Jelly

Chocolate Refrigerator Cake

Iced Coffee

Chicken Timbales

Melt three tablespoons of butter; add one-half cup soft bread crumbs and one cup of milk; cook for five minutes, stirring constantly. Add one-half teaspoon of salt, a little pepper and paprika, one tablespoon chopped parsley, one and one-half cups cooked chicken cut in dice, and three eggs slightly beaten. Mix well and turn into individual buttered timbale molds, filling them two-thirds full. Set molds in pan of hot water, cover with greased paper, and bake at 325° F. for thirty minutes. Serves 6.

Chocolate Refrigerator Cake

5 tablespoons cocoa	2 tablespoons cold water
⅓ cup powdered sugar	2 cups heavy cream
2 tablespoons hot water	2 tablespoons vanilla
2 teaspoons granulated gelatine	1 tin chocolate wafers

Combine cocoa, powdered sugar and hot water to make smooth paste. Soak one teaspoon gelatine in one tablespoon cold water, dissolve over hot water and add to cocoa mixture. Add one cup cream and vanilla and whip to consistency of whipped cream. Soak remaining one teaspoon gelatine in one tablespoon cold water and dissolve over hot water. Add to remaining cream and whip till stiff. Stand wafers on edge, facing each other, and spread alternately with the chocolate and plain whipped cream. The filling between each layer should be one-quarter inch thick. Mask outside of loaf with

plain whipped cream and let stand several hours in the refrigerator. Before serving garnish with remainder of chocolate and plain whipped cream and slice diagonally to show
layers of wafers. Serves 6 to 8.

Jellied Chicken Soup
Molded Tuna Salad with Cucumber Dressing
New Peas
Brown Bread Fingers
Sponge Cake   Peaches with Sunshine Sauce
Iced Tea

Molded Tuna Salad

To one can of flaked tuna, add one cup stiff mayonnaise, one
chopped, hard-cooked egg, one-fourth cup chopped olives,
one tablespoon capers and one teaspoon chopped chives.
Soften one-half tablespoon gelatin in one-fourth cup cold
water, place over hot water until dissolved, then add to the
fish mixture and stir lightly with a fork, being careful not
to break the fish. Put in cold wet molds and chill. Six individual molds.

Cucumber Dressing

To one-half cup thick cream, add one-fourth teaspoon salt,
a speck of pepper and two tablespoons vinegar. Beat until
stiff. Just before serving add one cucumber which has been
pared, chopped very fine and drained.

Sunshine Sauce

Boil one cup sugar with one-third cup water to 238° F.
or the soft-ball stage. Pour this sirup over the stiffly-beaten
yolks of two eggs. Continue beating until creamy. Add two
tablespoons vanilla. Just before serving, fold in one cup stiffly-
beaten cream.

YELLOW AND GREEN LUNCHEON

Orange Mint Cocktail
Buttered Asparagus   Fried Chicken
Baking Powder Biscuits
Stuffed Egg Salad
Golden Parfait
Yellow and Green Mints   Coffee

Stuffed Egg Salad

6 hard-cooked eggs   Mayonnaise
¼ cup minced ham   Lettuce

Remove the yolks from the hard-cooked eggs and combine
with the minced ham and sufficient mayonnaise to moisten.
Fill the eggs with this mixture and place one stuffed egg in
each nest of lettuce. Sardines, parsley, chives, anchovy or
minced bacon may be used instead of the ham. Serves 6.

Golden Parfait

1 cup sugar   1 tablespoon vanilla
½ cup water   6 egg yolks
2 cups cream whipped

Boil the sugar and water to 238° F. Pour slowly on beaten
egg yolks. Cook in the top of a double boiler until the mixture thickens. Cool and then fold in the cream which has
been beaten stiff. Add the vanilla and pour into a mold as
previously directed. Freeze in two parts of ice to one part
of salt for four hours. This recipe serves about eight.

A PINK AND GREEN LUNCHEON

Watermelon Balls with Ginger Ale
Mint Garnish
Salmon with Mayonnaise
Marinated Cucumbers
Green Peas   Tiny Parker House Rolls
Strawberry Velvet Ice Cream
Cakes Iced with Pale Green Frosting
Coffee

Strawberry Velvet Ice Cream

2 cups fresh strawberry pulp   2 cups cream
1 cup sugar

Wash and hull and put strawberries through potato ricer;
measure 2 cups. Add the sugar (the quantity depends on
the sweetness of the berries), and then the cream. Blend
thoroughly and freeze in either freezer or mechanical refrigerator. Makes about three pints.

Be sure, of course, to add a drop or two of green vegetable
coloring to the mayonnaise—before serving with the pink
salmon.

A TROPICAL LUNCHEON
Chicken and Mushroom Curry
Alligator Pear Salad
Macedoine Fruit Cocktail   Cocoanut Cake
Coffee

Chicken and Mushroom Curry (East Indian)

Slice one pound mushrooms and saute in four tablespoons of
butter or margarine about five minutes. Stir in the curry
sauce as made below; add two cups of cooked chicken cut
in cubes and mix thoroughly but gently. When well heated,
place in a serving dish and surround with two very ripe
bananas cut in lengthwise pieces. Serves 6.
For the Curry Sauce in the above recipe, melt two tablespoons
of butter or margarine in the top of double boiler, add one
medium onion chopped and cook about two minutes, but do
not brown. Add one tablespoon of curry and two tablespoons
of flour mixed together; stir until smooth. Stir in one cup
of milk, cook until tickened stirring constantly; add one-half
tablespoon of lemon juice. Place over boiling water in lower
part of double boiler and let cook five minutes longer. Keep
hot until served.

Alligator Pear Salad

Cut each pear in halves, remove the weed and pour into each
cavity two tablespoons of French Dressing. See that the fruit
and the dressing are ice cold.

Macedoine Fruit Cocktail

Carefully remove the fleshy sections from three grapefruit, leaving all membrane. Measure and then add half as much diced, canned pineapple and orange sections. Chill and serve garnished with finely chopped pistachio nuts. Serves 6.

LUNCHEON FOR A SPECIAL GUEST

Grapefruit Sections with Grapejuice
Nut and Pickle Salad
Cold Sliced Lamb
Cloverleaf Biscuits
Spanish Coffee Cream   Stuffed Celery
Iced Cakes   Salted Nuts
Tea

Nut and Pickle Salad

2½ tablespoons granulated gelatin
1 cup chopped walnut meats
2 cups sweet pickles
2 cups cold water
12 cloves

2 cups sugar
1 cup cider vinegar, medium strength
Mayonnaise
Lettuce

Boil together the vinegar, sugar, and cloves till the mixture threads. Then remove from the heat, remove the cloves, and add the gelatin, which has been soaked in the cold water for five minutes. Cool, and when beginning to set, stir in the chopped nut-meats and the pickles sliced thin. Pour into cold, wet, individual molds and set aside for a few hours to stiffen. Serve on lettuce with mayonnaise. Serves 6.

Spanish Coffee Cream

2 tablespoons granulated gelatin
1 teaspoon vanilla
1 cupful cream or evaporated milk

¼ teaspoon salt
3 cups coffee infusion
3 eggs
½ cupful sugar

Heat the coffee infusion to the boiling point. Pour it over the sugar, egg-yolks and salt well beaten together. Cook in the top of a double-boiler for about five minutes stirring constantly. Then add the gelatin which has been softened in the cream or evaporated milk and heat well again. Remove from the heat and allow to cool and partially stiffen. Then fold in the egg whites stiffly beaten and turn into a cold wet mold. Serve cold with cream. Serves 6 to 8.

AFTER BRIDGE REFRESHMENTS

It is now a charming gesture of hospitality for one to serve a very simple repast after bridge or, in fact, after any party. Happily, too, these little after-party snacks are being welcomed by hostesses and guests alike. They are much less work to prepare—often less expensive as well. And guests can partake of them gayly without fear of spoiling a later meal at home or upsetting seriously any calorie calculations they have made for the day.

The following menus suggest a number of simple after-bridge snacks in which tomato, clam and sauerkraut juice cocktails are served accompanied by assorted canapés or hors d'oeuvres. The cocktails may be purchased ready to serve or they may be prepared at home using the recipes which follow. The canapés which may be limited to two or three varieties or as many as the hostess has time to prepare, may be made from mixtures purchased ready to use or prepared by the hostess. Packaged crackers make a quick and easy foundation for these spreads. Serve the cocktails in small glasses and pass the canapés from a platter or tray.

If the weather seems too chilly for such cocktails, tea, cocoa, chocolate or cocoa-flavored malt drink may be served with the canapés or a fruit salad. But whatever you serve, keep it simple.

AFTER BRIDGE SNACKS
Apple Cider
Open Cheese Sandwiches of Whole Wheat Bread
Date and Nut Sandwiches

———

Avocado En Surprise
Clam Juice Cocktail
Toasted Rolled Cheese Sandwiches   Cashew Nuts

Sauerkraut Juice Cocktail
Assorted Canapés
Celery Curls

———

Ham & Cheese Roulades

Olives   Tiny Pickled Onions
Tomato Juice Cocktail

———

Ginger Fruit Salad   Lime French Dressing
Chocolate Parfait
Hot Rolls

Coffee   Wafers

Avocado en Surprise

Fill the centers of well-chilled, previously salted, large, ripe
avocado pears with sections of grapefruit, orange and peeled
grapes. Cover with French dressing made rosy with paprika
and Chili sauce. Garnish with mint leaves and surround with
watercress or serve on lettuce.

Ham and Cheese Roulades

1 package lemon flavored   6 tablespoons prepared horse-
  gelatin dessert   radish
2 cups boiling water   ½ tablespoon salt
2 bouillon cubes   Speck cayenne pepper
2 3-oz. package cream cheese   ⅓ cup cream
                                  14 thin slices cooked ham

Add the boiling water to the lemon-flavored gelatin and the
bouillon cubes, stir until completely dissolved and chill. Meanwhile rub the cream cheese to a smooth paste, add the prepared horseradish, salt, cayenne pepper and cream which has
been whipped stiff. Have the ham sliced very thin, then trim
each slice to a four-inch square. Spread one tablespoon of
the cheese mixture on each slice of ham and roll as com-
pactly as possible, allowing the cheese to project slightly over
the ends. Place the rolls, seam side down, in a shallow pan,
and when the gelatin mixture is cold and slightly thickened,
put a thin coating of it over each ham roll by using a teaspoon.
Set in the refrigerator to chill thoroughly. When the first

coating of gelatin has set, apply a second and chill again. In serving use a sharp knife to free the rolls from the thin layer of gelatin in the pan. Serves 14.

Chocolate Parfait

1 cup sugar	2 squares unsweetened chocolate
1 cup water	2 cups cream whipped
Whites 3 eggs	1 tablespoon vanilla

Boil the sugar and water to 238° F., or to soft ball stage. Pour slowly over the stiffly beaten whites, beating constantly; beat until cool. Fold in the chocolate that has been melted and cooled, cream, and vanilla. Pour into refrigerator trays, and freeze without stirring. Serves 8.

Ginger Fruit Salad

8 medium red apples	1 cup seedless white grapes
Juice 1 lemon	1 head lettuce
½ cup nut meats	2 bananas
1 cup candied ginger, chopped	Lime French Dressing
2 medium oranges	

Core apples and dice without peeling. Sprinkle with lemon juice at once to prevent discoloration. Add sliced bananas, orange sections, stemmed grapes, chopped nutmeats and chopped ginger. Serve on lettuce with Lime French Dressing, made as follows:

Lime French Dressing

Add bottled lime juice and powdered sugar to taste to French Dressing.

A "SPREAD YOUR OWN" PARTY

Let canapés run riot in your after-bridge refreshment menus —indeed, they have to the extent that hostesses are now having "spread your own" parties. By that we mean they simply provide the canapé spreads, the crackers, and let the guests help themselves. Unsalted crackers are favored for the canapé spread—toasted if you wish, or some prefer Melba Toast, which it is possible to buy if you do not wish to go to the trouble of making it.

Celery, olives, marinated in salad oil, and perhaps salted nuts will add sufficient variety to satisfy anyone's appetite. However, if a more elaborate menu is desired, one creamed hot dish with tiny biscuits, followed by a simple dessert may be included.

THE CANAPE SPREADS

These serve from 6 to 8 persons:

Roquefort and Cream Cheese Spread

Mash one four-ounce package roquefort cheese with one three-ounce package cream cheese, one tablespoon minced onions, and one-quarter cup top milk or cream.

Cottage Cheese and Green Pepper Spread

Combine one-half pound fresh cottage cheese with two tablespoons minced green pepper, one tablespoon minced onion, a dash of cayenne and one tablespoon garlic flavored French dressing. (For the latter allow one cut clove of garlic to stand in the French dressing for several hours or longer.)

Lobster Spread

Combine one six-ounce can of lobster, minced, one tablespoon lemon juice, one and a half tablespoon mayonnaise and one tablespoon garlic flavored French dressing.

Minced Ham and Egg Spread

Combine one-eighth pound minced cooked ham (two-thirds cup) with three shelled hard-cooked eggs, minced, two tablespoons minced onion, one and a half teaspoon prepared mustard, one teaspoon bottled condiment sauce and two tablespoons mayonnaise.

Almond and Olive Spread

Combine one-fourth pound of finely chopped salted almonds with one-fourth cup chopped minced stuffed olives, two tablespoons, mayonnaise and one teaspoon French dressing.

Sardine and Egg Spread

Combine 4 hard-cooked egg-yolks minced fine with one three and three-quarter ounce can sardines mashed. Add one table-spoon lemon juice, two tablespoons mayonnaise and one table-spoon garlic flavored French dressing.

Pineapple and Chicken Spread

Combine one-quarter cup canned crushed pineapple with one-half cup chopped cooked chicken and two tablespoons mayon-naise.

Crabmeat Spread

Mix one six and a half ounce can of crabmeat, minced with one-half cup chopped celery, one-quarter cup minced pimiento, one-quarter cup garlic flavored mayonnaise, one-eighth tea-spoon salt and one-eighth teaspoon paprika.

THE COCKTAILS

Tomato Juice Cocktail, No. 1

1 No. 3 can tomato juice or canned tomatoes	½ teaspoon salt
	1 teaspoon minced parsley
1 small onion, thinly sliced	1 bay leaf
1 teaspoon granulated sugar	1 stick of celery, bruised

Combine the ingredients listed and allow to chill fifteen min-utes or longer. Strain and serve very cold. To bruise the celery, twist with the fingers so as to break some of the fibers. Serves from 6 to 8.

Tomato Juice Cocktail, No. 2

Add one teaspoon lemon juice, one teaspoon bottled condiment sauce and one teaspoon Chili sauce to Tomato Juice Cocktail No. 1, and proceed as directed. This makes a more highly seasoned cocktail.

Clam Juice Cocktail

For making clam juice cocktail at home, the juice may be

purchased from the fish market. Or you can buy clam juice in bottles, to be seasoned by the following recipe:

2 cups clam juice or bouillon
⅓ cup catsup
1 tablespoon powdered sugar
3 drops Tobasco
2 tablespoons lemon juice
Celery salt to taste

Combine all ingredients. Chill thoroughly, strain and serve. Serves 4 to 6.

Sauerkraut Juice Cocktail

Sauerkraut juice can be purchased in cans, and prepared for serving in the following manner:

1 No. 3 can sauerkraut juice
1 teaspoon bottled condiment sauce
¼ teaspoon prepared mustard
Salt to taste
Speck of pepper

Combine the ingredients listed. Stir well, chill and serve. Serves 4 to 6.

WHEN THE YOUNG PEOPLE ENTERTAIN

Young people are always bringing home guests for the week end, and that's a problem to Mother who must plan the food for several days. Perhaps first of all there will be a Saturday afternoon tea, so we will start with a menu suitable for that. If the day is warm, of course, it will be served on the porch —with iced tea or punch as a beverage—if cool weather then hot coffee must be substituted.

Quince Sandwiches

Open-faced Peanut Butter and Banana Sandwiches

Fruit Punch   Salted Almonds

Crystallized Ginger

Quince Sandwiches

Half cup quince jelly, half cup chopped pecan meats, one package cream cheese, butter, whole wheat bread.

Mix the jelly and chopped nutmeats, and spread on thin slices of buttered bread. Top with slices of bread generously spread with softened cream cheese.

Open-Faced Sandwiches

> White bread.
> Peanut butter.
> Bananas, thinly sliced crosswise.
> Lemon juice.

Butter thin triangular slices of white bread. Spread thinly with peanut butter. Dip banana slices in lemon juice and arrange them on the triangles, pressing them lightly into the peanut butter. Brush with lemon juice.

Fruit Punch

1½ cups sugar	½ cup lime juice
1½ cups water	1½ cups grated pineapple
Juice 4 oranges	Juice 1 lemon

Combine the sugar and water and simmer for five minutes. Cool. Meanwhile combine the orange juice, lemon juice and lime juice. Add to the cooled syrup and just before placing in the refrigerator add the grated pineapple. When cold and ready to serve, dilute with mineral water or ice-water. This recipe makes about two quarts.

> Pineapple and Cucumber Salad, Cream Dressing
> Watercress Sandwiches
> Sparkling Grape Punch
> Fresh Peach Ice Cream
> Chocolate Wafers

Pineapple and Cucumber Salad

Two and a half tablespoons granulated gelatin, one-half cup cold water, one-half cup boiling water, juice one lemon, one-third cup vinegar, one teaspoon salt, one-half cup sugar, three cups grated pineapple, one-half cup finely diced cucumber, one pimiento, chopped.

Soak gelatin in the cold water five minutes. Add the boiling water and stir until gelatin is dissolved Add lemon juice, vinegar, salt and sugar. Chill. When it has begun to set add pineapple, cucumber and pimiento. Pour into six wet individual molds and chill. Turn out on crisp lettuce leaves and serve with the following dressing:

Cream Dressing

One teaspoon dry mustard, one teaspoon salt, one-sixteenth teaspoon cayenne pepper, two tablespoons fat or oil, one teaspoon sugar, two eggs, beaten, one-half cup hot vinegar, one cup cream.

Beat eggs, add dry ingredients, cream and hot vinegar, slowly. Cook over hot water in a double boiler, stirring constantly until thickened. Add fat and stir until well blended.

Sparkling Grape Punch

One pint bottle sparkling white grape juice, one pint bottle carbonated water, one pint bottle pale dry ginger ale, ice cubes tinted green, mint leaves.

Chill and mix just before serving. Garnish with sprigs of mint. Color the water to be frozen into ice cubes with green vegetable coloring matter, pour into trays and freeze as usual. Or freeze one of the many carbonated fruit beverages in cubes.

Frozen Pistachio Cheese Salad

Olives   Clover-leaf Rolls

Raspberry Fizz   Frosted Cake

Frozen Pistachio Cheese Salad

Three three-ounce packages cream cheese, one two-ounce package roquefort cheese, one-half cup chopped pistachio nuts, one-half teaspoon salt, one tablespoon lemon juice, one-quarter cup cream, whipped, green vegetable coloring.

Mix the cream cheese and roquefort cheese with a fork until soft. Tint a delicate green with vegetable coloring. Add the chopped nuts, salt and lemon juice. Fold in the whipped cream. Turn into one of the trays of a refrigerating unit and spread smooth with a spatula to a thickness of about three-quarter-inch. Chill until firm. Cut into small squares. Serve on crisp lettuce. Garnish with radish roses, and cucumber slices. Serve with French dressing. Serves 8.

Raspberry Fizz

One quart vanilla ice cream.
Three pints raspberry carbonated beverage.

Put a scoopful of vanilla ice cream into eight tall glasses, Pour the carbonated beverage over the ice cream and serve at once. Any other desired flavor may be used.

Creamy Corn Chowder
Crisp Whole Wheat Wafers
Hot Gingerbread   Cheese Cubes
Chocolate or Cocoa flavored Malt Drink

Creamy Clam Chowder

2 cups canned corn
2 cups canned tomatoes
2 cups diced celery
1 quart water
1/4 cup chopped pimiento
1 cup evaporated milk

3 tablespoons butter
2 teaspoons salt
3 tablespoons flour
1/4 cup grated cheese
1-16 teaspoon soda

Combine corn, tomatoes, celery and water and cook for 30 minutes. Add all other ingredients in order given. Allow the chowder to come to a boil. Serves 8.

If you have a sandwich toaster, this rainy day menu will surely appeal to you.

Toasted Boston Sandwiches
Toasted Epicurean Sandwiches
Chocolate or Cocoa flavored Malt Drink
Sliced Peaches   Sponge Cake

Toasted Boston Sandwiches

1 can baked beans, drained
  and sieved
2 stalks celery, minced
Canned Boston brown bread

1 teaspoon horseradish
6 sweet gherkins, sliced
Tomato catsup

Mix the sieved beans, celery, horseradish, and sliced pickles.

Toasted Epicurean Sandwiches

2 medium tomatoes,
  minced
3 green peppers, minced
1 small onion, minced
1/4 teaspoon salt

Cooked salad dressing
Lettuce hearts
White bread
Olives

Mix the minced and drained vegetables with enough of the cooked salad dressing to spread easily. Add salt. Spread between slices of bread. Butter sandwiches on the outside and toast in a sandwich toaster. Garnish with lettuce hearts and olives. Makes 6 to 8 sandwiches.

Here is another delicious drink, suitable for refreshment on a warm afternoon or evening:

Orange Nogg

Dissolve two-thirds cup of sugar in two cups of orange juice and chill. When ready to serve, pour the orange juice slowly into one and one-third cups chilled evaporated milk diluted with one and one-third cups ice water. Shake vigorously in a glass jar and serve when cold. Serves four generously.

Since young people make merry late Friday and Saturday nights, they nearly always want to sleep late Sunday morning, and then are ready for something tempting by way of breakfast. A leisurely breakfast on the porch, in summer, is always delightful.

BREAKFAST MENU

Honey-dew Melon Balls in Grapefruit Juice
Crisp Ready-to-Eat Cereal in Cream
Hot Crunchy Blueberry Muffins
Bacon Curls   Coffee

Blueberry Muffins

¼ cup shortening
½ cup sugar
1 egg well beaten
1½ cups all-purpose flour
½ teaspoon salt

3 teaspoons tartrate or phosphate baking powder, or
1½ teaspoons phosphate-sulphate baking powder
2 cups milk
1 cup blueberries

Cream the shortening, add the sugar, and blend thoroughly. Add the well-beaten egg. Mix and sift flour, salt, and baking powder, and add alternately with the milk to the first mixture. Fold in the blueberries. Pour into hot greased muffin pans and bake in a hot oven of 400 degrees F. for 25 minutes. In this recipe, as in all Institute recipes diluted evaporated milk may be substituted for bottled milk.

Melons in Grapefruit Juice

Cut Honey Dew melons in halves and remove the seeds. Scoop out in balls. Cover with grapefruit juice, either fresh or canned, arrange in cocktail glasses and chill until served. Garnish with fresh mint if desired. Any kind of melon may be used instead of Honey Dew if desired. The balls are made by using the half-teaspoon in your measuring set.

Or perhaps you have served an early breakfast and there will be need of a hearty dinner.

SUNDAY DINNER

Squash Soup
Toasted Cheese Rolls
Corn Custard   Ginger Ale Salad
Roast Beef with Browned Potatoes
Peach Parfait
Coffee

Squash Soup

When summer squash first appear in the markets, they are expensive, but only a small one will be needed for Squash Soup. Prepare and cut into dice two cups of summer squash. Add one onion chopped fine and cook in three cups of boiling water until the squash is tender. Mash the squash slightly and add one cup of top milk. Thicken with two tablespoons of flour mixed with three tablespoons melted fat, while stirring constantly. Season with one teaspoon salt and one-eighth teaspoon white pepper. Serve very hot, garnish with whipped cream. Serves six.

Toasted Cheese Rolls

Mix the following ingredients into a smooth paste: Two cups soft sharp cheese, one-half teaspoon salt, speck cayenne, one teaspoon prepared mustard, and three tablespoons cream.

Remove the crusts from a fresh loaf of bread and cut in lengthwise slices one-fourth inch thick. Butter the large slices with a small amount of butter and spread with the cheese mixture. Roll the slices lengthwise like a jelly roll. Wrap the rolls of bread and cheese firmly in a damp cloth and place in the refrigerator for several hours. Just before serving, cut the rolls into one and one-half inch lengths and toast in the broiling oven or on the electric grill. If cut small, these rolls are delicious served with soup or salad or make a hearty sandwich for Sunday night tea.

Ginger Ale Salad

¾ cup diced, canned pine-
  apple
¾ cup chopped grape-fruit
  pulp
⅓ cup blanched shredded
  almonds
¼ cup seeded malaga grapes
1 cup ginger ale

2 tablespoons granulated
  gelatin
½ cup cold water
Few grains salt
Few grains paprika
Mayonnaise
Lettuce

Soak the gelatin in the cold water for five minutes, then dissolve it over hot water. Add one-fourth cup of the ginger ale. Combine the diced pineapple, grapefruit pulp, malaga grapes, shredded almonds, salt and pepper and then add the remaining three-fourths cup of ginger ale. Add the gelatin mixture, stir thoroughly and pour into individual molds which have been dipped in and out of cold water. Chill thoroughly, unmold and serve on lettuce leaves, garnished with mayonnaise. Serves six.

Peach Parfait

1 cup mashed fresh or
  canned peaches
1 cup sugar
⅛ cup water

2 egg whites
Juice 1 orange
1 pint heavy cream,
  whipped

Few drops bitter almond

Boil the sugar and water together to 238° F. or until it threads, and pour gently into the egg-whites, which should be beaten stiff, whipping constantly. Combine the peaches and orange-juice. Beat in the egg-white mixture. Stir briskly until cool, and then fold in the whipped cream and almond, which should be used sparingly. Pour into a mold, cover with wax paper and press on the lid. If this does not fit very tightly, dip a cloth in melted paraffin or fat, and bind the edge. Pack in two parts of ice to one part of salt for four hours. If canned peaches are used, the amount of sugar should be reduced to three-fourths of a cup.

SUNDAY DINNER

Piquant Fruit Cocktail
Roast Lamb with Mint Sauce
Fresh Green Peas   Celery and Olives
Raw Vegetable Salad
Pineapple Delight
Coffee

Piquant Fruit Cocktail

Mix together one-half cup of powdered sugar, one-half cup of orange juice, and one-third cup of grapefruit juice and chill. Remove pits from one cup of canned cherries, either white or red, and cut canned pears in cubes to the amount of one cup. Place the fruit in cocktail glasses, alternating cherries and pears, fill with the liquid, and sprinkle each service with one-half tablespoon of chopped, crystallized ginger.

Raw Vegetable Salad

Marinate separately in enough mayonnaise to bind one cup finely chopped green pepper, one cup finely chopped cabbage, and one cup finely chopped raw carrots. On a leaf of lettuce place a mound of carrots, place a mound of cabbage on top of the carrots, and a mound of green pepper on the cabbage. Top with a layer of grated cheese—one-fourth pound of American cheese, grated, will be needed. Serve with a Savory Dressing made as follows: beat with an eggbeater until thoroughly combined one tablespoon of dry mustard, one and one-half tablespoons of Worcestershire sauce, two teaspoons of sugar, one-half teaspoon of salt, one-eighth teaspoon of celery salt, a dash of cayenne pepper, one-third cup of catsup, one cup of salad oil and one-half cup of vinegar. Serves six.

Pineapple Delight

½ cup pineapple, diced
1 pint whipping cream
12 marshmallows, diced
12 maraschino cherries, diced

½ cup chopped nuts
1 teaspoon vanilla
1 tablespoon confectioners' sugar

Whip cream until stiff, then fold in the pineapple, marshmallows, cherries, nuts, sugar and vanilla. Chill and serve in sherbet glasses.

SUNDAY NIGHT SUPPER

Chicken Creole Style, in Bread Cases
Sliced Tomatoes in French Dressing
Hot Graham Muffins
Ice Cream   Coffee   Cookies

Chicken Creole Style

3 tablespoons fat or margarine
2 tablespoons chopped green pepper
½ teaspoon salt
½ cup tomato pulp
1 teaspoon lemon juice

1 tablespoon chopped onion
3 tablespoons flour
1 cup canned chicken broth
1 tablespoon horseradish
1½ cups canned chicken meat

Melt the fat in a frying pan, add chopped onion and green pepper, and saute until golden brown. Add salt and flour, and stir until well blended. Add chicken broth and tomato pulp. Stir until mixture reaches the boiling point, then add horseradish, lemon juice and chicken. Keep hot in a double boiler. Serve in bread cases. Serves six.

Bread Cases

Remove crusts from a loaf of sandwich bread. Cut loaf in slices about 2½ inches thick. Remove bread from center of each slice, causing cup-like depressions. Spread with melted fat and brown under the broiler heat. Fill with Chicken Creole Style.

SUNDAY NIGHT SUPPER
Cheese and Lobster Delight
Watercress Salad
Peppermint Ice Cream
Wafers   Coffee

Cheese and Lobster Delight

1 teaspoon chopped onion
3 tablespoons chopped green
  pepper
3 tablespoons butter or margarine
2 tablespoons flour
½ teaspoon prepared
  mustard
¼ teaspoon salt

1 cup canned, strained
  tomatoes
½ cup grated cheese
1 egg, slightly beaten
¾ cup heated milk
1 cup canned or fresh-
  cooked lobster
Toast

Cook the onion and green pepper in the butter until tender, about five minutes. Then add the flour, stir well, and next add the mustard, salt, tomatoes, cheese, and beaten egg. When blended, add to the hot milk and continue cooking, while stirring, until the sauce is smooth and thickened. Then fold in the lobster meat and serve on buttered toast. Canned or fresh cooked crabmeat or shrimp may be substituted for the lobster called for in the above recipe. Serves six.

Watercress Salad

1 bunch watercress
¼ pound bacon

6 hard-cooked eggs
French dressing

Wash the watercress, dry thoroughly, and arrange on salad plates. Cut the bacon in dice and fry until crisp; drain from the fat and cool. Slice the eggs and arrange one on each bed of watercress. Scatter the bacon dice over the egg. Serve with French dressing.

Peppermint Ice Cream

9 sticks peppermint candy
3 cups whipping cream
2 tablespoons sugar

1 tablespoon granulated
  gelatin
¼ cup cold water
¼ cup hot milk

Soak gelatin in cold water five minutes. Add sugar and gelatin to scalded milk. Stir until gelatin is dissolved. Add one-half of the crushed candy. When cool, add to stiffly whipped cream. Add balance of crushed candy. Put in inset pans of refrigerator and freeze three to five hours.

SCHOOL GIRL PARTIES

Whether you are planning an afternoon snack a-la-teatime or having school friends in for the evening, the following menus will be found helpful. They are inexpensive and easy to prepare, so that little help from mother or the family cook will be needed.

Celery and Olive Sandwiches

Mock Paté de Foie Gras Sandwiches

Open-Face Guava Sandwiches

Pecan Cookies   Cocoanut Date Strips

Tea

Celery and Olive Sandwiches

1 cup finely-diced celery	Mayonnaise
¼ cup chopped, stuffed olives	1 loaf whole-wheat bread

Mix chopped celery and olives with enough mayonnaise to spread. Spread between slices of buttered whole-wheat bread. Cut into squares and garnish each sandwich with a slice of stuffed olive. Makes 18 small sandwiches.

Mock Pate de Foie Gras Sandwiches

¼ pound liverwurst	1 loaf white bread
¼ cup minced parsley	Watercress or Parsley
2 tablespoons mayonnaise	

Remove casing from liverwurst and mash. Add parsley and mayonnaise and mix well. Spread between slices of buttered white bread. Cut into diamond-shaped sandwiches. Garnish plate with parsley or watercress. Makes 18 small sandwiches.

Open-Face Guava Sandwiches

1 loaf white bread
1 3-oz. pkg. cream cheese
Cream

½ cup chopped walnut
  meats
Mayonnaise
1 glass Guava jelly

Cut bread into ¼ in. slices and then into rounds about 2 in. in diameter. Mix cream cheese with enough cream to make it spread easily. Spread the top of the bread rounds with this mixture, and spread the sides with mayonnaise. Press chopped nuts firmly around the edge. Just before serving drop ½ teaspoon guava jelly in the center of each sandwich. Makes 24 sandwiches. Serve on galax leaves from the florist's.

Pecan Cookies

¾ cup shortening
1½ cup brown sugar
1 egg
½ teaspoon salt

2 cups cake or pastry flour
⅛ teaspoon soda
¼ cup chopped pecan meats
½ cup whole pecan meats

Cream the shortening. Add the sugar, and blend well. Add the whole egg, and mix thoroughly. Sift flour with soda and salt and add to the shortening mixture gradually. Add chopped nutmeats. Cover and let stand overnight in the refrigerator. Form into tiny balls (½ in. in diameter). Press a whole nut-meat on top of each cooky. Bake in a moderate oven of 375° F. for 8 to 10 minutes. Makes 5 dozen cookies.

Cocoanut Date Strips

Plain pastry
2 tablespoons butter or
  margarin
Top milk

¼ cup brown sugar
¼ cup shredded cocoanut
¼ cup shredded dates

Make once the recipe for plain pastry, using 1½ cup flour as the basis. Roll out to ⅛ in. thickness. Spread with the softened butter. Mix the sugar, cocoanut, and dates cut in shreds. Spread on half of the buttered pastry. Fold over the other half, and press firmly in place. Cut into strips ¾ in. wide by 3 in. long, and place on greased baking sheets. Brush with top milk and bake 10-15 minutes in a very hot oved of 500° F. or until delicately browned. Makes about 2 dozen strips.

Garnishes for Tea

We recommend these: lemon slices stuck with whole cloves and garnished with candied ginger or fruit peel; half slices or oranges garnished with rose geranium leaves; maraschino cherries filled with sprigs of mint; tiny gum drops or rock candy.

Or perhaps it's a birthday party, and you will want something a little more elaborate:

BIRTHDAY PARTY MENU

Almond Sandwiches   Chicken and Pineapple Sandwiches
Open Lobster Sandwiches
Golden Punch   Petits Four

Almond Sandwiches

1 3-oz. pkg. cream cheese   ¼ pound salted almonds
2 tablespoons lemon juice   2 loaves whole-wheat bread

Mash the cream cheese, and mix thoroughly with the lemon juice to a spreading consistency. Chop salted almonds and add. Spread between buttered slices of whole-wheat bread. Cut in "fingers." Makes 50 small sandwiches.

Chicken and Pineapple Sandwiches

1 cup canned crushed pine-   2 loaves white bread
  apple   ½ pound walnut meats
1 cup chopped cooked **or**   ½ cup mayonnaise
  canned chicken

Drain pineapple, and mix with the chopped chicken and mayonnaise. Spread between buttered slices of white bread. Cut each sandwich into quarters diagonally, forming triangles. This recipe makes 50 sandwiches.

Open Lobster Sandwiches

1 12-oz. can lobster, minced   3 tablespoons French
2 tablespoons lemon juice   dressing
3 tablespoons mayonnaise   2 loaves white bread

Combine all ingredients adding additional seasoning to taste. Spread on buttered rounds of white bread. Garnish each with a sprig of parsley. Makes 50 sandwiches.

Golden Punch for 50

2 No. 2½ cans apricots
4 cups orange juice
2 cups lemon juice

4 quarts carbonated lime beverage
Fresh mint

Put the apricots and juice through a strainer, then combine with the orange and lemon juice. Pour over ice cubes or ice, and add the carbonated lime beverage just before serving. Garnish with the fresh mint. Serves 50.

Here is a delightful birthday dinner menu, planned to be served buffet style.

BIRTHDAY BUFFET DINNER

Apple Juice or Grapefruit Juice
Stuffed Celery   Green and Ripe Olives   Gherkins
Crisp Crackers
Escalloped Chicken and Oysters
Buttered Finger Rolls   Cranberry Jelly
Salad Bowl of Mixed Greens with French Dressing
Molded Ice Cream   Cakes
Coffee

Escalloped Chicken and Oysters

4 cups diced cooked or canned chicken
1 pound mushrooms, sautéed
1 quart oysters
2 cups cooked or canned rice
2 cups cooked or canned peas

3 cups white sauce made with milk, oyster liquor, chicken, and mushroom stock
2 cups soft bread crumbs

4 tablespoons melted butter or margarine

Arrange the chicken, mushrooms, oysters, rice, and peas in layers in 2 large casseroles. Pour the sauce over all. Top with the crumbs mixed with the melted butter, and bake in a hot oven of 425° F. for 20 minutes or until the mixture is heated and the crumbs brown. Serves 12-16.

For entertaining just a few guests, cozy Sunday night suppers are unsurpassed. Here is a menu that is both unusual and delicious:

SUNDAY NIGHT SUPPER

Curried Shrimp with Rice and Chutney
Orange Muffins
Peach Temptation   Marble Cake

Orange Muffins

4 cups all-purpose flour

8 teaspoons tartrate or phosphate baking powder or 4 teaspoons combination-type baking powder

1 teaspoon salt

½ cup grated orange peel

2 eggs

2 cups bottled milk or 1 cup evaporated milk and 1 cup water

½ cup melted fat

½ cup granulated sugar

Sift and measure the flour, then sift it with the baking powder, salt, and sugar, and add the orange peel. Beat the eggs, add the milk and the melted fat, and turn into the dry ingredients all at one time, and stir quickly and vigorously until the dry ingredients are just mixed, and have a lumpy appearance. Fill greased muffin pans ⅔ full, and bake in a hot oven of 425°F. for 25 minutes. Makes 3 dozen muffins.

Peach Temptation

4 teaspoons granulated gelatin

6 tablespoons cold water

⅔ cup boiling water

¾ cup marshmallow whip

2 cups sieved canned peaches or sweetened fresh peaches

½ pint cream, whipped

Slices of canned or fresh peaches

Soak gelatin in a cup with the cold water for 5 minutes. Stand cup in boiling water until gelatin dissolves. Add boiling water to marshmallow whip and mix well. Add the sieved peaches and the dissolved gelatin to the whip mixture. Line individual cold wet molds with slices of peaches, and fill with above mixture. Chill until firm. Serve with whipped cream. Makes 12 individual molds.

A garden or lawn is a lovely setting for a party, and the food must be delectable to meet the occasion:

GARDEN PARTY MENU

Dainty Sandwiches

Lace Cookies   Assorted Ices

Iced Tea   Iced Coffee   Iced Chocolate

Lace Cookies

¼ cup molasses
¼ cup shortening
¼ cup granulated sugar
½ cup pastry or cake flour
⅛ teaspoon soda

¼ teaspoon tartrate or phosphate baking powder or ⅛ teaspoon combination-type baking powder
¼ cup chopped walnut meats

Slowly bring molasses, shortening, and sugar to boiling point. Boil one minute and remove from heat. Add mixed and sifted dry ingredients. Add nuts. Drop mixture by ¼ teaspoon on greased cookie sheets, 3 inches apart. Bake in a moderate oven of 350° F. for 10 minutes. Cool slightly, then remove carefully with a thin knife or spatula. Makes 75 cookies.

Formal luncheons are the answer to many an entertainment problem. Here's a delightful one for you to serve:

FORMAL LUNCHEON

Tomato Juice Cocktail
Whole-Wheat Crackers Spread with Cream Cheese
Molded Crabmeat Salad
Cucumber Mayonnaise
Buttered Green Beans   Hot Rolls
Sponge Cake with Sliced Peaches and Foamy Sauce

Cucumber Mayonnaise

3 medium cucumbers   ¹⁄₁₆ teaspoon pepper
½ teaspoon salt   3 cups mayonnaise

Pare cucumbers, chop, and drain thoroughly. Add to remaining ingredients. Serves 16.

Foamy Sauce

6 tablespoons butter   2 cups powdered sugar
4 eggs, separated   1 teaspoon vanilla
     2 cups cream, whipped

Cream butter and sugar. Add well-beaten egg yolks; beat thoroughly over hot water in a double-boiler. Remove from the heat and fold in the stiffly-beaten egg whites, vanilla, and whipped cream. Serves 16.

BRIDAL PARTIES

From the moment the bride is engaged until the wedding breakfast is served, there are no end of festivities in her honor. First, of course, is the engagement party.

A color scheme gives an added air of festivity. Perhaps you have a lace table cover. If so, spread it over pale green sateen. Be sure to have napkins to match the cloth.

A centerpiece of flowers—sweet peas or rosebuds, to carry out your color scheme—in a low silver or crystal bowl, is charming. Candlesticks to match in glass or silver, and bon bon dishes filled with pink and green mints, complete the picture.

A pair of silver hearts in front of each plate, tied together, serve two purposes—on the top heart write the guest's name —making a pretty place card. On the bottom heart mount small pictures of the engaged couple, and write the announcement.

ENGAGEMENT LUNCHEON

Cream of Celery Soup
Croutons Cut in Heart Shapes
Chicken or Ham Mousse

or

Creamed Lobster with Mushrooms
Green Peas   Shoestring Potatoes
Heart Shaped Biscuits
Molded Beet Salad
Strawberry Velvet Ice Cream
Green Frosted Cakes
Coffee

Chicken or Ham Mousse

3 egg yolks
1½ cups milk
¼ cup cold water
1 cup heavy cream

½ cup hot chicken broth
Salt, pepper and paprika
1 cup minced white meat of
  chicken or ham

Beat yolks, add milk and cook in double boiler until a light custard. Soak gelatin in cold water, add the hot chicken broth, stir until dissolved, then add to the custard, then the minced chicken. Season to taste and when cool add the cream, whipped. Put into greased individual molds; let stand in ice box several hours or over night.

Creamed Lobster with Mushrooms

1 quart flaked lobster
1 small can mushrooms or
  one cup grated cheese

2 eggs
1 cup cream sauce
Salt and pepper

Beat up the eggs and stir into the lobster; add the mushrooms and the lobster; add the mushrooms and the cream sauce, which should be well seasoned. Place in a baking dish, sprinkle over with grated cheese and buttered bread crumbs.

Molded Beet Salad

2 cups tiny beets
2 tablespoons vinegar
⅔ cup hot water
1 teaspoon salt
1 teaspoon sugar
2 tablespoons grated horse-
    radish

1½ tablespoons granulated
    gelatin
¼ cup cold water
¾ cup mayonnaise
1 head lettuce

Scrub the beets thoroughly and boil until tender; rub off the skin. Pour over them the vinegar, salt, sugar, horseradish, and hot water. Place over the heat and bring to the boiling point. Then add the gelatin, which has been softened in the cold water, and stir until dissolved. Pour into a shallow pan which has been previously wet with cold water. Set away to chill, cut in cubes, and serve on lettuce or cress with mayonnaise. This recipe will serve at least eight. Large beets may be used and cut into cubes about an inch in diameter after cooking. Serves six.

ANNOUNCEMENT TEA PARTY

Fruit Salad with Cheese Dressing
Pimento Sandwiches
Chopped Ham Sandwiches
Golden Glow Ice Cream   Tiny Cakes
Salted Almonds   Coffee

Fruit Salad with Cheese Dressing

Remove the pulp in sections from two grapefruit. Chop one-third cup of pecan meats coarsely and add them with three-fourths cup of seeded Tokay grapes to the grapefruit sections. Add a cheese dressing made by mixing together in a bowl four tablespoons of salad oil, one tablespoon of grapefruit juice, one-half tablespoon of vinegar, one teaspoon of salt, one-eighth teaspoon of pepper, one-fourth teaspoon of paprika, and one tablespoon of finely chopped Roquefort cheese. Beat with a fork until thoroughly blended. Serves six.

Golden Glow Ice Cream

2 quarts milk	2 cups sugar
1 tablespoon flour	1 cup hot water
1 quart can apricots	2 oranges

1 cup grated pineapple

Boil the sugar and water together five minutes. Add the grated pineapple, apricots cut fine with juice, and juice and pulp of the oranges. Scald the milk, add the flour moistened with two tablespoons of milk, and cook two minutes. Blend the milk and fruit mixture, cool, and freeze using eight parts of ice to one part of salt. This recipe makes a gallon.

AFTERNOON OR EVENING SHOWER FOR THE BRIDE-TO-BE

Chicken Neptune
Olives   Pickles
Orange Cream Cheese Sandwiches
Apricot Cream Sherbet   Cakes with White Frosting
Coffee

Orange Cream Cheese Sandwiches

Mix one package of cream cheese with one teaspoon of grated orange rind, and add enough juice to spread. Use as a filling for very thin sandwiches of white or whole wheat bread—preferably cut in heart shapes with a cookie cutter.

Pineapple cheese sandwiches may be made the same way by using crushed pineapple, or by buying pineapple cream cheese already mixed.

Apricot Cream Sherbet

3 cups canned sieved apricots	1 cup sugar
	2 cups cream

Measure the apricots, which have been put through a potato ricer, cover with the sugar and let stand three hours. Fold in the cream whipped stiff. Freeze, using eight parts of ice to one of salt. This recipe makes about two quarts.

WEDDING BREAKFAST

Halves of Grapefruit or Melon
Minced Chicken with Vegetable Border
Tiny Cloverleaf Rolls
or
Cheese Sticks
Currant Jelly or Preserves
Bride's Cake   White Parfait
Coffee

Minced Chicken with Vegetable Border

6 medium-sized potatoes
2 cups medium white sauce
1½ cups minced cooked
   chicken
1 cup sliced canned or
   fresh mushrooms
2 tablespoons fat or oil
1 tablespoon minced
   pimientoes

2 hard-boiled eggs
2 tablespoons minced
   parsley
1 medium-sized can
   asparagus tips
Pimiento strips
6 stuffed olives

Pare and cook potatoes until tender and drain. Meanwhile
prepare medium white sauce to which add the minced chicken,
mushrooms, which have been soutéed for 3 minutes in the
fat, and minced pimientoes. Rice and mash the potatoes, add
the hard-cooked egg yolks finely chopped, and minced parsley.
Arrange the chicken mixture in the center of a heat-proof
platter. Then, using a pastry bag, or a spoon, make a border
of the mashed-potato mixture around the platter. Place the
platter under the broiler heat long enough to brown the
potatoes. Then arrange on top of the chicken the contents
of 1 heated, drained, can of asparagus tips, in bunches of 4.
Garnish each boquet of asparagus with a strip of pimiento,
and place 1 stuffed olive in the center of the creamed chicken.
Serves 6.

White Parfait

1 cup sugar
½ cup water
Whites 3 eggs
1 pint cream

½ teaspoon gelatin
1 tablespoon cold water
1 tablespoon vanilla

Boil the sugar and water to 238° F. Pour slowly on to the egg whites, which have been beaten stiff. Add the gelatin which has been soaked for five minutes in one tablespoon of cold water. Beat until cool and fold in the cream, which has been beaten stiff. Add the vanilla, pour into the refrigerator pans, and freeze without stirring. This recipe serves six to eight.

WEDDING BUFFET SUPPER

Chicken Neptune
Heart Shaped Sandwiches
New Orleans Bisque Ice Cream
Bride's Cake   Coffee

Chicken Neptune

2 dozen fresh shrimp
2 dozen large oysters
1 small can crab meat
2 cups cooked, white chicken meat, diced
6 fresh mushrooms, sliced
½ green pepper chopped fine

4 tablespoons fat or oil
3 tablespoons flour
1 pint cream or top milk
1½ teaspoons salt
¼ teaspoon paprika
¼ teaspoon pepper
½ pimiento, chopped fine

Wash shrimp and cook for 20 minutes in boiling water; shell, and remove the viscera. Wash oysters, cook slowly in their own juice until edges curl. Carefully clean the crab meat and combine with diced chicken. Combine sliced mushrooms and chopped green pepper and sauté for 3 minutes in 2 tablespoons fat. Meanwhile prepare a white sauce by placing 2 tablespoons of the fat in the top of a double boiler. When melted, add flour gradually, stirring constantly. When smooth, add cream slowly and seasonings, still stirring mixture, and cook until thoroughly blended. Then combine with previously prepared ingredients, using a fork. Heat thoroughly and serve on small slices of toast. Serves 10.

New Orleans Bisque Ice Cream

1 cup milk	2 cups thin cream
1 teaspoon cornstarch	½ cup sugar
1 teaspoon vanilla	1 dozen macaroons

Heat all but one tablespoon of the milk in the top of the double boiler. Add the cornstarch mixed with the cold milk and continue cooking twenty-five minutes. Remove, strain, and cool. Then add the cream, sugar and vanilla. Pack in a freezer in the usual way. Freeze in eight parts of ice and one of salt, until half done and then stir in the macaroons which have been crumbled. Finish the freezing. This recipe makes about three pints.

SANDWICHES

Apple Sandwiches

1 large apple
Lemon juice
⅛ cup raisins

Graham bread
Butter

Peel, core and chop the apple. Add the raisins and chop finely together. Butter thin slices of graham bread; spread some of the mixture on one slice, sprinkle with lemon juice, and cover with another slice.

Baked Bean Sandwiches

½ cup baked beans
2 tablespoons grated American cheese
Salt

2 teaspoons orange juice
Butter
Brown bread

Mash the baked beans. Add the grated cheese and salt to taste. Moisten with the orange juice and spread between slices of buttered brown bread.

Banana Sandwiches

Bananas
Lemon juice
Brown or maple sugar

Whole wheat bread
Butter
Chopped nuts

Peel and cut bananas into thin length-wise slices. Arrange a layer of sliced bananas on thin slices of buttered whole wheat bread; squeeze a little lemon juice over the bananas and sprinkle with a little brown or grated maple sugar and a few finely chopped nuts. Put on the top slices of buttered bread, press together, trim and cut.

Cheese, Olive and Green Pepper Sandwiches

1 cup grated American cheese
¼ cup minced green peppers
Bread

¼ cup chopped stuffed olives
2 tablespoons mayonnaise
Butter

Mix together the cheese, finely chopped olives, minced green peppers and mayonnaise. Butter slices of bread, spread half of them with the filling and cover with the other slices of bread.

Chicken Almond Sandwiches

1 cup chopped chicken
8 tablespoons cream
¾ teaspoon salt
White or Graham bread

1 cupful chopped blanched
  almonds
¼ teaspoon paprika
Dash pepper
Butter

Blend the chicken and almonds together with the cream and add the seasoning. Spread between buttered slices or bread. Either white or graham bread may be used.

Creole Sandwiches

4 tablespoons butter
2 tablespoons tomato catsup
6 stuffed olives

½ cup flaked sardines
1 tablespoon lemon juice
Whole wheat crackers

Soften the butter; add the sardines finely flaked, the tomato catsup, lemon juice and the olives chopped fine. Spread on crisp whole wheat crackers.

Chicken King Sandwiches

1 cup cold chicken
1 tablespoon butter
About 6 tablespoons thick
  white sauce
⅛ teaspoon paprika
Bread
Butter

¼ cupful skinned
  mushrooms
¼ teaspoon salt
1 tablespoon sweet red
  peppers
½ teaspoon parsley
Dash cayenne pepper
½ teaspoon chopped onion

Wash and cut up the mushrooms and cook for five minutes in the tablespoon of butter. Mince the chicken, red pepper, parsley and onion. Add to the mushrooms together with the seasonings, and moisten with the highly seasoned thick white sauce. Spread between buttered slices of bread.

Chicken Giblet Sandwiches

Giblets 1 chicken
1 tablespoon cream
1 hard-cooked egg
Rye bread
Butter

½ teaspoon Worcestershire
  sauce
1 teaspoon tomato
  catsup
½ teaspoon salt

Boil the giblets in salted water until tender. Put them together with the hard-cooked egg through a meat chopper. Add the seasonings and cream; spread between buttered slices of rye bread.

Cream Cheese Sandwiches

Cream cheese
Boston brown bread

Horseradish
Butter

Mix equal parts of cream cheese and prepared horseradish. Spread on buttered slices of Boston brown bread and press another slice of bread on top of each.

Lobster and Olive Sandwiches

½ cup lobster meat
Mayonnaise
8 stuffed olives

Bread
Butter

Either canned or fresh lobster meat may be used. Combine the lobster and stuffed olives and chop fine. Moisten with mayonnaise or thick boiled salad dressing and spread between slices of buttered bread.

Mock Deviled Ham Sandwiches

3 frankfurters.
¼ teaspoon prepared
  mustard

3 tablespoons mayonnaise
Butter
Bread

Boil the frankfurters, chill, remove skins, and put through the food chopper. Mix with mayonnaise and mustard and spread between slices of buttered bread. This recipe will make five large, full-sized sandwiches.

Peanut Butter and Banana Sandwiches

3½ oz. jar peanut butter   2 bananas
Buttered bread

Spread lightly with peanut butter, the buttered slices of bread. Over each place a layer of thinly sliced bananas. Cover with slices of buttered bread.

Pepper Sandwiches

4 green peppers	1 lemon
½ teaspoon onion	2 tablespoons cooked
2 tablespoons salad oil	salad dressing
¼ teaspoon salt	1 large cream cheese
4 walnuts	4 stuffed olives
Bread	Butter

Seed and chop the peppers fine. Cover with the juice of the lemon and let stand one hour. Add the finely chopped onion, salad dressing, oil, salt, cream cheese, chopped walnuts and olives. Mix together well. Spread between slices of buttered bread.

Pimiento Sandwiches

White bread	Graham bread
Canned pimientos	Butter

Butter slices of white and graham bread. Arrange strips of pimiento over the surface of the bread and put a white and graham slice together for each sandwich. Cut in heart shapes.

Tuna Sandwiches

½ cupful tuna fish	½ teaspoonful Worcester-
2 tablespoons tomato	shire sauce
catsup	Mayonnaise
Butter	White or graham bread

Mince the tuna fish, add the Worcestershire sauce and catsup and enough mayonnaise to moisten liberally—about two tablespoons. Mix to a paste and spread daintily on thin buttered white or whole wheat bread. Cover, press and cut in triangles or strips.

Tomato Sandwiches

Tomato
Salt
Bread

Paprika
Onion salt
Butter

Place slices of tomato on slices of buttered bread and sprinkle with paprika, salt and onion salt. Top with more buttered bread.

Welsh Rarebit Sandwiches

Welsh rarebit
Butter

Spanish or Bermuda onions
Bread

Make Welsh rarebit by any preferred method and cool. Spread one slice of bread with the cheese mixture and the other with butter. Sprinkle the buttered slice with finely sliced or shredded Spanish or Bermuda onions. The amount of onion used may be varied according to one's liking for them. Then put the two slices together. The same idea may be used when serving the rarebit hot. Place the onion on the toast and then cover with the hot cheese mixture.

HOT SANDWICHES

There are occasions when the midnight snack MUST be more than a fancy tid-bit—when the young folks return from horseback riding, for instance, or skating. Hot sandwiches, also, may be served as the main course for lunch.

English Muffin Savory

English muffins
Ham

Butter
Eggs

Hollandaise, cheese or rich white sauce

Split large English muffins, toast and butter them. Lay a thin round of fried or boiled ham on each and on top of this a poached egg. Last top the egg with a liberal spoonful of Hollandaise, cheese or rich white sauce. To simplify the last minute preparation of this dish, two halves of a hot, hardcooked egg may be substituted for the poached egg.

Fraternity Specials

Slices white bread	Tomatoes
Bacon	Salt and pepper
American cheese	Onion salt

Cut the desired number of slices of bread one-half inch thick. Lay two or three slices of bacon of the right length on each slice of bread. Then cover the bacon with thin slices of fresh tomatoes and sprinkle with salt, pepper and onion salt. Cover the tomatoes with thin slices of cheese and arrange another layer of bacon slices on top. Bake at 450° F. for twenty minutes; then place under broiler heat to brown top. Serve at once.

Green Pepper Sandwiches

6 large green peppers	½ cup sliced onion
6 medium sized tomatoes	3 tablespoons salad oil, butter or bacon drippings
Fresh buns, white or entire wheat bread	
	Salt and pepper to taste

Cook the sliced onions in the oil for five minutes. Remove seeds and stem from peppers and peel the tomatoes. Chop coarsely together, add to the onion and oil and cook until thick—about forty-five minutes. Season to taste with salt and pepper and serve as a hot filling for sandwiches made of the desired bread. To make this very substantial, insert two slices of cooked bacon or a slice of cooked ham in each sandwich.

Ham Sandwiches

1 cup minced ham	1-2 teaspoons prepared mustard
Bread	
1 egg	Butter
½ teaspoon salt	1 cup milk
Fat	⅛ teaspoon pepper

Mince left-over ham including some fat. Season with the mustard. Spread on slices of buttered bread, which have been cut a little thicker than for ordinary sandwiches. Cover each with a slice of buttered bread; press firmly together, and cut into good-sized oblongs or squares. Dip these in a mixture made of the egg, milk, salt and pepper beaten together.

Sauté quickly to a rich brown on both sides in a little melted fat. Lay on a hot platter, garnish with parsley and serve at once. A salad of shredded cabbage and apple dressed with mayonnaise with which has been mixed one tablespoon of catsup, is excellent to serve with these sandwiches.

Lou's Sandwiches

White bread   Butter
                 Snappy or piquant cheese

Spread thinly sliced, buttered, white bread with softened "snappy" or other piquant cheese. Make it into sandwiches, press together firmly, trim off crusts, toast, cut in triangles and serve hot.

Picnic or Camping Sandwiches

1 can pimientoes   Cheese
1 tablespoon butter   Buttered bread

Sauté pimientoes quickly in the butter and remove from pan. In the same butter place thin slices of cheese and hold this over the campfire until the cheese is pliable but not melted. Place between buttered slices of bread a layer of pimiento and a layer of cheese. Serve while hot.

Salem Sandwiches

1/2 cup cheese sauce   1 egg
1/2 teaspoon salt   1 cup milk
1 cup salmon   1/8 teaspoon pepper
Bread   Butter

Flake fresh or canned salmon and mix with the cheese sauce to moisten. With this as a filling make sandwiches of buttered bread. Trim the sandwiches, cut them and dip in a mixture made of the egg, milk, salt and pepper beaten together. Sauté quickly in hot butter. Serve with potato and beet salad laid on lettuce nests.

HORS D'OEUVRES

Hors d'Oeuvres are appetizers and the addition of one often changes an uninteresting meal to an appetizing one. They solve the problem of a Sunday night supper—served with canapes or sandwiches—you have an appetizing spread that differs a little from the usual "meal."

Fruity Hors d'Oeuvres

Watermelon balls   Pears
Peaches   Lemon juice
Chopped pistachio nuts   Maraschino cherries
Pineapple   Orange
Mint leaves   White grapes

For the summer luncheon the hors d'oeuvres dish may be filled with the above fruits. Marinate the watermelon balls in French dressing; slice the pears thin, cut in scalloped disks with a scalloped cutter, sprinkle with lemon juice and garnish in center with finely chopped maraschino cherries. Stone the peaches, cut in eighths, dip in lemon juice or orange juice and roll in finely chopped pistachio nuts. Dip the segments of sliced pineapple in powdered mint leaves. Bits of grapefruit or oranges or halved white grapes may be used to make a quintet of delicate, mouth watering appetizers.

Orlys d'Anchois

Small jar anchovies   1 tablespoon minced
1 tablespoon olive oil   parsley
1 teaspoon grated onion   1 cup bread flour
Pepper   ½ teaspoon salt
2 eggs   ⅔ cup milk
                     Paprika

Bone and dry the anchovies. Lay them on a plate and pour over them the olive oil. Sprinkle with grated onion, minced parsley, and a little pepper. Let them stand for one hour. Then make a batter as follows: Mix and sift together the flour, salt and pepper. Add the milk gradually and the eggs well beaten. Dip the anchovies in the batter and fry in hot fat at 360° F. Dust with paprika and serve very hot as a savory.

Tomato Savory

6 tomatoes	½ cup heavy cream
1 teaspoon salt	½ tablespoon flour
⅛ teaspoon pepper	½ tablespoon butter
1 teaspoon sugar	Crisp crackers

Cut a cone-shaped piece from the stem end of each tomato. Mix salt, pepper and sugar together and sprinkle over tomatoes. Bake in oven at 375° F. until tomatoes are soft but not broken. Remove the tomatoes to individual serving dishes and keep hot. Heat the cream mixed with the juice left in the pan after baking tomatoes. Thicken slightly with the flour blended with the butter. Pour this sauce over the tomatoes and serve hot accompanied by crisp crackers.

Stuffed Cucumbers

Cucumbers	2 boned sardines
French dressing	2 hard cooked eggs
1 tablespoon butter	Sprig parsley

Cut a cucumber in pieces about one and one-half inches in length. Then cut away strips of peel horizontally, leaving a striped green and white effect. Now scoop out the centers of the cucumber slices to form cups, place a marinate of French dressing and let stand in the refrigerator for an hour. Meanwhile chop the pulp very fine. Chop the yolks of the hard-cooked eggs and add butter, the sardines and parsley. Mix well and add the cucumber pulp at the last moment. Fill the cucumber cups with the mixture piled high in the centers and top with a star of pimiento.

Summer Hors d'Oeuvres

6 slices raw tomato	3 hard-cooked eggs
1½ teaspoon chopped chives	Well seasoned French dressing

The eggs should be sliced in halves lengthwise. Put one-half with the sliced side down on each tomato slice. Pour over the French dressing and sprinkle with chives, allowing one-fourth teaspoon for each egg.

Winter Hors d'Oeuvres

Frankfurter sausages	Onion
French dressing	Hard-cooked eggs
Pickled beets	Parsley
Green pepper	Celery
Lemon juice	Cream cheese
Smoked salmon	Pimiento

For the winter luncheon fill the first compartment of the Hors d'oeuvres dish with frankfurter sausages which have first been steamed, cut in half inch slices and peeled, and marinated with French dressing for one hour. After arranging slices in dish top each slice with an infinitesimal disk of onion. Slice the hard-cooked eggs very thin, marinate in French dressing and dip in powdered parsley. Slice the beets, cut with a scalloped cooky cutter and garnish in center with a dot of finely chopped green pepper mixed with French dressing. Cut the celery in stalks one inch long, and soak in iced lemon water to blanch. Dry and fill with cream cheese mixed with pimientoes. Slice the smoked salmon as thin as paper and cut in small pieces. For the center, chopped pickles or pickled red cabbage is nice. About the entire dish scatter a thin ring of finely chopped parsley. Place it in the refrigerator to permit the hors d'oeuvres to chill thoroughly.

SALADS

Apple and Watercress Salad

3 large apples	Bar-le-Duc or currant
1 small cream cheese	jelly
Watercress	French Dressing

Wash and core apples, leaving the skin on, and cut crosswise into inch thick slices. Mix the Bar-le-Duc with cream cheese until a smooth paste is formed; spread this mixture on the slices of apple, allowing one slice to each portion. Mix French Dressing with the watercress, lay it on one side of the salad-plate and place the apple slices on the other. Serves 6.

Banana and Mint Salad

6 small bananas
1 tablespoon lemon juice
Lettuce

2 tablespoons chopped mint
¼ cup chopped nuts
½ cup mayonnaise

Skin the bananas and cut them in halves, lengthwise. Place them on beds of crisp lettuce and sprinkle with the lemon-juice and chopped mint. Garnish with the Mayonnaise and the nuts combined. Serves 6.

Deviled Egg Salad

4 eggs, hard-cooked
6 tablespoons deviled ham
2 tablespoons chopped chives

1 teaspoon vinegar
¼ teaspoon prepared mustard
¼ teaspoon sugar

Chill eggs and cut in halves lengthwise. Mash yolks, add other ingredients. Refill egg whites, serve on cut salad greens with Cooked Dressing. Serves 4.

Emerald Salad

Shredded green pepper
Chopped chives
Lettuce

Radishes
French Dressing
Watercress

Line a salad bowl with crisp, cold leaves of lettuce or romaine. Sprinkle these with shredded green pepper, then arrange a second layer of leaves in the bowl, sprinkled with chopped chives. In the very center of the bowl, place the heart of the lettuce, surrounded by a ring of watercress. If a second jewel is desired for the sake of color, let it take the form of tiny, crimson, globe radishes, crisped in ice-water, for an hour. Serve with French or Piquant Dressing. For a more elaborate salad the tips of cooked green asparagus may be added to this foundation. Serves 6.

Egg and Asparagus Salad

6 hard-cooked eggs
2 tablespoons chopped nut meats
1 cup cooked asparagus tips

1 teaspoon minced parsley
French Dressing
Extra nut-meats, parsley, and asparagus tips
Lettuce

Shell the eggs and cut in halves lengthwise. Mash the yolks, add the nutmeats, the asparagus-tips, and the parsley, and blend with four tablespoons of French Dressing that is not very sour. Fill the egg-halves with this mixture, arrange on lettuce leaves, and garnish with the extra asparagus-tips, parsley, and nutmeats. If any of the asparagus-mixture is left over, it can be blended with a mayonnaise or a bland cooked dressing and passed with the salad. Serves 6.

Ginger Fruit Salad

8 red apples
1 lemon, juice
½ cup nutmeats
1 cup candied ginger, chopped

2 bananas
2 oranges
1 cup seedless white grapes
1 bunch watercress

Lime French Dressing

Core apples and dice without peeling. Sprinkle with lemon juice at once to prevent discoloration. Add sliced bananas, orange sections, stemmed grapes, chopped nutmeats and chopped ginger. Serve on watercress with Lime French Dressing. Serves 8.

Jellied Fruit Salad

1 package lemon gelatine
2 tart red apples

4 slices canned pineapple
2 bananas
Fruit salad dressing

Prepare the lemon gelatine as directed on the package. While it is cooling, dice the unpeeled apple and the pineapple, and slice the bananas. Mix the fruit and place in it a cold, wet ring mold or individual molds. When the jelly begins to thicken pour it over the fruit. Serves 8.

Jellied Chicken and Vegetable Salad

2 tablespoons granulated gelatine
3 cups hot chicken broth or canned chicken soup
2 cups cooked vegetables (peas, string beans, carrots, beets, asparagus, etc.)

½ cup cold water or chicken broth
¾ teaspoon salt
1 cup diced chicken meat
1 tablespoon chopped pimiento
1 green pepper, minced

Soak gelatine in cold water or broth 5 minutes. Add hot broth and stir until gelatine is dissolved, add salt and cool. Pour a thin layer of this mixture into a cold wet mold, and let it stiffen slightly. Add some of the vegetables and chicken meat, more jelly, etc., continuing until all ingredients are used. Chill until firm, unmold on lettuce leaves and garnish with parsley or watercress and Mayonnaise. Serves 6.

Jellied Spring Salad

1 package lemon flavored
   gelatine
1 teaspoon salt
1 cup diced cucumbers
1 cup diced, tender young
onions
2 cups boiling water
1 teaspoon vinegar
1 cup thinly sliced radishes.
   Watercress

Dissolve gelatine in the boiling water. Add salt and vinegar. When slightly thickened stir in the vegetables. Turn into cold, wet molds and chill until set. Serve on watercress. Serves 8.

Jellied Pineapple and Crabmeat Salad

2 teaspoons granulated
   gelatine
⅓ cup cold chicken
   stock or
1 chicken bullion cube dissolved in ⅓ cup boiling
   water, and cooled
1 tablespoon tarragon
   vinegar
1 cup mayonnaise
1 cup drained and diced
   canned pineapple
½ cup diced celery
1 cup crab meat
3 cups shredded cabbage
½ cup French dressing

Soak gelatine in the cool chicken stock for five minutes. Dissolve over hot water, add the tarragon vinegar and cool. When cold, add slowly to one-half cupful of Mayonnaise, beating thoroughly. Meanwhile combine the pineapple, crab meat and the diced celery and add to the gelatine mixture. Pack in cold, wet molds and chill. When firm, remove from molds and arrange on the shredded cabbage that has been marinated in the French dressing for five minutes just before serving. Garnish with radish roses and serve with remaining Mayonnaise. Serves 6.

May Fruit Salad

6 slices fresh or canned pineapple
1 large orange

Sprigs fresh mint
1 banana
6 strawberries

Honey Salad Dressing

Wash and crisp the mint, arrange, stem-ends toward the center, on individual salad plates. Place a slice of pineapple on each bed of mint. On this put a slice of orange, then a layer of banana sliced into disks, and top with a strawberry. Pour over it the salad dressing. If fresh pineapple is used it should be sprinkled with sugar and allowed to stand in a cold place for at least an hour. Serves 6.

Pineapple and Chicken Salad

1 cup drained and diced
  canned pineapple
2 cups diced cooked
  chicken

¾ cup diced celery
1 head lettuce
1¼ cups Mayonnaise
8 ripe olives

Combine the pineapple, chicken, celery and one-third cupful Mayonnaise. Arrange on lettuce, garnish with ripe olives and serve with the remaining Mayonnaise. Serves 6.

Pomegranate Salad

6 canned pear halves
⅛ cup pecan meats, chopped
Pomegranate seeds

2 packages cream cheese
Watercress
Cream Mayonnaise
Lettuce

Arrange crisp lettuce on individual salad plates. Place half a canned pear on each. Mix cream cheese and chopped nut meats and form into balls. Place one ball in center of pear. Place a few sprigs of watercress at blossom end of pear. Serve with Cream Mayonnaise sprinkled lightly with pomegranate seeds. Serves 6.

Shrimp and Pineapple Salad

1½ cups canned or fresh
  cooked shrimp
1 cup canned or fresh
  pineapple, diced
⅛ teaspoon paprika

2 sprigs chives, chopped
6 tablespoons French
  Dressing
Romaine
½ teaspoon salt

Combine the shrimp, pineapple, salt, paprika and chives. Chill thoroughly, and just before serving, pour over the French dressing. Toss until well mixed, then arrange on crisp romaine or endive leaves and serve. Serves 6.

Novel Potato Salad

10 small potatoes
½ large green pepper
2 tablespoons chopped
  walnuts
2 hard-cooked eggs
3 small cooked beets
6 spiced, pickled cucumbers

Parsley
Salt
Pepper
Paprika
Cooked salad dressing
5 small gherkins
Lettuce

Combine cold cooked potatoes with the green pepper, hard-cooked eggs, cooked beets, pickled cucumbers, and walnut meats. Chop all quite fine, and add salt, pepper and paprika to taste. Moisten with cooked dressing to a consistency that will mold. Pack in a wet mold, and set away to chill. When ready to serve, turn the salad out on a bed of lettuce. With a broad knife, mask the whole of the salad with the dressing, as though icing a cake. Halve the gherkins and place them star fashion on top of the mold; stick a sprig of parsley or tiny inside-leaves of lettuce in the very center. Serve the salad very cold and pass cooked salad dressing. Serves 6.

Salami Salad

1 cup diced salami
½ cup French dressing

2 cups shredded cabbage
¼ cup grated cheese

Mix salami and cabbage. Add cheese to dressing and marinate salami and cabbage, 30 minutes. Sliced radishes may be added if desired. Serve on crisp lettuce. Serves 6.

Spring Salad

Lettuce   Cream cheese
Yellow cheese   Minced parsley
2 hard-cooked eggs   French dressing
Radishes   Crisp crackers

Arrange beds of lettuce on a shallow salad dish and cover with
radish-roses. Make small balls of both yellow and cream cheese,
dip one side of the latter in finely minced parsley and arrange
on salad. Meanwhile dice a border of the hard-cooked eggs
around the edge. Pour French dressing over all and serve
with crisp crackers.

Strawberry Salad

2 cups ripe strawberries   ½ cup chopped pecan
1 cup celery cubes   meats
Heart leaves of lettuce   ½ cup French dressing
                                 Whipped cream

Combine the strawberries, chopped nut meats, and celery cubes.
Marinate the dressing, arrange on lettuce, and top with whipped
cream and whole nut meats, or a sprig of fresh mint. Serves 6.

Veal Salad, Summer Style

2 cups cold veal, diced   4 tablespoons salad oil
1 cup diced stringbeans or   1½ tablespoons vinegar
   celery or equal parts of   3 tomatoes
   each   Mayonnaise
6 hard-cooked eggs   Parsley
½ teaspoon salt   Lettuce
Few grains pepper

Chop the eggs rather coarsely, and combine them with the veal,
stringbeans, oil, vinegar, salt and pepper. Let stand thirty minutes to marinate. Then add Mayonnaise to moisten. Arrange
the salad in a mound on a large platter, cover with Mayonnaise,
border with lettuce and sliced tomatoes. Serves 6.

SALAD DRESSINGS

Golden Dressing

4 eggs
1½ teaspoons flour
1 cup sugar

8 tablespoons lemon juice
2 cups canned pineapple juice

Beat eggs, add sugar, flour and lemon juice and beat again. Add pineapple juice and cook in top of double boiler until it thickens, stirring constantly. Cool. Fold in one cup of cream, whipped. Serves 10-12.

Honey Salad Dressing

3 tablespoons salad oil
2 tablespoons honey

1 tablespoon lemon juice
⅛ teaspoon salt

Beat together the salad oil, honey, lemon juice and salt until well blended. Use at once.

Piquant Salad Dressing

1 tablespoon dry mustard
½ tablespoon Worcestershire sauce
⅓ cup catsup
½ cup vinegar

2 teaspoons sugar
½ teaspoon salt
⅛ teaspoon celery salt
Dash cayenne pepper
1 cup salad oil

Mix all ingredients and beat with an egg-beater until thoroughly combined. This dressing is particularly good with sliced cucumber. Serves 6.

This page is purposely left blank in order that you may insert such recipes (not already appearing in this Cook Book) as may have a special appeal.

Recipes appear daily in the DETROIT TIMES and may add variety to the menu.

This page is purposely left blank in order that you may insert such recipes (not already appearing in this Cook Book) as may have a special appeal.

Recipes appear daily in the DETROIT TIMES and may add variety to the menu.

This page is purposely left blank in order that you may insert such recipes (not already appearing in this Cook Book) as may have a special appeal.

Recipes appear daily in the DETROIT TIMES and may add variety to the menu.

This page is purposely left blank in order that you may insert such recipes (not already appearing in this Cook Book) as may have a special appeal.

Recipes appear daily in the DETROIT TIMES and may add variety to the menu.

This page is purposely left blank in order that you may insert such recipes (not already appearing in this Cook Book) as may have a special appeal.

Recipes appear daily in the DETROIT TIMES and may add variety to the menu.

This page is purposely left blank in order that you may insert such recipes (not already appearing in this Cook Book) as may have a special appeal.

Recipes appear daily in the DETROIT TIMES and may add **variety** to the menu.

This page is purposely left blank in order that you may insert such recipes (not already appearing in this Cook Book) as may have a special appeal.

Recipes appear daily in the DETROIT TIMES and may add variety to the menu.

This page is purposely left blank in order that you may insert such recipes (not already appearing in this Cook Book) as may have a special appeal.

Recipes appear daily in the DETROIT TIMES and may add variety to the menu.

This page is purposely left blank in order that you may insert such recipes (not already appearing in this Cook Book) as may have a special appeal.

Recipes appear daily in the DETROIT TIMES and may add variety to the menu.

This page is purposely left blank in order that you may insert such recipes (not already appearing in this Cook Book) as may have a special appeal.

Recipes appear daily in the DETROIT TIMES and may add variety to the menu.

This page is purposely left blank in order that you may insert such recipes (not already appearing in this Cook Book) as may have a special appeal.

Recipes appear daily in the DETROIT TIMES and may add variety to the menu.

This page is purposely left blank in order that you may insert such recipes (not already appearing in this Cook Book) as may have a special appeal.

Recipes appear daily in the DETROIT TIMES and may add variety to the menu.

This page is purposely left blank in order that you may insert such recipes (not already appearing in this Cook Book) as may have a special appeal.

Recipes appear daily in the DETROIT TIMES and may add variety to the menu.

This page is purposely left blank in order that you may insert such recipes (not already appearing in this Cook Book) as may have a special appeal.

Recipes appear daily in the DETROIT TIMES and may add variety to the menu.

This page is purposely left blank in order that you may insert such recipes (not already appearing in this Cook Book) as may have a special appeal.

Recipes appear daily in the DETROIT TIMES and may add variety to the menu.

This page is purposely left blank in order that you may insert such recipes (not already appearing in this Cook Book) as may have a special appeal.

Recipes appear daily in the DETROIT TIMES and may add variety to the menu.

This page is purposely left blank in order that you may insert such recipes (not already appearing in this Cook Book) as may have a special appeal.

Recipes appear daily in the DETROIT TIMES and may add variety to the menu.

This page is purposely left blank in order that you may insert such recipes (not already appearing in this Cook Book) as may have a special appeal.

Recipes appear daily in the DETROIT TIMES and may add variety to the menu.

This page is purposely left blank in order that you may insert such recipes (not already appearing in this Cook Book) as may have a special appeal.

Recipes appear daily in the DETROIT TIMES and may add variety to the menu.

This page is purposely left blank in order that you may insert such recipes (not already appearing in this Cook Book) as may have a special appeal.

Recipes appear daily in the DETROIT TIMES and may add variety to the menu.

This page is purposely left blank in order that you may insert such recipes (not already appearing in this Cook Book) as may have a special appeal.

Recipes appear daily in the DETROIT TIMES and may add variety to the menu.

This page is purposely left blank in order that you may insert such recipes (not already appearing in this Cook Book) as may have a special appeal.

Recipes appear daily in the DETROIT TIMES and may add variety to the menu.

This page is purposely left blank in order that you may insert such recipes (not already appearing in this Cook Book) as may have a special appeal.

Recipes appear daily in the DETROIT TIMES and may add variety to the menu.

This page is purposely left blank in order that you may insert such recipes (not already appearing in this Cook Book) as may have a special appeal.

Recipes appear daily in the DETROIT TIMES and may add variety to the menu.

This page is purposely left blank in order that you may insert such recipes (not already appearing in this Cook Book) as may have a special appeal.

Recipes appear daily in the DETROIT TIMES and may add variety to the menu.

This page is purposely left blank in order that you may insert such recipes (not already appearing in this Cook Book) as may have a special appeal.

Recipes appear daily in the DETROIT TIMES and may add variety to the menu.

This page is purposely left blank in order that you may insert such recipes (not already appearing in this Cook Book) as may have a special appeal.

Recipes appear daily in the DETROIT TIMES and may add variety to the menu.

This page is purposely left blank in order that you may insert such recipes (not already appearing in this Cook Book) as may have a special appeal.

Recipes appear daily in the DETROIT TIMES and may add variety to the menu.

This page is purposely left blank in order that you may insert such recipes (not already appearing in this Cook Book) as may have a special appeal.

Recipes appear daily in the DETROIT TIMES and may add variety to the menu.

This page is purposely left blank in order that you may insert such recipes (not already appearing in this Cook Book) as may have a special appeal.

Recipes appear daily in the DETROIT TIMES and may add **variety to the menu.**

This page is purposely left blank in order that you may insert such recipes (not already appearing in this Cook Book) as may have a special appeal.

Recipes appear daily in the DETROIT TIMES and may add variety to the menu.